Intellectual Property Law in Turkey

Intellectual Property Law in Turkey

Ergun Özsunay
Murat R. Özsunay

This book was originally published as a monograph in the International Encyclopaedia of Laws/Intellectual Property Law.

Founding Editor: Roger Blanpain
General Editor: Frank Hendrickx
Volume Editor: Hendrik Vanhees

Wolters Kluwer

Published by:
Kluwer Law International B.V.
PO Box 316
2400 AH Alphen aan den Rijn
The Netherlands
E-mail: lrs-sales@wolterskluwer.com
Website: www.wolterskluwer.com/en/solutions/kluwerlawinternational

Sold and distributed by:
Wolters Kluwer Legal & Regulatory U.S.
920 Links Avenue
Landisville, PA 17538
United States of America
E-mail: customer.service@wolterskluwer.com

ISBN 978-94-035-2987-5

e-Book: ISBN 978-94-035-2997-4
web-PDF: ISBN 978-94-035-3007-9

The Authors

Professor Dr Ergun Özsunay was born in Istanbul. He graduated from Istanbul University Faculty of Law. After his graduation, he joined the faculty staff as a research assistant. He assisted Mr Alfred F. Conard (the University of Michigan, School of Law), visiting professor of law at Istanbul University from 1958 to 1959. Then he attended Graduate Studies at Harvard Law School in 1959–1960 and obtained his LLM degree. On his return home, he assisted Mr E. Alan Farnsworth, Colombia University, School of Law, visiting professor of law at Istanbul University in 1961–1962.

In 1961, he obtained the SJD degree (the doctor of science of law). During 1962–1963, he attended *Faculté International pour l'Enseignement de Droit Comparé* in Strasbourg for advance legal studies on comparative law (*Diplome de droit comparé and Diplome d'études superieurs de droit comparé*). He studied at the *Max Planck Institut für auslaendisches-und internationales Privatrecht* in 1963/1964 on his *Habilitationsschrift* (Prof. Dr Konrad Zweigert).

He became an associate professor of civil law and comparative law in 1965.

In 1972, he studied for ten months at the Freiburg/Br University as a researcher and worked on patent licensing agreements and 'joint stock corporation (*société anonyme*) of European type' (Prof Dr Ernst von Caemmerer).

He became a full professor of civil and comparative law in 1973.

He served seven years as the director of the Institute of Comparative Law at the Istanbul University (1978–1985).

He is a member of the following associations or organizations: German Association of Comparative Law (corresponding member), International Association of Legal Science (A.I.S.J.) (former President), Titular Member of the International Academy of Comparative Law, member of the International Association for Procedural Law, UNIDROIT (corresponding member).

He represented the Turkish governments at the following diplomatic conferences: Convention on Agency in International Sale of Goods (Geneva, 1983); Convention on the Law Applicable to Contracts in the International Sale of Goods (The Hague, 1985); Convention on International Factoring and Financial Leasing (Ottawa, 1988).

At present, he is the Turkish delegate at DH-BIO (former Steering Committee on Bioethics) at the Council of Europe. He is a member of the International Chamber of Commerce (ICC) Commissions on Competition and on Commercial Law and Practice. He has also served as the Turkish representative at the UNCITRAL Working Groups II (Arbitration and Conciliation), III (Online Dispute Resolution) and VI (Secured Transactions).

He has been practising law for thirty-five years as a legal consultant. Further, he has been serving for many years as an international arbitrator in commercial disputes.

He has written several books and more than one hundred forty articles, essays, national reports, general reports, etc. in the fields of law of obligations (contracts and torts), cartel law, competition law, arbitration law, intellectual property law, commercial law, associations and foundations and comparative law.

Murat R. Özsunay, a dual citizen of Türkiye and Germany, is an Attorney-at-Law (*Avukat*) of the Istanbul and Frankfurt/M Bars. He is also a European and Turkish Patent & Trademark Attorney (European Patent Institute – epi, *Türk Patent Enstitüsü – TPE*), a licensed mediator and an ICC arbitrator based in Istanbul.

A graduate of Quartz Hill High School, California (American Field Service – AFS Scholar) and *Kadiköy Anadolu Lisesi* (Istanbul), Istanbul University Law Faculty (1985), Academy of American & International Law (Dallas) and U.T. Austin (Master of Comparative Jurisprudence – MCJ), he worked in Istanbul, Frankfurt/M and at the Registry of the ECHR in Strasbourg.

He has an international practice and occasionally teaches, *inter alia*, civil law, contracts, torts, foreign investments, intellectual property (IP), civil procedure, mediation-arbitration, and European Court of Human Rights – ECHR litigation at J.W. Goethe University – *Juridicum* (Frankfurt/M), Bahcesehir University (Istanbul), Istanbul Bar Apprentice Training Centre – SEM, Georgia State University College of Law Summer School (Linz), American University Washington School of Law.

Moreover, he attends conferences worldwide and generally presents national or comparative reports on related topics.

He publishes in English and Turkish primarily on arbitration, civil-commercial law, civil procedure and IP. He is a member of, *inter alia*, the International Bar Association (IBA), European Patent Institute (epi), International Chamber of Commerce (ICC-WBO), Association of German Chambers of Industry and Commerce (AHK) (listed arbitrator), International Association for the Protection of Intellectual Property (AIPPI-Germany), *Gesellschaft für Rechtsvergleichung* (GfR, German Comparative Law Society), International Association of Procedural Law (IAPL), *Deutsch-Türkische Juristenvereinigung e.V.* (German-Turkish Lawyers Association), *Deutscher Anwaltverein (DAV-Avukatlar Dernegi*, German Bar Association), Austrian Arbitration Association (ArbAut), Vienna International Arbitral Centre (VIAC) (listed practitioner). He speaks English, German and Turkish; he can read Azeri and French.

Table of Contents

List of Abbreviations

AMedC	Act on Mediation in Civil Law Disputes, No. 6325 (*Hukuk Uyusmazliklarinda Arabuluculuk Kanunu = HUAK*),
APIL	Act on Private International Law and Procedural Law (2007), No. 5718 (*Milletlerarasi Özel Hukuk ve Usul Hukuku Kanunu = MÖHUK*)
Auflage	ed.
Band	Volume
C	*Cilt* (Volume)
C.Cass.	Court of Cassation (*Yargitay*)
CBK	Presidential Decree, abbreviation in Turkish
CCP	Code of Civil Procedure (2011), No. 6100 (*Hukuk Muhakemeleri Kanunu = HMK*)
CCrimP	Code of Criminal Procedure (2004), No. 5271 (*Ceza Muhakemesi Kanunu = CMK*)
CEB	Code of Enforcement and Bankruptcy (1932), No. 2004 (*Icra ve Iflas Kanunu = IIK*), last amendment by the Law, No. 7445 of 28 March 2023
Cf.	Compare
Ed.	Editor
EPÜ	*Europäisches Patentübereinkommen*
Eu.Pat-TR-Reg.	Implementing Regulation concerning the Validation of European Patents related to European Patent Convention in Türkiye (2001), *Avrupa Patentlerinin Verilmesi ile İlgili Avrupa Patent Sözlesmesinin Türkiye'de Uygulama Seklini Gösterir Yönetmelik*
FSEK	Law on Intellectual and Artistic Works (1951), No. 5846 (*Fikir ve Sanat Eserleri Kanunu*), amended several times, last by Act, No. 7346 of 25 December 2021, abbreviation in Turkish
Gen. Ed.	General Editor
ICC	International Chamber of Commerce
IPR	Intellectual Property Right

List of Abbreviations

ICOC	The Istanbul Chamber of Commerce (*Istanbul Ticaret Odasi = ITO*)
KHK	Governmental decree having the Power of Law (*Kanun Hükmünde Kararname*), abbreviation in Turkish
OR	*Obligationenrecht* (Swiss Code of Obligations)
PL	Press Law (2004), No. 5187 (*Basin Kanunu*)
Para.	Paragraph
PatTM-AttyL	Law on Patent and Trademark Attorneyship and Some Other Arrangements (2003), No. 5000 *(Patent ve Marka Vekilligi ile Bazı Düzenlemeler Hakkında Kanun)*
PICTopoL	The Protection of Integrated Circuit Topographies Law (2004), No. 5147 *(Entegre Devre Topografyalarinin Korunmasi Hakkinda Kanun)*
PPlantL	Protection of Rights of Breeders on New Varieties of Plants Law (2004), No. 5042 *(Yeni Bitki Çesitlerine Ait Islahci Haklarinin Korunmasina Iliskin Kanun)*
PPP	Purchasing Power Parity
SMK	Industrial Property Law (*Sinai Mülkiyet Kanunu*), No. 6769 of 22 December 2016 (Official Gazette, No. 29944 of 10 January 2017, last amended 28 July 2020), abbreviation in Turkish
SMK-Yön	Implementing Regulation of Industrial Property Law, *6769 Sayılı Sınai Mülkiyet Kanununun Uygulanmasına Dair Yönetmelik (2017),* abbreviation in Turkish
TBMM	*Türkiye Büyük Millet Meclisi*
TCC	Turkish Civil Code (2001), No. 4721 (*Türk Medeni Kanunu = TMK*)
TCO	Turkish Code of Obligations (2001), No. 6098 (*Türk Borçlar Kanunu = TBK*)
TComC	Turkish Commercial Code (2011), No. 6102 (*Türk Ticaret Kanunu = TTK*)
TPC	Turkish Penal Code (2004), No. 5237 (*Türk Ceza Kanunu = TCK*)
TürkPatent	Turkish Patent and Trademark Office [or Authority] *(Türk Patent ve Marka Kurumu)* (previously named Turkish Patent Institute = TPI, *Türk Patent Enstitüsü = TPE)*
TRIPS	Trade-Related Aspects of Intellectual Property Rights
UPOV	International Convention for the Protection of New Varieties of Plants
URG	*Bundesgesetz über das Urheberrecht und verwandte Schutzrechte*
Vol.	Volume
WIPO	World Intellectual Property Organization
WTO	World Trade Organization
ZGB	*Zivilgesetzbuch* (Swiss Civil Code)

General Introduction

§1. General Background of Türkiye (Turkey)[1]

I. Geography and Political Orientation

1. Türkiye covers an area of 783.562 m^2 (302.535 sq mi) (European part in Thrace: 23.506 sq km, Asian part in Anatolia: 760.05 sq km). The country lies between Europe and Asia, as a crossroads between Eastern Europe, Asia, and the Middle East. Thrace in the northwest of Türkiye is in Europe. Trace separated from her Asian part, Asia Minor (Anatolia), by the Marmara Sea and by two straits: the Bosporus in Istanbul, and the Dardanelles in Çanakkale (historically also known as Troy). Asia Minor (Anatolia) is a peninsula surrounded by four different seas: in the north, the Black Sea and Marmara Sea, in the west, the Aegean Sea, and in the south, the Mediterranean Sea.

2. Türkiye shares her western borders in Europe (Trace, the Balkans) with Greece Bulgaria and Greece, and her eastern borders in Asia Minor with Georgia, Armenia, Azerbaijan, Iran, Iraq and Syria. Turkish Airlines carried 72 million passengers in 2022 alone, connecting 293 destinations in 128 countries.

3. Istanbul (Constantinople) had been the capital of the East Roman Empire (Byzantium) and after 1453, it had become the capital of the late Ottoman Empire. It is the largest city of Türkiye although the capital of the Turkish Republic is Ankara.

4. Since 1995, Türkiye has been the only country without full EU membership which is in the EU Customs Union, applying all relevant EU rules and regulations. She is a significant North Atlantic Treaty Organization (NATO) member with the second largest armed forces in NATO after the USA. She has also established close

1. Following an official letter submitted to the United Nations by the Republic of Türkiye in 2022, the country's name has been officially changed to Türkiye at the UN. A letter had been received on 1 June from the Turkish Foreign Minister addressed to the UN Secretary-General, requesting the use of 'Türkiye' instead of 'Turkey' for all affairs. The country name change became effective from the moment the letter was received, https://turkiye.un.org/en/184798-turkeys-name-changed-turkiye For its reasons, *see* 'Turkey officially changes name at UN to Türkiye' in Guardian, https://www.theguardian.com/world/2022/jun/03/turkey-changes-name-to-turkiye-as-other-name-is-for-the-birds For the use of the name 'Türkiye' as a trademark, *see* Official Gazette, No. 31679 of 4 Dec. 2022.

ties with Russia, which enabled her to act as the sole mediator accepted by both parties in the Russia-Ukraine crisis. She has close ties with the Islamic world as well as the non-aligned African countries.

II. Population Statistics as of 2021

5. Türkiye has 84.7 million inhabitants.[2] The Turkish population has been increasing. The annual population growth rate in the first two years of the 2020s is 5.5‰ and 12.7‰. 15.3% of the population is between 15–24 years old which is considered a young population. The total fertility rate is around 1.70. Nearly 77 % of the total population lives in urban areas. The rate of urbanization is 1.4% annually.[3]

III. Cultural Composition

6. Ethnic groups living in present-day Türkiye could roughly be listed below:

> Turkic-speaking peoples: Turks, Azerbaijanis, Tatars, Karachays, Uzbeks, Crimean Tatars and Uyghurs; Indo-European-speaking peoples: Kurds, Zazas, Megleno-Romanians, Bosniaks, Albanians, Pomaks, Ossetians, Armenians, Hamshenis, Goranis and Greeks; Semitic-speaking peoples: Arabs, Jews and Assyrians/Syriacs; Caucasian-speaking peoples: Circassians, Georgians, Lazs and Chechens. Turkish is the official as well as the most spoken mother language.

7. After the dissolution of the multi-ethnic Ottoman Empire (1299–1923) at the end of World War I and following the Turkish War of Independence (1919–1922), an exodus by the large portion of Turkish (Turkic) and Muslim peoples from the Balkans (Balkan Turks, Albanians, Bosniaks, Pomaks), Caucasus (Abkhazians, Ajarians, Circassians, Chechens), Crimea (Crimean Tatar diaspora), and Crete (Cretan Turks) took refuge in present-day Türkiye. Most of these immigrants had previously lived as citizens of the Ottoman Empire and their arrival also affected fundamental features of the Turkish Republic.

8. Presently, Türkiye receives many economic migrants from nearby countries such as Armenia, Moldova, Georgia, Iran, and Azerbaijan but also from Central Asia, Ukraine, and Russia. During the 2010s, high numbers of people fleeing especially from the Syrian civil war and arriving in Türkiye caused a migrant crisis.

9. For newcomers, Turkish citizenship can be obtained on a range of legal grounds. These include reunification with their family, marriage to a Turkish citizen,

2. 2021 TUIK Address Based Population Registry System, Türkiye Istatistik Kurumu Haber Bülteni (Turkish Statistical Institute News Bulletin), No. 45866 of 19 Dec. 2022, https://data.tuik.gov.tr/Bulten/Index?p=Nufus-ve-Konut-Sayimi-2021-45866.
3. https://data.worldbank.org/indicator/SP.URB.TOTL.IN.ZS?contextual=default.&locations=TR.

for the purchase of real estate worth USD 400,000 from a Turkish citizen or company. The minimum investment amount had been attractive until recently.

10. Turkish citizens are predominantly Muslim as the traditional non-Muslim ethnic groups of the country consist of about 0.2% of the population. Despite formal declarations that about 99.8% of the population are Muslims, academic research and polls suggest that it may in fact be lower.

11. According to unofficial figures,[4] about 90% of Turkish Muslims are Sunni Muslims. Shia-Aleviler (Alevis, Ja'faris and Alawites) denominations in the total form up to 10% of the Muslim population. In recent times, there appear to be some citizens who identify themselves as 'non-practicing Muslim' or 'spiritual but not religious' whereas a few openly declare to be 'someone with no religious conviction'.[5]

12. Regardless of ethnic or religious background, 'Everyone bound to the Turkish State through the bond of citizenship is a Turk (Constitution, Article 66).' The Republic of Türkiye recognizes the concept of 'minorities' (*azinlik*) only as defined by the Treaty of Lausanne (1923); these are strictly limited to Greeks, Armenians, and Jews only on religious matters. The Kurds who make up roughly 15% of the country, Alevis, Assyrians/Syriacs of various Christian denominations and all the others are Turkish citizens who are not deemed as 'minorities'.

13. The non-Muslim religious population or ethnic groups in present-day Türkiye can be listed as Christians (Greek Orthodox, Oriental Orthodoxy, Armenian Apostolic, Roman Catholic, etc.) and Jews (Sephardi). Turkish citizens of the Jewish community are mainly descendants of the Sephardic Jews who were expelled from Spain in 1492 and found refuge in the Ottoman Empire.

IV. Turkish Economy, Its Main Sectors and Foreign Trade[6]

14. Based on macro-economic indicators, Türkiye seems to be performing good, however, she is currently facing problems in the following issues: inflation, interest rates, Credit Default Swap (CDS) ratings, unemployment rate and foreign trade deficit. According to some critics, these problems are the result of an unorthodox

4. As Türkiye does not conduct official censuses about religious denominations, precise figures are unavailable.
5. *See* 'Religion in Turkey' in Wikipedia.
6. Turkish Statistical Institute (TUIK), Turkish Exportes Union (TIM), Trademap, IMF World Economic Outlook Database, 2022 October, TR Investment Office, TR Ministry of Trade General Directorate of Exports, TR Ministry of Industry and Technology General Directorate of Industry, TR Ministry of Tourism, TR Banking Regulation and Supervision Agency, Sustainable Economy and Finance Research Association (SEFiA), Automotive Manufacturers Association (OSD), Turkish Clothing Manufacturers Association (TGSD), Turkish Chemical Manufacturers Association, Turkcimento, Cement, Glass, Ceramics, Ceramics and Soil Products Exporters Association, Bloomberg HT, An Analysis of Global Foodstuffs Trade and Turkey, Palacioglu, T., *Economic and Financial Analysis of Global and National Developments*, Ekin Yayin, 2022.

approach of the government which briefly claims that 'interest rate is the reason and inflation rate is the outcome'. This approach together with the FED interest rises due to increasing global inflation, and hikes in energy and foodstuff prices. The recession expectations in the European Union (EU) following the Russia-Ukraine war deteriorated the FX values (USD appreciated 42%) and CDS ratings (jumped to 513) at the end of 2022. These events carried Türkiye to the top 5 in the inflation league with 64.27%.

15. Despite high unemployment and the recent pandemic years, Türkiye has succeeded to create 479 thousand jobs annually between 2005 and 2020.

16. As for the 110 USD billion foreign trade deficit, this occurred mainly due to two extraordinary developments: (a) 100 billion USD for *energy imports* which were more than doubled as a result of increasing energy prices, (b) over *140 tons of gold imports in the first nine months* of 2022. On the other hand, Türkiye could compensate for this deficit with a record level of *tourism income.*

17. This unorthodox approach defined as the new Turkish economic model, on the other hand, has given its fruits to economic growth. According to the International Monetary Fund (IMF) World Economic Data, Türkiye has positively been separated from the developing economies even in times of economic crises with robust economic growth. Between 2000–2022, *the Turkish GDP increased 3.48* times. For many years, Türkiye's growth ranked in the top 5 of the developing economies. The GDP which is given *as USD 853,5 billion* in nominal figures (20th highest in the world, end of 2022) is calculated as more than *USD 3,3 trillion* (11th highest) in terms of *Purchasing Power Parity* (PPP), that is 90 % of that of France and well above of Italy, Mexico, Korea, Canada and Spain. In other words, Turkish per capita income which is only USD 9.961 is in fact USD 38.759 in PPP.

18. Türkiye's net *government debt* which stands at *30.5 % of Gross Domestic Product (GDP)*, far less than that of the EU's 87.9% and the US's 94.7%, gives room for further monetary easing measures. Despite all expenditures and trade deficits, Türkiye has maintained to keep the *budget and current account deficits, 5.9% and 5.6% in order*, thanks to increasing tax, tourism, international construction and logistics revenues. These figures point out that Türkiye's CDS rating is a pure contradiction to its real payment power.

19. Türkiye has a *strong industrial base, skilled, hardworking and inexpensive work force* (minimum wage which was around USD 320 in 2022 is announced as USD 450 but subject to a decrease in line with inflation), *financial institutions, infra and over structure of any kind. 82% of Turkish exports* which reached a total of USD *226.6 billion* in 2022 are industrial products. Moreover, 50.3% of it is destined for Europe (41.3% to the EU) and 7.5% to NAFTA countries. On the import side of the coin, USD *364.4 billion in imports* took Türkiye to the 20th main importer in the world.

Top 10 export destinations (as of 2022)

20. Germany (18.9 USD bn), USA (14.4 USD bn), UK (12.3 USD bn), Italy (11.2 USD bn), Iraq (10.5 USD bn), Spain (9.1 USD bn), France (8.9 USD bn), Russia (7.7 USD bn), Netherlands (7.4 USD bn), Israel (6.7 USD bn).

Top 10 import suppliers (as of November 2022)

21. Russia (54.3 USD bn), China (37.7 USD bn), not declared (31.3 USD bn), Germany (211.6 USD bn), USA (14.1 USD bn), Switzerland (12.9 USD bn), Italy (12.7 USD bn), India (10.1 USD bn), France (8.5 USD bn), Korea (8.3 USD bn).

§2. Legal Background of Türkiye

I. Political and Legal System

A. History of the Political and Legal System

1. The Ottoman Legal System *(Shari'a)*

22. The Republic of Türkiye was founded in 1923, following the abolition of the Ottoman Empire. Until the nineteenth Century, the legal order of the Ottoman Empire was primarily religious law based on Islam. It was called *Shari'a*, the holy law of Islam.

23. *Shari'a* was a theocratic law aimed at the regulation of relationships between individuals as well as between individuals and State and State organizations. This part of *Shari'a* was called *fiqh*.

24. The principles of *Shari'a* were by their nature, absolute, mandatory, and unchangeable.

25. The Ottoman Sultans were not only the heads of the Empire but also caliphs (*halife*), Prophet Muhammad's successors as heads of Islam.[7]

7. For details *see* Özsunay, Ergun, Legal Science During The Last Century: Türkiye, *Inchieste Di Diritto Comparato*, 6, Legal Science During The Last Century, Padova, 1976, pp. 695–728; Özsunay, Ergun, Some Remarks on the Amendments Proposed by the Preliminary Draft of the Turkish Civil Code, '*Liber Memorialis* François Laurent 1810–1887', (Editors: J. Erauw/B. Bouckkaert/H. Bocken/H. Gaus/M. Storme), E. Story-Scientia, Bruxelles, 1989, pp. 605–641; Özsunay, Ergun, Religious Fundamentalism: Turkish Experience, Universidade da Coruna, *Nacionalismo en Europa – Nacionalismo en Galicia, La religion como elemento impulsar de la ideologia nacionalista, Simposo internacional celebrado en: Pazo de Marinan a Coruna*, 4–6 Septiembre 1997, NINO Centro de Impresion Digital, 1997, pp. 116–128; Özsunay, Ergun, Legal Culture and Legal Transplants-Turkish National Report, (Editor: Jorge A. Sanchez Cordero), Legal Culture and Legal Transplants / *La culture juridique et l'acculturation du droit*, Vol. II, Mexico, 2012, pp. 1035–1050.

2. The Ottoman Reform Period *(Tanzimat)*

26. The first movement of secularization in the Ottoman Empire began after 1839 (Promulgation of the Decree on '*Tanzimat*' [Reforms]).[8]

27. During the '*Tanzimat* Period' several west European codes, particularly French laws were adopted to modernize and secularize the legal system in the Ottoman Empire.

28. On the other hand, in the nineteenth century, some codifications of religious and national character were achieved. The Ottoman '*Mejelle*' (*Mecelle*) was the first important codification in the world of Islam covering several fields of private law (law of obligations and property, but not family and inheritance law).

29. Another important enactment was the 'Family Law Decree' of 1917 which dealt with relationships in the field of family law.

3. Promulgation of the Republic and Secularization Movement

30. A turning point in Turkish history was 29 October 1923. On this date, Türkiye became a Republic.

31. After the promulgation of the Republic in Türkiye, the process of secularization was carried out by the founders of the Republic with determination:

> First, the caliphate was abolished by the Act on Abrogation of Caliphate, No. 431 of 3 March 1924 (*Hilafetin Ilgasina ve Hanedani Osmaninin Türkiye Cumhuriyeti Memaliki Haricine Çikarilmasina Dair Kanun*). At the same time, religious education was also abolished by the Act on Unification of Education, No. 430 of 3 March 1924 (*Tevhidi Tedrisat Kanunu*).

32. It was followed by Act No. 677 of 30 November 1925 abolishing dervish lodges and cells and prohibiting the use of some titles related to sects (*Tekke ve Zaviyelerle Türbelerin Seddine ve Türbedarliklar ile Bir Takim Unvanlarin Men ve Ilgasina Dair Kanun*).

33. In the Constitution of 20 April 1924, it was stated that the religion of the Turkish State was Islam (Article 2). This provision was abolished by Act No. 1222 of 10 April 1928. In 1937, the principle of secularism was inserted into the Constitution by Act No. 3115.

8. For details *see* Berkes, Niyazi, *Teokrasi ve Laiklik* (Theocracy and Secularism), Istanbul, 1984, pp. 29 et seq.; Bulut, Faik, *Ordu ve Din* (Military and Religion), Istanbul, 1995, pp. 21 et seq.

4. Westernization of the Legal System Through Global Adoptions of Foreign Law

34. In 1926, the Swiss Civil Code (*ZGB*) and Code of Obligations (*OR*) were adopted with only some slight amendments and alterations.

35. Thus, important steps were taken especially in family and inheritance laws (equality between man and woman, rights to divorce and parental authority to women, etc.).

36. Adoption of the Swiss Civil Code and Code of Obligations was followed by the adoptions of other foreign laws in several fields: Turkish Code of Civil Procedure from Swiss Canton Neuchatel [later several amendments]; Turkish Enforcement and Bankruptcy Law from Switzerland [later several amendments]; Turkish Penal Code from Italy [later several amendments]. Türkiye departed definitely from the Islamic law sphere and joined the western (continental west European) legal system. Thus, Islamic law became a part of its '*droit ancien*'.[9]

37. In Türkiye, the Civil Code (*MK*) of 1926 was replaced by the new Turkish Civil Code (TCC = *TMK*), No. 4721 of 22 November 2001 (Official Gazette, No. 24607 of 8 December 2001). Likewise, the first Code of Obligations of 1926 (*BK*) was replaced by the new Turkish Code of Obligations (TCO = *TBK*), No. 6098 of 11 January 2011 (Official Gazette, No. 27836 of 4 February 2011). Both Codes have been revised in light of the recent Swiss legislation. Moreover, some EU legislation and international conventions have been considered in the revision works.

5. Türkiye – European Union (EU) Relations

38. Relations between Türkiye and the European Union (EU) take place within the framework of the Association Agreement, referred to as the Ankara Agreement signed on 12 September 1963 and effective 1 January 1973.[10]

39. The Ankara Agreement provided the possibility of Türkiye's eventual membership in the EU. A preparatory stage, during which the Community gave support to Türkiye to strengthen its economy was followed by a transitional stage, aimed at preparing both Türkiye and the Community (EU) for an eventual customs union.

40. The transitional stage was followed by the *Additional Protocol* signed on 23 November 1970.

9. For details *see* Özsunay, Ergun, *supra* n. 2, at pp. 699 et seq.; Özsunay, Ergun, *Karsilastirmali Hukuka Giris* (Introduction to Comparative Law), Istanbul, 1976, pp. 270 et seq. Further *see* Lipstein, K, The Reception of Western Law in Turkey, in *Annales de la Faculté de Droit d'Istanbul*, 1956, No. 6, pp. 11–27.
10. For details on Türkiye-EU relations *see* Özsunay, Ergun, *Avrupa Birligi Hukuku ve Türkiye-AB Iliskileri* (EU Law and Türkiye-UE Relations), Istanbul, 2015, pp. 385–425 and 451–455.

41. Türkiye applied for full membership to the Community (EU) on 14 April 1987. Türkiye and the EU signed an Agreement on 6 March 1995 in Brussels (decision of EC-Türkiye Association Council) for the customs union between Türkiye and the EU. It came into force on 1 January 1996. This agreement stipulated the removal of all customs duties, tariffs, quotas or any restrictions having an equivalent effect; measures to enhance political and economic cooperation and harmonization of Turkish law with the EU law in several fields.[11]

42. Türkiye attached particular importance to the European Union's Enlargement Process. Despite the satisfactory functioning of the Customs Union, the Commission excluded Türkiye from the enlargement process in its Report 'Agenda 2000'. In the Luxembourg Summit, Türkiye's eligibility for membership was confirmed but the development of Türkiye-EU relations was made conditional on certain economic, political and foreign policy questions.

43. The recognition of Türkiye as a candidate for accession at the Helsinki European Council in December 1999 ushered in a new area in the relations between Türkiye and the EU. For both parties, Helsinki marks a qualitatively new beginning and a process of strategic mutual transformation. Following the Helsinki Summit, the EU Commission started to prepare an Accession Partnership for Türkiye. The EU Council confirmed in 2004 that Türkiye fulfils the Copenhagen political criteria for opening the accession negotiations with Türkiye.

44. Accession negotiations have been launched on 3 October 2005 with the adoption of the 'Negotiation Framework Document' that consists of tree fundamental elements on which negotiations will carry out: (i) fulfilling the Copenhagen political criteria with no exceptions and assimilating and speeding up the political reforms; (ii) undertaking and applying the EU *acquis*; (iii) establishing and strengthening the dialogue with civil society and in this regard undertake a communication strategy aimed at both the European and the Turkish public.

45. The EU *acquis* has been categorized under thirty-five chapters as follows: free movement of goods, free movement of workers, right of establishment and freedom to provide services, free movement of capital, public procurement, company law, intellectual property law, competition policy, information society, energy, taxation, social policy and monetary policy, etc. Several Chapters have been negotiated but there are still rather important Chapters to be opened and negotiated. The Screening Reports approved at the Council of the EU with benchmarks show the situation of negotiations between Türkiye and the EU on several Chapters.

46. Türkiye has issued a *'National Program'* regarding the adoption of '*acquis communautaire*'. The first Decree of the Council of Ministers was the Decree dated 19 March 2001 on *'Türkiye's National Program for the Adoption of the Acquis of the EU'* and *'Decree concerning the Implementation, Coordination and Following-up of the Türkiye's National Program on the Adoption of the Acquis of the EU'* (Official

11. *See* Art. 37: approximation of laws.

Gazette, No. 24352 *Mük.* of 24 March 2001). The second Decree of the Council of Ministers was the Decree dated 23 June 2003 (No. 2003/5930) on *'Türkiye's National Programme for the Adoption of the Acquis of the EU'* and *'Decree concerning the Implementation, Coordination and Following-up of the Türkiye's National Programme on the Adoption of the Acquis of the EU'* (Official Gazette, No. 25178 *Mük.* of 24 July 2003). The Third Decree of the Council of Ministers of 31 December 2008 (No. 2008/14481) on *'Türkiye's National Program'* was promulgated on 31 December 2008 (Official Gazette, No. 27097 of 31 December 2008).

47. There are four *'Accession Partnership Documents'* (2001, 2003, 2006 and 2008) under which negotiations have been carried out. Further from 1998 until 2013 *'Regular Progress Reports'* have been prepared and announced. Regarding the situation of negotiations between the EU and Türkiye the *'European Parliament Resolutions'* of 10 February 2010, 9 March 2011, 29 March 2012 and 12 March 2014 on the Progress Reports indicate the situation of the developments of the EU-Türkiye relations.

48. To carry out its undertaking, Türkiye has been continuing to adopt EU legislation in several fields of law and endeavours to adopt the EU *acquis*. New laws or decrees having the power of law in several important fields have been drafted in the light and under the influence of the EU legislation.[12]

49. It was during the *migration crisis* that the EU decremented its political gap with the Turkish Republic. This forward step was committed whilst negotiations on the *'Agreement between Turkish Republic and European Union on Readmission of Persons Residing without Authorization'* so that probability for mobility without visa perquisite was about to arise.

50. In 2016, a peculiar *coup d'etat* attempt with terrorist methods aiming at the destruction of Turkish democracy luckily failed. A clear condemnation of these illegal events from the EU seemed to arrive later than it was expected in Türkiye, causing disappointment. Political discussions in Türkiye for a reinstatement of the abolished death penalty–which soon faded away–also damaged the political relations with the EU.

51. In November 2016, a resolution by the European Parliament voted in favour of a non-binding resolution to request that the European Commission temporarily suspend membership negotiations due to the 'disproportionate repressive measures' of the government regarding various persons who have allegedly all been involved in the events leading to the failed 2016 coup.

12. For example, *see* Act on Protection of Competition *(Rekabetin Korunmasi Hakkkinda Kanun)*, No. 4054 and the secondary legislation for the implementation of this law. Further *see* the abolished governmental decrees having the power of law on protection of industrial designs (*KHK*/554), geographical indications (*KHK*/555), trademarks (*KHK*/556), patents (*KHK*/551). At present all these governmental decrees were replaced by Industrial Property Law (*Sinai Mülkiyet Kanunu*), No. 6769 of 22 Dec. 2016 (Official Gazette, No. 29944 of 10 Jan. 2017). As regards copyright *see* Acts No. 4110 of 7 Jun. 1995 and No. 4630 of 21 Feb. 2001.

52. On 13 December 2016, the European Council resolved that it would not open any new areas in Türkiye's membership talks in the 'prevailing circumstances'.

53. In 2017, EU officials expressed that planned Turkish policies violate the Copenhagen criteria of eligibility for an EU membership, but especially in April of that year the Parliamentary Assembly of the Council of Europe voted to reopen its monitoring procedure against Türkiye.

54. On 26 June 2018, the EU's General Affairs Council stated that 'the Council notes that Türkiye has been moving further away from the European Union. Türkiye's accession negotiations have therefore effectively come to a standstill and no further chapters can be considered for opening or closing and no further work towards the modernization of the EU-Türkiye Customs Union is foreseen.' The Council added that it is 'especially concerned about the continuing and deeply worrying backsliding on the rule of law and on fundamental rights including the freedom of expression'. The bottom-line view as of 2022 read: 'Overall, in many areas, significant further work is needed on legislative alignment with the EU acquis. In all areas, implementation and enforcement needs substantial improvement. Ensuring the independence of regulatory authorities and developing administrative capacity are key for Türkiye to achieve further progress.'[13]

B. Current Political and Legal System under the Constitution

55. Under the 1982 Turkish Constitution (*Anayasa*),[14] the Turkish State is a republic (Article 1). The Republic of Türkiye is a democratic, secular (*laik*, Turkish adaptation of French *laïcité*, i.e., without a state religion) and social State governed by the rule of law; bearing in mind the concept of public peace, national solidarity, and justice; respecting human rights; loyal to 'nationalism of [the Republic's founding-father] Atatürk' and based on the fundamental tenets set forth in the Preamble (Constitution, Article 2).

56. According to the Constitution, the provision establishing the State as a republic (Article 1) and the provision on the characteristics of the Republic (democratic, secular, and social state) (Article 2) may not be amended. Even their amendment may not be proposed (Article 4).

57. One of the basic characteristics of the Republic of Türkiye is secularism defined in the Preamble of the Constitution as no interference whatsoever of 'sacred religious feelings' in state affairs and politics. The principle of secularism is one of the pillars of modern Türkiye. Nevertheless, Türkiye has a peculiar system of providing religious services to her Sunni Muslim citizens as a public service, financed

13. 'Key findings of the 2022 Report on Türkiye', https://ec.europa.eu/commission/presscorner/detail/en/country_22_6088.
14. Official Gazette, No. 2709 of 9 Nov. 1982, amended many times, last in 2017.

also from the general budget. The Presidency of Religious Affairs (*Diyanet Isleri Baskanligi*), which is within the general administration, exercises its duties prescribed in its particular law in accordance with the principles of secularism removed from all political views and ideas and aims at national solidarity and integrity. (Constitution, Article 136). Accordingly, Sunni Muslim imams are civil servants, employed and paid by the state as other civil servants.

58. Like other contemporary constitutions, the Turkish Constitution also guarantees several basic freedoms, categorized in the Constitution as 'rights and duties' in three groups: (a). 'individual', (b). 'social and economic', and (c) 'political' (Articles 12–74). Under the Constitution, everyone has, *inter alia*, the right to freedom of conscience, religious belief and conviction, thought and opinion as well as the expression and dissemination of thought (Articles 24–26). (Cf. Articles 9 and 10 of the European Convention for the Protection of Human Rights and Fundamental Freedoms [European Convention of Human Rights] of 4 November 1950).[15]

59. Turkish democracy is based on the principle of the separation of powers: the legislative, the executive and the judicial powers.

The Legislative

60. The Grand National Assembly of Türkiye (*Türkiye Büyük Millet Meclisi = TBMM*) shall be composed of six hundred deputies elected by universal suffrage (Constitution, Article 75). Elections for *TBMM* and presidential elections shall be held every five years and on the same day (Article 77). Members of *TBMM* shall not represent their own constituencies or constituents, but the nation as a whole (Article 80). The duties and powers of *TBMM* are to enact, amend, and repeal laws; to debate and adopt the budget bills and final accounts bills; to decide to issue currency and declare war; to approve the ratification of international treaties, to decide with the majority of three-fifths of *TBMM* to proclaim amnesty and pardon; and to exercise the powers and carry out the duties envisaged in the other articles of the Constitution (Article 87).

61. The President of the Republic shall promulgate the laws adopted by *TBMM* within fifteen days. He/she shall send the laws that he/she deems, in whole or in part, unsuitable for promulgation, along with the justification, back to *TBMM* for reconsideration in the same period. In case of being partially deemed unsuitable by him/her, *TBMM* may discuss only those articles. Budget laws shall not be subject to

15. The Turkish Constitution of 1982 has been translated into English by the Prime Ministry Directorate General of Press and Information as 'The Constitution of the Republic of Türkiye, 1982', Ankara, 1982. Its German translation has been made by Prof Dr E. Hirsch. *See 'Die Verfassung der Türkischen Republik vom 9. November 1982', Jahrbuch des Öffentlichen Rechts der Gegenwart, Neue Folge, Band 32*, Tübingen, 1983. For details on Turkish constitutional law *see* Teziç, Erdogan, *Anayasa Hukuku, 2. Basi* (Constitutional Law, 2nd ed.), Istanbul, 1991; Özbudun, Ergun, *Türk Anayasa Hukuku, 2. Basi* (Turkish Constitutional Law, 2nd ed.), Ankara, 1992, Biçak, Vahit / Arslan, Zühtü, International Encyclopaedia of Laws, Constitutional Law (Türkiye), The Hague, London, New York, 2004.

this provision. If *TBMM* adopts the law sent back for reconsideration without any amendment with an absolute majority, the law shall be promulgated by the President of the Republic; if the Assembly makes a new amendment to the law, he/she may send the amended law back for reconsideration. Provisions relating to constitutional amendments are reserved. (Constitution, Article 89)

62. In conformity with the conditions set forth in the law, citizens have the right to vote, to be elected, to engage in political activities independently or in a political party, and to take part in a referendum (Constitution, Article 67). Citizens have the right to form political parties and duly join and withdraw from them. One must be over eighteen years of age to become a member of a party. Political parties are indispensable elements of democratic political life. Political parties shall be formed without prior permission and shall pursue their activities in accordance with the provisions set forth in the Constitution and laws. The statutes and programmes, as well as the activities of political parties, shall not be contrary to the independence of the State, its indivisible integrity with its territory and nation, human rights, the principles of equality and rule of law, the sovereignty of the nation, the principles of the democratic and secular republic; they shall not aim to promote or establish class or group dictatorship or dictatorship of any kind, nor shall they incite citizens to crime (Constitution, Article 68). The activities, internal regulations and operation of political parties shall be in line with democratic principles. Political parties shall not engage in commercial activities. The dissolution of political parties shall be decided finally by the Constitutional Court after the filing of a suit by the Office of the Chief Public Prosecutor of the High Court of Appeals. The permanent dissolution of a political party shall be decided when it is established that the statute and programme of the political party violate the provisions of Constitution Article 68. A party which has been dissolved permanently shall not be founded under another name. Political parties that accept aid from foreign states, international institutions and persons and corporate bodies of non-Turkish nationality shall be dissolved permanently (Constitution, Article 69).

63. As of early 2023, the main political parties in Türkiye are as follows: *Adalet ve Kalkinma Partisi* (*AKP*, Justice and Development Party, having the majority in the Parliament and governing the country), *Cumhuriyet Halk Partisi* (*CHP,* Republican People's Party), *Milliyetçi Hareket Partisi* (*MHP,* Nationalist Movement Party), Iyi (Good) Party and *Halklarin Esitlik ve Demokrasi Partisi* (HEDEP, Peoples' Equality and Democracy Party), BBP (Great Unity Party), Saadet (Felicity) Party and Vatan (Patriotic) Party, There are also a small number of independent (*bagimsiz)* members of the Parliament.

The Executive

64. Since April 2017, Türkiye is no longer a 'parliamentary' democracy. The Office of the Prime Ministry (*Basbakanlik*) has been abolished and there is no Government (*Hükümet*) which needs to obtain a vote of confidence (*güven oyu*) from the parliament, i.e., *TBMM*. In a referendum, the Turkish voters approved a constitutional transition from a parliamentary system to a *quasi-presidential system*, by

51.4% to 48.6%. Unlike the previous system with a 'Counsel of Ministers (*Bakanlar Kurulu*)' in the Executive Power (*Yürütme*), under Article 101 of the Constitution (as amended on 16 April 2017; Act No. 6771), the Executive Power is now exercised by 'one' real (physical) person: 'President of the Republic' (*Cumhurbaskani*). Unlike the former 'Counsel of Ministers', the one-person Executive branch, i.e., the President is now elected personally and directly by the public for five years, from among Turkish citizens over forty years of age who are eligible to be a deputy and have completed higher education. He/she may be elected for two terms at most. On 9 July 2018, the first president of the 'presidential' Turkish Republic took this new Office, understandably without the existence of a prime minister. The next general elections are to be held in 2023 which marks the hundredth Anniversary of the Turkish Republic.

65. Duties and powers of the President are defined under Article 104 of the Constitution (as amended by Act No. 6771 of 16 April 2017): The President of the Republic is the head of the State. The executive power shall be vested in him/her. In his/her capacity as the Head of State, he/she shall represent the Republic of Türkiye and the unity of the Turkish Nation; he/she shall ensure the implementation of the Constitution and orderly and harmonious functioning of the organs of the State.

66. The President of the Republic (Cumhurbaskani) shall *inter alia*, promulgate laws; send laws back to the Grand National Assembly of Türkiye (TBMM) to be reconsidered; appeal to the Constitutional Court for the annulment of all or certain provisions of laws and the Rules of Procedure of the Grand National Assembly of Türkiye on the grounds that they are unconstitutional in form or in content; appoint and dismiss the deputies of the President of the Republic and the ministers; appoint and dismiss the high ranking executives; ratify and promulgate international treaties; submit laws regarding amendment to the Constitution to referendum, if he/she deems it necessary. Furthermore, the President may– with exceptions– issue presidential decrees (*Cumhurbaskanligi kararnamesi = CBK*) on the matters regarding executive power (*yürütme yetkisi*); issue regulations (*yönetmelik*) in order to ensure the implementation of laws, provided that they are not contrary thereto. Finally, the President perform various other duties conferred on him/her by the Constitution (Article 104) and laws.

The Judiciary

67. Judicial power shall be exercised by independent and impartial courts on behalf of the Turkish Nation (Constitution, Article 9).

Council of Judges and Prosecutors (Hakimler ve Savcilar Kurulu, HSK)

68. Council of Judges and Prosecutors (Constitution, Article 159) is established and exercises its functions in accordance with the principles of the independence of the courts and the security of the tenure of judges. The Council is composed of thirteen members; and comprises two chambers. The President of this Council is the Minister of Justice and the Undersecretary to the Ministry of Justice is an ex officio member.

69. A total of four Council members are elected by the President of the Republic among highly qualified civil and administrative judges and public prosecutors. The other Council members are elected by the Grand National Assembly of Türkiye (*TBMM*) among the candidates of the High Court of Appeals; the Council of State, also among teaching staff working in the field of law at higher education institutions and lawyers. The applications for membership of the Council to be elected by the Grand National Assembly of Türkiye are made to the Office of the Speaker of the Assembly. The Council takes final decisions on proposals of the Ministry of Justice concerning the abolition of a court, or changes in the territorial jurisdiction of a court; it also exercises the other functions given to it by the Constitution and laws. The Council's authority includes supervising whether the judges and public prosecutors perform their duties in accordance with relevant laws; investigating whether they have committed offences in connection with, or in the course of their duties, and whether their behaviour and conduct are in conformity with the requirement of their status and duties. The decisions of the Council, other than dismissal from the profession, shall not be subject to judicial review. (Constitution, Article 159).

70. 'Judges shall be independent in the discharge of their duties; they shall give judgment in accordance with the Constitution, laws, and their personal conviction conforming to the law.' 'Legislative and executive organs and the administration shall comply with court decisions; these organs and the administration shall neither alter them in any respect, nor delay their execution.' (Constitution, Article 138). 'Judges and public prosecutors shall not be dismissed, or unless they request, shall not be retired before the age prescribed by the Constitution; nor shall they be deprived of their salaries, allowances or other rights relating to their status, even as a result of the abolition of a court or a post.' (Constitution, Article 139).

High Courts

The Constitutional Court (Anayasa Mahkemesi)

71. The Constitutional Court examines the constitutionality, in respect of both form and substance, of laws, presidential decrees and the Rules of Procedure of TBMM, and decides on individual applications. Constitutional amendments are examined and verified only with regard to their form. However, presidential decrees issued during a state of emergency or in time of war shall not be brought before the Constitutional Court alleging their unconstitutionality as to form or substance (Constitution, Article 148).

72. The Constitutional Court is composed of fifteen members.

73. The Constitution requires that each of the institutions below nominate three candidates for each Constitutional Court member.

74. A total of three members among the candidates of the Court of Accounts and Presidents of the Bars are elected by the Grand National Assembly of Türkiye (*TBMM*) as the Legislative branch.

75. A total of eight members among the candidates of the High Court of Appeals, Counsel of State and Council of Higher Education are appointed by the President who is the one-person Executive branch and may– if so elected– at the same time happen to be the President of his/her political party.

76. A total of four members from among high-level executives, self-employed lawyers, first-category judges and public prosecutors or rapporteurs of the Constitutional Court having served as rapporteur for at least five years are elected also by the President who is the one-person Executive branch and may– if so elected– at the same time happen to be the President of his/her political party.

Administrative Court System: Judicial Review of the Actions and Acts of the Administration

77. The administration is liable to compensate for damages resulting from its actions and acts. Türkiye has a specialized three-instance administrative court system (*idari yargi*) with its own rules of procedure. As the highest court within that specialized system, the Council of State (*Danistay*) monitors, *inter alia*, the outcome of administrative law disputes. Recourse to judicial review is available against all actions and acts of administration including taxation. In concession, conditions and contracts concerning public services and national or international arbitration may be suggested to settle the disputes arising from them. Only those disputes involving an element of foreignness may be submitted to international arbitration (*tahkim*).

78. Judicial power of administrative courts is limited to the review of the legality of administrative actions and acts, and in no case may it be used as a review of expediency. No judicial ruling shall be passed which restricts the exercise of the executive function in accordance with the forms and principles prescribed by law, which has the quality of administrative action and act, or which removes discretionary powers.

79. A justified decision of an administrative court regarding the suspension of execution of an administrative act may be issued, should its implementation result in damages which are difficult or impossible to compensate for and, at the same time, the act would be clearly unlawful (Constitution, Article 125).

80. As for the three-instance civil law and criminal law court system, the Constitution naturally lists among the high courts also the High Court of Appeals (*Yargitay*) which consists of specialized chambers for matters of civil law and criminal law disputes.

81. The Court of Jurisdictional Disputes (*Uyusmazlik Mahkemesi*) is empowered to deliver final judgments in disputes between civil and administrative courts concerning their jurisdiction and judgments (Constitution, Article 158).

82. Finally, the Court of Accounts (*Sayistay*) is a specialized quasi-court and examines budgetary issues in the name of the Grand National Assembly of Türkiye (Constitution, Article 160).

C. Legal Family or Tradition Regarding Especially Private Law

83. As summarized above, the Republic of Türkiye is a civil law country which belongs to the Romano-Germanic legal system. Enacted law is the main source of law.

84. The most important current legal sources in Turkish private law are the Turkish Civil Code *(Türk Medeni Kanunu)*, No. 4721 of 22 November 2001; Turkish Code of Obligations *(Türk Borçlar Kanunu)*, No. 6098 of 11 January 2001; Turkish Commercial Code *(Türk Ticaret Kanunu)*, No. 6102 of 13 January 2011; Law on Consumer Protection *(Tüketicinin Korunmasi Hakkinda Kanun)*, No. 6502 of 7 November 2013; Law on Product Safety and Technical Regulations *(Ürün Güvenligi ve Teknik Düzenlemeler Kanunu)*, No. 7223 of 5 March 2020; Act on Protection of Competition *(Rekabetin Korunmasi Hakkinda Kanun)*, No. 4054 of 7 December 1994 (as amended); Law on Intellectual and Artistic Works *(Fikir ve Sanat Eserleri Kanunu)*, No. 5846 of 5 December 1951 (as amended); Industrial Property Law (*Sinai Mülkiyet Kanunu*), No. 6769 of 12 December 2016.[16]

85. Turkish civil procedure is regulated by the Code of Civil Procedure *(Hukuk Muhakemeleri Kanunu)*, No. 6100 of 12 January 2011.[17] This Code has been enacted in light of recent developments in the field of civil procedure.[18]

86. Issues related to the enforcement of court decisions and to bankruptcy are regulated by the Code of Enforcement and Bankruptcy, No. 2004 (CEB, *Icra ve Iflas Kanunu; IIK*).[19] This Code was modelled upon Swiss Federal Code of Enforcement and Bankruptcy (*BG betreffend Schuldbetreibung and Konkurs, SchKG*). IIK has been amended several times with the aim of serving the changing economic needs of the country.

---

16. TCC and TCO are modelled upon Swiss Civil Code and Code of Obligations. TComC has been drafted partly under the influence of Swiss Code of Obligations, and partly in the light of EU legislation.
17. Official Gazette, No. 27836 of 4 Feb. 2011.
18. The former Code of Civil Procedure, No.1086 of 18 Jun. 1927 *(Hukuk Muhakemeleri Kanunu)* was modelled upon the Swiss Canton Neuchatel's Code of Civil Procedure.
19. Official Gazette, No. 2128 of 19 Jun. 1932; as amended various times, last amended by Law No. 7343, Official Gazette of 30 Nov. 2021.

87. As regards the issues related to private international law, Act on Private International Law and Procedural Law, No. 5718 *(*APIL, *Milleterarasi Özel Hukuk ve Usul Hukuku Hakkinda Kanun; MÖHUK)* and Law on International Arbitration No. 4686 *(Milletlerarasi Tahkim Kanunu)* were enacted. These laws, along with related international treaties to which Türkiye is a party, regulate the issues of private international law, conflict of jurisdictions, recognition and enforcement of foreign courts and foreign arbitral awards, and international arbitration.

88. As for primary sources of criminal law and criminal procedure, the Turkish Penal Code (TPC - *Türk Ceza Kanunu* - *TCK*), No. 5237 of 26 September 2004 (as amended) and Criminal Procedure Code, (CCrimP – *Ceza Muhakemesi Kanunu* - *CMK*), No. 5271 of 4 December 2004 (as amended) respectively are to be mentioned before any other relevant Law.

II. Relation and Hierarchy Between the Sources of Law

89. The Turkish Constitution (*Anayasa*), No. 2709 of 18 October 1982 has priority in the hierarchy among the sources of law.[20] Under Turkish law, constitutional provisions prevail over all codes and laws (statutes). According to the Turkish Constitution, laws cannot conflict with the Constitution (Article 11).

90. International treaties to which the Republic of Türkiye is a party should be ratified by the Turkish Grand National Assembly by the enactment of law. They become enforceable after their publication in the Official Gazette as with the other laws. Nevertheless, some international treaties enter into force without the approval of parliament. These are 'the treaties which regulate economic, commercial, and technical relations and which are not effective for a period longer than one year'. They may be put into effect through promulgation in the Official Gazette provided that they do not entail a financial commitment of the state and provided that they do not infringe upon the status of individuals or upon the right of ownership of Turkish citizens in foreign countries. Nevertheless, such treaties are to be brought to the attention of the Parliament within two months following their promulgation.

91. International treaties ratified by the enactment of law have the same effects as other laws. Nevertheless, where a contradiction arises between a provision of an

20. Official Gazette, No. 17863 Mük. of 9 Nov. 1982. Turkish Constitution has been amended by several laws. The most important last amendment has been made by Law on Amendment in the Constitution of the Republic of Türkiye, No. 6771 of 21 Jan. 2017 (Official Gazette, No. 29976 of 11 Feb. 2017). The amendment was approved by the Referendum held on 16 Apr. 2017. Articles 101 et seq. of the amended Constitution regulates the *'Executive Power.'* By this amendment Türkiye has adopted a sui generis presidential regime. Law, No. 6771 has amended the following Articles of the Constitution: 8, 9, 15, 17, 19, 73, 75, 76, 77, 78, 82, 87, 88, 89, 91, 93. For details of the new constitutional regime in Türkiye *see* TBB (Union of Turkish Bar Associations), Law, No. 6771 relating to amendments in the Constitution of the Republic of Türkiye (6771 sayili T.C. Anayasasinda Degisiklik Yapilmasina Dair Kanun Hakkinda Mukayeseli Açiklamalar), www.tbb.gov.tr. Regarding qualifications, duties and powers of the President, *see* Arts 100 et seq.

existing statute and the statute ratifying an international treaty the judge should solve the conflict in accordance with the general principles of law. Thus, the subsequently enacted law shall prevail over the earlier one (*lex posterior derogate legi prior*) and a particular rule shall prevail over the general rule (*lex specialis derogate legi generali*).

92. As regards the treaties related to fundamental rights and freedoms of the individuals in cases of conflict between international law and domestic law, the provisions of international treaties shall prevail (Constitution, Article 90 as amended on 7 May 2004).[21]

93. Laws have the characteristics of generality and abstractness and are applied until they are repealed by a subsequent law. Nevertheless, some laws are enacted only for a certain period (e.g., law related to yearly budget) or for some exceptional events (catastrophes like earthquakes and floodings).

94. Since the recently introduced presidential system, another source of law in Turkish law is the 'presidential decree' (*Cumhurbaskanligi Kararnamesi = CBK*). The President of the Republic (Cumhurbaskani) may, if he/she deems it necessary, issue presidential decrees (*CBK*) on the matters regarding executive power (*yürütme yetkisi*). However, there are exceptions to the scope of presidential decrees. No presidential decree may regulate the following: fundamental rights, individual rights and duties and political rights and duties; the matters which are stipulated in the Constitution to be regulated exclusively by law (*kanun*); the matters explicitly regulated by law *(kanun)*. In the case of a discrepancy between the provisions of the presidential decrees (*CBK*) and the laws (*kanun*), the provisions of the laws shall prevail. A presidential decree shall become null and void if the Grand National Assembly of Türkiye (*TBMM*) enacts a law on the same matter. As with laws, the presidential decrees may judicially be examined by the Constitutional Court regarding their 'constitutionality' as to form or substance except during a state of emergency or in time of war (Constitution, Article 148).

95. A presidential decree (Constitution, Article 104) may historically be compared to a 'decree having the power of law' (*kanun hükmünde kararname = KHK*), i.e., the decree-laws prior to the introduction of the presidential system. These had been made possible by a 1971 amendment to the previous 1961 Constitution: The Turkish Grand National Assembly could previously authorize the Council of Ministers (*Bakanlar Kurulu*), by a special statute, to issue such decrees having the power of law. In the special statute, the principles, scope, and duration of decree-laws were stated. Unlike the current presidential decrees, the former decree-laws had to be submitted to the review and approval of *TBMM* on the day of their publication in the Official Gazette (Constitution, Article 91, abolished).

96. The legal terms in English 'by-law' or 'regulation' refer to the same type of rules in Turkish law (*yönetmelik*): These can be issued by the President of the Republic, the ministries, and public corporate bodies to ensure the implementation

21. For details *see* Ansay/Wallace (Eds.), Introduction to Turkish Law, pp. 6–7.

of laws and presidential decrees relating to their jurisdiction, provided that they are not contrary to these laws and decrees. In this monography, we prefer to use the commonly used term 'regulation' which may also have been referred to as 'by-law' in some other legal translations from Turkish to English. The regulations (by-laws) which should also be published in the Official Gazette shall be designated by law. Annulment of a regulation (by-law) can be requested from the Council of State (*Danistay*) (Law on the Council of State, No. 2575, Article 24).

97. Other than the above-mentioned regulations (by-laws, *yönetmelikler*), previous versions of Turkish constitutions had accepted a similar type of rules known as *'tüzük', or 'nizamname'* as one of the sources of law. As the above-mentioned regulations (by-laws), these specific regulations (*tüzük, nizamname*) were also dependent upon a law (statute) but could not contain provisions contrary to the law on which they were dependent. They contained implementation details of particular laws and were issued by the Council of Ministers. This particular source of law has been abolished by a constitutional amendment on 21 January 2017; however such regulations (*tüzük, nizamname*) issued earlier continue to remain in force. In this monography, we prefer to translate the original Turkish terms '*yönetmelik*' as well as the relatively older terms '*tüzük*' / '*nizamname*' into English simply as 'regulation'.

§3. Background of the Turkish Intellectual Property Law

I. National Legal Sources

A. Legal Terminology

98. In Turkish intellectual property law, two terms have been used for a long time to define different kinds of intellectual works: 'intellectual rights' (*fikri haklar*) for the author's rights such as copyright, moral rights, financial rights and neighbouring rights (*komsu haklar*) on works of intellectual and artistic rights, and 'industrial property' (*sinai mülkiyet*) for rights on inventions (patents), utility models, industrial designs, geographical designations, trademarks.

99. The current doctrine prefers to use a general term, namely 'intellectual property' (*fikri mülkiyet*) to express all kinds of intellectual and industrial rights. The term 'intellectual property' is used to bring together not only the above-mentioned intellectual rights and industrial property, but also computer programs, databases, chips, and plant variety rights. This new tendency in the doctrine seems to be in harmony with the system accepted by the WIPO Treaty (section 6 No. 40) and the Trade-Related Aspects of Intellectual Property Rights (TRIPS) Agreement (section 6 No. 5).[22]

22. *See* Tekinalp, Ünal, *Fikri Mülkiyet Hukuku, Güncellestirilmis ve Genisletilmis 5. Basi* (Intellectual Property Law, Updated and Enlarged 5th ed.), Istanbul, 2012, pp. 1–5; Keyder, Virginia B., *Fikri Mülkiyet Haklari ve Gümrük Birligi* / Intellectual Property Rights and Customs Union, Istanbul, 1996.

100. Likewise, it is observed that the term 'intellectual, industrial and commercial property' has been used by the Council decision dated 6 March 1995 relating to a common position by the Community in the EC-Türkiye Association Council implementing the final phase of the Customs Union.[23]

101. The term 'intellectual law' (*fikri hukuk*) is used in the law school curricula in the narrow sense and usually covers the author's rights.

102. Within the broadest sense of the term 'intellectual property' (*fikri mülkiyet*) under the current doctrine, it is possible to distinguish 'the law on intellectual and artistic works' and the 'law on trade names, undertaking names (enterprise, business names, *isletme adi*) and geographical indications':

> The first category comprises usually the author's rights, patent and trademark rights as its subject matters are 'works of intelligence'.

103. As regards the second category, it is obvious that trade names, undertaking (enterprise, business) names and geographical indications are only distinctive signs. They are not 'works of intelligence'. They only distinguish the owner of an undertaking from another one or the goods and services of an undertaking from another one.

104. Moreover, it is also possible to distinguish some 'intellectual works' from others:

- Normally, pure rights on intellectual works do not need any registration for their protection while registration is required for the other kinds (e.g., patents, utility models, etc.).
- Likewise, 'moral rights' are peculiar only to intellectual and artistic works.
- Compulsory licensing is peculiar to patents in spite of some restrictions on 'intellectual and artistic works for the public interest.

B. Historical Background

105. Protection of intellectual property is not new to Türkiye. In the early days of the Republic of Türkiye (1923), one can find the governments' endeavours for the protection of intellectual property, e.g., the Republic's first government programme of 5 September 1923 relating to the 'development of arts and national creation'.

23. Compare The Decree of the Council of Ministers dated 13 Mar. 2001 on the 'Türkiye's National Program for Adoption of the *Acquis* of the EU' and 'Decree concerning the Implementation, Coordination and Following-up of the Türkiye's National Program on the Adoption of the *Acquis* of the EU' (Official Gazette, No. 24352 *Mük.* of 24 Mar. 2001).

106. Regarding the legislation related to recent Turkish intellectual property law, the two most important sources of law are *Fikir ve Sanat Eserleri Kanunu* (*FSEK*): Law on Intellectual and Artistic Works, No. 5846 of 5 December 1951 (as amended) and *Sinai Mülkiyet Kanunu (SMK)*: Industrial Property Law, No. 6769 of 22 December 2016. These two primary sources are abbreviated in this monography according to their original Turkish titles in italics.

107. Nevertheless, it should be noted that these laws should be examined in the light of the Turkish Constitution (No. 2709 of 7 November 1982) as amended by several recent laws which transformed the Republic of Türkiye from a parliamentary system to a Presidency regime in 2017. The amended provisions of the Constitution have an impact on the above-mentioned laws regulating the Turkish intellectual property regime. The first law is the *Law*, No. 6771 of 21 January 2017 regarding the harmonization of the amendments made in the Constitution. It was followed by another Law, No. 7142 of 10 May 2018 which granted the *Authorization to amend Various Laws and Decrees having the Power of Law for the purpose of harmonization with the amendments of the Turkish Constitution made by Law*, No. 6771. Regarding the adaptation of the provisions of the amended Constitution the *Decree having the Power of Law* (*KHK*/700), was issued on 2 July 2018 by the Council of Ministers. It deals with *Amendments in Some Laws and Decrees having the Power of Law for the purpose of providing Harmony with the Amendments in the Constitution made by the Law*, No. 7142.[24]

1. Copyright Law

108. The first endeavours to draft a specific Law for the protection of intellectual and artistic works can be found in the early 1940s (The 'Hirsch's Draft').

109. Following intensive drafting works, the first Law on Intellectual and Artistic Works (*Fikir ve Sanat Eserleri Kanunu – FSEK*) was finally enacted on 5 December 1951.[25]

110. Several amendments have been made to it since 1951, in 1983 by Act, No. 2936 of 1 November 1983, Act, No. 4110 of 7 June 1995 and Act, No. 4630 of 21 February 2001 as the result of new technical developments and international agreements relating to the protection of industrial property. These amendments were followed by other amendments relating to new issues and solutions in intellectual property law by Act, No. 5101 of 3 March 2004, Act, No. 5217 of 14 July 2004; Act, No. 5571 of 28 December 2006; Act, No. 5718 of 27 November 2007 and Act, No. 5728 of 23 January 2008.

24. For the impact of the amended Constitution upon Industrial Property Law, No. 6769 *see* Art. 209 of *KHK*/700.
25. *See* Official Gazette, No. 7931 of 13 Dec. 1951.

111. Thus, provisions protecting computer programs, databases and neighbouring rights were included in *FSEK*.[26]

112. Recently *a draft law* has been presented to the *Presidency of the Grand National Assembly* to amend *FSEK* in light of current developments in this area.

113. According to the *Turkey 2018 Report* by the European Commission (2018 Communication on EU Enlargement Policy), 'Türkiye has a good level of preparation in the intellectual property law area. In the coming year, Türkiye would adopt copyright legislation in line with the "acquis"; improve enforcement measures to combat industrial and intellectual property infringements and sustain a constructive dialogue with intellectual property right (IPR) owners, increase awareness regarding counterfeiting and piracy and focus on the benefits of a strong IPR protection system for economic growth. With regard to copyright and neighbouring rights, the draft copyright law remains to be adopted. Collective rights management remains an outstanding issue that the new copyright law would address, particularly in relation to foreign producers, public performance rights and reproduction rights.'[27]

114. We will not go into details here on the historical background and amendments of intellectual property rights as they are explained in the following chapters. Therefore, we refer to our explanations in the relevant chapter on Copyright Law.

2. Patent Law

115. The previous Turkish patent law was regulated by the Decree Having the Power of Law on the Protection of Patent Rights (*Patent Haklarinin Korunmasi Hakkinda Kanun Hükmünde Kararname*, *KHK*/551) of 27 June 1995.[28]

116. At present, this *KHK* was abolished and replaced by 'Industrial Property Law' (*Sinai Mülkiyet Kanunu: SMK*), No. 6769 of 22 December 2016[29]

117. The historical developments of the Turkish patent law can be found in Chapter 2.

---

26. For the Act, No. 2936: Official Gazette, No. 18210 of 3 Nov. 1983; Act, 4110: Official Gazette No. 22311 of 12 Jun. 1995, and Act, No. 4630: Official Gazette, No. 24335 of 3 Mar. 2001.
27. *See* European Commission, Turkey 2018 Report, Ch. 7 (5.7.), p. 69.
28. It should be noted that the following solutions were brought by *KHK*/551 to the Turkish patent law: (i) regulation of utility models; (ii) introduction of a patent system based on examination and non-examination; (iii) criteria for patentability (novelty, inventive step, susceptibility of industrial applicability); (iv) publication of applications; (v) opposition by third parties; (vi) protection terms (seven years for non-examined patents; ten years for utility models, and twenty years for patents granted upon examination); (vii) employee inventions; (viii) compulsory licensing which is compatible to the TRIPS Agreement; (ix) a system of satisfactory protection against infringements; (x) specialized court for patent infringements.
29. *See* Official Gazette, No. 29944 of 10 Jan. 2017. For patents and utility models *see* Arts 82–141; 142–145. Regarding the common provisions of all industrial property *see* Arts 146 et seq.

3. Trademark Law

118. Previously the Turkish trademark law was regulated by the Decree Having the Power of Law for Protection of Trademarks (*Markalarin Korunmasi Hakkinda Kanun Hükmünde Kararname, KHK*/556) of 24 June 1995.[30]

119. This *KHK* was subsequently abolished and is now replaced by 'Industrial Property Law' (*SMK*), No. 6769 of 22 December 2016 (for trademarks *see* Articles 4–32 and 146 et seq.).[31]

120. Further 'the Implementing Regulation of Industrial Property Law' (*SMK-Yön*) was promulgated.[32]

121. According to the *European Commission Turkey 2018 Report*: *SMK* ensures inter alia, greater alignment with the IPR 'acquis' in relation to trademarks and designs and updates the Turkish IPR system in line with international agreements and practices. Simplified registration procedures were introduced. The new law does not include specific provisions for biotechnological inventions. An *IPR Academy* was set up in 2017, which will be responsible for all IPR training for civil servants. Further in 2017, the 'Regulation on the Code of Conduct and Disciplinary Measures for Patent and Trademark Attorneys' *(Türk Patent ve Marka Kurumu Patent Vekilleri ve Marka Vekilleri Disiplin Yönetmeligi)* entered into force. On judicial enforcement, *SMK* aims to ensure a higher level of legal alignment with the EU Enforcement Directive.[33]

122. The historical background of the Turkish Trademark Law can be found in Chapter 3.

4. Trade Names

123. Trade names and business names are regulated by the provisions of the 'Turkish Commercial Code', No. 6102 *(*TComC – *Türk Ticaret Kanunu: TTK)* of 13 January 2011 (Articles 39 et seq.). We refer to Chapter 4 for details.

---

30. It should be noted that *KHK*/556 had introduced to the Turkish intellectual property law (i) protection of service marks; (ii) protection of guarantee and collective marks; (iii)absolute and relative grounds for refusal; (iv) exhaustion of rights conferred by the registered trademark; (v) publication of applications; (vi) opposition by third parties; (vii) strong and satisfactory remedies for infringements; (viii) specialized courts for intellectual property law matters.
31. *See* Official Gazette, No. 29944 of 10 Jan. 2017. This law entered into force on the date of its promulgation in the Official Gazette with exceptions relating to the provisions of its Art. 23(2); Art. 69(4), and Art. 26 (seven years later).
32. *See* Official Gazette, No. 30047 of 24 Apr. 2017.
33. Nevertheless, 'the implementation of the accelerated destruction procedure and the functioning of IPR criminal courts need to be improved' (European Commission, Turkey 2018 Report, Ch. 7 (5.7), p. 69).

5. Designs

124. Previously, designs were regulated in Turkish law under the term 'industrial design' by the 'Decree having the Power of Law for Protection of Industrial Designs' (*Endüstriyel Tasarimlarin Korunmasi Hakkinda Kanun Hükmünde Kararname*, *KHK*/554) of 27 June 1995.[34]

125. *KHK*/554 was later abolished and replaced by 'Industrial Property Law' (*Sinai Mülkiyet Kanunu: SMK*), No. 6769 of 22 December 2016. This Law no longer uses the term 'industrial design' (sinai tasarim), it simply refers to *'design'* (tasarim).[35]

126. The historical background and drafting works relating to 'designs' can be found in Chapter 5.

6. Geographic Indications and Traditional Product Names

127. Previously geographical indications were regulated in Turkish law by the 'Decree having the Power of Law for Protection of Geographical Indications' *(Cografi Isaretlerin Korunmasi Hakkinda Kanun Hükmünde Kararname*, *KHK*/555) of 27 June 1995.[36]

128. This *KHK* was later abolished and replaced by 'Industrial Property Law' (*Sinai Mülkiyet Kanunu: SMK*), No. 6769 of 22 December 2016. *SMK* has added 'traditional product names' to 'geographical indication' (*cografi isaret ve geleneksel ürün adi*).[37]

129. The historical background and development of the protection of 'geographical indications' can be found in Chapter 6.

---

34. *KHK*/554 had been drafted in the light of the TRIPS Agreement as well as EC legislation. *KHK*/554 had introduced the following points into Turkish industrial property law: (i) a system for industrial designs based on registration; (ii) non-examination as to the substance; (iii) publication of industrial designs; (iv) deferment of publication; (v) possibility of multiple applications; (vi) opposition by third parties; (vii) better protection against infringements on the rights of industrial design; (viii) specialized courts for cases relating to industrial designs.
35. *See* Official Gazette, No. 29944 of 10 Jan. 2017. For 'designs' *see* Arts 55-81. Regarding the common provisions of all industrial property *see* Arts 146 et seq.
36. Several new solutions relating to geographical indication were introduced by *KHK*/555 to Turkish law: (i) protection of designation of origin and geographical indications; (ii) publication; (iii) opposition by all interested parties; (iv) relations of geographical indications with trademarks; (v) better protection against infringements; (vi) specialized courts.
37. *See* Official Gazette, No. 29944 of 10 Jan. 2017. For 'geographical indications and traditional products names' *see* Arts 33–54. Regarding the common provisions for all industrial property *see* Arts 146 et seq.

7. Plant Variety Protection

130. In Türkiye, breeder's rights on new varieties of plants are protected by the 'Protection of Rights of Breeders on New Varieties of Plants *Law' (Yeni Bitki Çesitlerine Ait Islahatçi Haklarinin Korunmasi Hakkinda Kanun)*, No. 5042 of 8 January 2004.[38]

131. The details on the protection of plant varieties can be found in Chapter 7.

8. Chip Protection

132. In Türkiye, the integrated circuit topographies are protected by the 'Protection of Integrated Circuit Topographies Law' *(Entegre Devre Topografyalarinin Korunmasi Hakkinda Kanun)*, No. 5147 of 22 April 2004. The aim of this Law is not only to protect the integrated circuit topography but also to encourage the development of industry and technology in this field. This Law covers the principles, rules and requirements for the protection of registered layout-designs (topographies) (Article 1). The details on the protection of integrated circuit topographies are explained in Chapter 8.

9. Trade Secrets and Confidential Information

133. Trade secrets and confidential information are protected by the provisions of the Turkish Commercial Code (TComC, *TTK*, No. 6102 of 13 January 2011 on *unfair competition* (Articles 54 et seq.). These provisions can also be invoked, under certain circumstances, to protect manufacturing and commercial secrets as well as know-how.

134. For further details, we refer to our explanations in Chapter 9.

II. International Legal Sources

135. Under the *Turkish Constitution* (Article 90), international agreements ratified by the *Turkish Grand National Assembly* are constituent parts of the Turkish law.

136. In the field of international intellectual property, Türkiye has signed and ratified various multilateral agreements. The foremost multilateral agreements are as follows:

38. *See* Official Gazette, No. 25347 of 15 Jan. 2004.

- Convention Establishing the World Intellectual Property Organization (WIPO) of 14 July 1967, as amended 1979. It was ratified by Türkiye.[39]
- Paris Convention for the Protection of Industrial Property of 20 March 1883, revised at Brussels (1900), Washington (1911), The Hague (1925), London (1934), Lisbon (1958) and Stockholm (1967), and amended in 1979. It was ratified by Türkiye.[40]

137. Türkiye has renounced reservation relating to Articles 1–12 by the Governmental Decree No. 94/5903.[41]

- Madrid Agreement for the Repression of False or Deceptive Indications of Source on Goods of 14 April 1891, revised at Washington (1911), The Hague (1925), London (1934) and Lisbon (1958), and supplemented by the Additional Act of Stockholm (1967). It was ratified by Türkiye.[42]
- Madrid Agreement Concerning the International Registration of Marks of 14 April 1891, revised at Brussels (1900), Washington (1911), The Hague (1925), London (1934), Nice (1957) and Stockholm (1967), and amended in 1979. Türkiye had ratified the Hague version (1925) of the Madrid Agreement (*see* Official Gazette, No. 1506 of 29 May 1930). It set aside however this Agreement in 1955 by the Decree, No. 4/5215.[43]
- Protocol relating to the Madrid Agreement concerning the International Registration of Marks (as signed in Madrid on 28 June 1989). Türkiye adhered to this Protocol by Decree No. 97/9731 of 5 August 1997.[44]
- Implementing Regulation Concerning the Madrid Agreement and Related Protocol for International Registration of Trademarks.[45]
- Nice Agreement Concerning the International Classification of Goods and Services for the Purposes of the Registration of Marks of 15 June 1957, revised at Stockholm (1967) and at Geneva (1977), and amended in 1979. It was ratified by Decree of 95/7094 of 12 July 1995.[46]
- Vienna Agreement Establishing an International Classification of the Figurative Elements of Marks of 12 June 1973 and amended on 1 October 1985. It was ratified by Decree No. 95/7094 of 12 July 1995.[47]
- Trademark Law Treaty (adopted at Geneva on 27 October 1994). Turkey ratified this Treaty by Law, No. 5118 of 7 April 2004. It entered into force in Türkiye on 1 January 2005.
- Hague Agreement Concerning the International Deposit of Industrial Designs of 6 November 1925, revised at London (1934) and The Hague (1960), supplemented by the Additional Act of Monaco (1961), the Complementary Act of

39. *See* Official Gazette, No. 15417 of 11 Nov. 1975.
40. *See* Official Gazette, No. 15418 of 20 Nov. 1975.
41. *See* Official Gazette, No. 22060 of 23 Sep. 1994.
42. *See* Official Gazette, No. 9529 of 7 Feb. 1957.
43. *See* Official Gazette, No. 9059 of 20 Jul. 1955.
44. *See* Official Gazette, No. 23088 (*Mük.*) of 22 Aug. 1997.
45. *See* Official Gazette, No. 23637 of 12 Mar. 1999.
46. *See* Official Gazette, No. 22373 of 13 Aug. 1995.
47. *See* Official Gazette, No. 22373 of 13 Aug. 1995.

Stockholm (1967) and the Protocol of Geneva (1975), and amended in 1979. Türkiye ratified this Agreement by Law, No. 5117 of 7 April 2004. It entered into force on 1 January 2005.

- Locarno Agreement Establishing an International Classification for Industrial Designs of 8 October 1968, as amended on 28 September 1979. Türkiye adhered to this Agreement by Decree, No. 97/9731 of 5 August 1997.[48]
- Patent Cooperation Treaty (PCT) of 19 June 1970 (Washington), amended in 1979 and modified in 1984. It was ratified by Law, No. 4115 of 7 July 1995.[49]
- Implementing Regulation concerning the Patent Cooperation Treaty (*Patent Isbirligi Antlasmasina Dair Yönetmelik*). This regulation is in force as of July 1992.[50]
- Convention on the Unification of Certain Points of Substantive Law on Patents for Invention of 27 November 1963.
- Convention on the Grant of European Patents (European Patent Convention) of 5 October 1973 as amended on 21 December 1978, 17 December 1991, 13 December 1994, 20 October 1995 and 5 December 1996. This Convention and its protocols were ratified by Türkiye by Law, No. 4504 of 27 January 2000.[51]
- Act Revising the Convention on the Grant of European Patents (European Patent Convention) of 29 November 2001. EPC 2000 entered into force on 13 December 2007. This Convention was ratified by Türkiye by Law, No. 5598 of 13 March 2007 (Official Gazette No. 26465 of 17 March 2007).
- Implementing Regulation concerning the Validation of European Patents related to European Patent Convention in Türkiye (Eu.Pat-TR-Reg)(Official Gazette, No. 24282 of 9 January 2001) and Amending Implementing Regulation of this regulation.[52]
- Strasbourg Agreement Concerning the International Patent Classification of 24 March 1971 as amended on 2 October 1979. It was ratified by Decree, No. 95/7094 of 12 July 1995.[53]
- Budapest Treaty on the International Recognition of the Deposit of Microorganisms for the Purposes of Patent Procedure of 28 April 1977, modified in 1980. Türkiye adhered to this Treaty by Decree, No. 97/9731 of 5 August 1997.[54]
- International Convention for the Protection of New Varieties of Plants of 2 December 1961, revised at Geneva (1972 and 1978) and revised again at Geneva in 1991.
- Berne Convention for the Protection of Literary and Artistic Works of 9 September 1886, completed at Paris (1896), revised at Berlin (1908), completed at Berne (1914), revised at Rome (1928), at Brussels (1948), at Stockholm (1967) and at Paris (1971) and modified in 1979. Paris version of the Convention was ratified by Türkiye by Act, No. 4117 of 7 July 1995.[55]

---

48. *See* Official Gazette, No. 23088 (1. *Mük.*) of 22 Aug. 1997.
49. *See* Official Gazette, No. 22341 of 12 Jul. 1995.
50. *See* Tutanak Dergisi (Review for Protocols, Period 19, Legislative Year 3, No. 665).
51. *See* Official Gazette, No. 23948 of 29 Jan. 2000.
52. *See* Official Gazette, No. 26883 of 22 May 2008.
53. *See* Official Gazette, No. 22373 of 12 Aug. 1995.
54. *See* Official Gazette, No. 23088 of 22 Aug. 1997 (*Mük*).
55. *See* Official Gazette, No. 22341 of 12 Jul. 1995.

- Universal Copyright Convention of 6 September 1952, revised in Paris (1971).
- International Convention for the Protection of Performers, Producers of Phonograms and Broadcasting Organizations (Rome Convention) of 26 October 1961. It was ratified by Act, No. 4116 of 7 July 1995.[56]
- Convention for the Protection of Producers of Phonograms against Unauthorized Duplication of Their Programs of 29 October 1971.
- Agreement Establishing the World Trade Organization (WTO) (List of Annexes 1–4); Annex 1/C: Agreement on Trade-Related Aspects of Intellectual Property (TRIPS Agreement). WTO Agreement was ratified by Act, No. 4067 of 26 January 1995.[57]

III. Turkish Patent and Trademark Office [‘Authority’] (TürkPatent), Patent and Trademark Attorneys, Dispute Resolutions

A. *Establishment of TürkPatent*

1. Overview

138. The recently renamed the Turkish Patent and Trademark Authority [or ‘Office’], i.e., TürkPatent is the continuation of the previous one known as Turkish Patent Institute (TPI, *Türk Patent Enstitüsü = TPE*) which had originally been established by the Decree of the Council of Ministers, No. *KHK*/544 of 24 June 1994.[58]

139. Later *KHK*/544 on TPI had been replaced by Act, No. 5000 of 6 November 2003.[59]

140. With the enactment of Industrial Property Law (*SMK*, No. 6769), the Law, No. 5000 was also amended by *SMK* Articles 166–191. The title of the Law, No. 5000 and the name of TPI were changed to *‘Türk Patent ve Marka Kurumunun Kurulus ve Görevleri Hakkinda Kanun’* (Law on Establishment and Duties of TürkPatent (*SMK*, Article 188)). After this amendment, the Law, No. 5000 was amended once again by *KHK*, No. 703 of 2 July 2018 (Article 86). The title of the amended Law, No. 5000 was *‘Patent ve Marka Vekilligi ile Bazi Düzenlemeler Hakkinda Kanun’* (Law on Patent and Trademark Attorneyship and Some Other Arrangements, PatTMAttyL). Lastly, the aims and duties and the organization of TürkPatent have been arranged by *CBK*, No. 4 of 15 July 2018.[60]

141. *CBK*, No. 4 Article 358 deals with ‘Establishment and aim of the Authority’ while Article 359 covers ‘Definitions’.

56. *See* Official Gazette, No. 22341 of 12 Jul. 1995.
57. *See* Official Gazette, No. 22213 of 25 Feb. 1995.
58. Official Gazette, No. 21970 of 24 Jun. 1994.
59. Official Gazette, No. 25294 of 19 Nov. 2003.
60. Official Gazette, No. 30479 of 15 Jul. 2018, Arts 358–383.

2. Duties and Functions

142. The Authority (TürkPatent) has been entrusted with the development and protection of industrial property rights (*CBK*, No.4 Article 360).

3. Organs, Units, Boards and Dispute Resolutions

143. TürkPatent's 'organs' are Board of Directors, Advisory Board and Presidency (*CBK*, No. 4 Article 361).

144. TürkPatent's 'service units' are Patent Department; Trademarks Department; Designs Department; European Union and Foreign Relations Department; Innovation and Promotion Department; Geographical Indications Department; Department for Re-examination and Evaluation; Personnel Department; Data Processing Department; Department for Strategy Development; Legal Advisory (*CBK*, No. 4 Articles 368–380).

4. Dispute Resolutions Before TürkPatent Re-examination and Evaluation Department Boards, Litigation

145. The formation and working principles of the Re-Examination and Evaluation Department are found in the Implementing Regulation *(Türk Patent ve Marka Kurumu Yeniden Inceleme ve Degerlendirme Dairesi Kurullari Yönetmeligi)* issued by TürkPatent.[61] Persons whose interests are affected due to a final decision of a relevant TürkPatent department may raise objections within two months. In case of an objection, a competent Board (*Kurul*) of the Re-Examination and Evaluation Department re-examines and evaluates the decision of the relevant department. These objections may pertain to a department decision regarding industrial property rights (e.g., trademarks, patents, utility models, designs, integrated circuit topographies) including geographical indications and traditional product names. A TürkPatent Board decision given upon an objection becomes the final decision of TürkPatent.

146. A lawsuit can be filed against a TürkPatent Re-Examination and Evaluation Department Board decision within two months from its notification before the Civil Court of Intellectual and Industrial Rights (*Fikri ve Sınai Haklar Hukuk Mahkemesi*) in Ankara, the Capital of Türkiye. It should be noted that, in Türkiye, unlike some other counties, the parties may choose to be represented before any court, including specialized courts, only by attorneys at law (*avukat*), and not by any patent attorney (*patent vekili*) or trademark attorney (*marka vekili*).

---

61. Official Gazette, No. 30064 of 12 May 2017.

5. 'The Academy for Intellectual Property and Training Center for Industrial Property Rights'

147. *CBK*, No. 4 Article 367 lays down the rules relating to the establishment and functions of *'The Academy for Intellectual Property and Training Center for Industrial Property Rights'*.[62] The Academy is engaged in training, consultancy and research activities related to intellectual property rights. The Training Centre has been established to conduct training activities related to industrial property rights.

B. Patent and Trademark Attorneys

148. Representation before TürkPatent for matters of patent and trademark may only be undertaken (i) by natural and legal persons or (ii) by registered patent or trademark attorneys (*patent vekili, marka vekili*) (*SMK*, Article 160(1)), i.e., not by attorneys at law (*avukat*).

149. Those who are domiciled outside the country can only be represented by patent or trademark attorneys (*SMK*, Article 160(3)).

150. Where a patent or trademark attorney has been appointed, all procedures are executed through the attorney and all notices are sent to the attorney (*SMK*, Article 160(4)).[63]

IV. Specialized Courts and Mediation

151. Legal proceedings relating to Turkish law on intellectual property rights are filed in 'specialised' courts of first instance. These are civil courts and criminal courts of intellectual and industrial property rights in Ankara and Istanbul, established by the Ministry of Justice.

152. However, an increasing number of intellectual property law disputes are subject to mediation. For particularly listed disputes, a pre-court mediation attempt is mandatory while it is voluntary for other specific disputes. The rules governing private law mediation in Türkiye may be summarized as follows: Mediation activities are conducted by real persons registered in the register of mediators organised by the Ministry of Justice. Mediators must have a law degree and five years' experience in their legal profession; they must also be trained before passing a formal

62. *See* Regulation on Academy for Intellectual Property (*Fikri Mülkiyet Akademisi Yönetmeligi*), Official Gazette, No. 30948 of 14 Nov. 2019.

63. For details regarding patent and trademark attorneys, *see* Regulation on Examination, Registration and Discipline of Patent and Trademark Attorneys (*Patent Vekilligi ve Marka Vekilligi Sınav, Sicil ve Disiplin Yönetmeligi*), Official Gazette, No. 31447 of 7 Apr. 2021 (as amended).

examination (Mediation Act on Private Law Disputes, Article 20).[64] The Directory of Mediation Department, which operates under the Ministry of Justice, has set up a commission to identify fields of expertise in mediation. Mediation of intellectual property law disputes is also identified as a field of special expertise which requires a mediator's proof of additional training.

153. For further explanations on specialised courts and mandatory mediation for each topic of Turkish IP law, *see* the heading 'Specialised Courts and Mediation' of the relevant section.

64. Act on Mediation in Civil Law Disputes (AMedC, *Hukuk Uyusmazliklarinda Arabuluculuk Kanunu, HUAK*), No. 6325, Official Gazette of 22 Jun. 2012.

Chapter 1. Copyright and Neighbouring Rights

§1. Legislative History

I. Background of *FSEK*

154. The main source of the law on copyright protection in Türkiye is the 'Law on Intellectual and Artistic Works' (*Fikir ve Sanat Eserleri Kanunu*, hereinafter '*FSEK*'), No. 5846 of 5 December 1951.[65]

155. Since its enactment, *FSEK* has been amended and updated several times. The emergence of new technologies, rapid technological changes, and innovations (e.g., transistor radios, stereo transmissions, cassette recorders, digital audio broadcasting, and widespread commercial use of colour TV) followed by the Internet necessitated amendments in *FSEK*.

156. On the other hand, EU-Türkiye relations have considerably affected the modernization endeavours in the field of copyright law.

157. The most important amendments in *FSEK* were realized by Act, No. 2936 of 1 November 1983 and Act, No. 4110 of 7 June 1995. In light of modern developments in the field of copyright law, several provisions were added to *FSEK* (e.g., authorship on cinematographic works, protection of neighbouring rights, protection of computer programs, databases, etc.). *FSEK* has also been amended by Act, No. 4630 of 21 February 2001. Several new concepts (e.g., interface, interoperability, related rights, neighbouring rights, etc.) relating to copyright law are defined and new solutions in this field have been transferred to Turkish copyright law (Article 1(B) added to *FSEK* by the Act, No. 4630).[66]

158. It should be noted that several *EC directives* and *resolutions* have been taken into account with regard to the *FSEK* amendments.

159. In this respect, the following *EU legislation* can be cited:

- Council Directive 91/250/EEC of 14 May 1991 on the legal protection of computer programs (EC Software Directive);[67]
- Council Resolution 92/C/138/01/EC of 14 May 1992 on increased protection for copyright and neighbouring rights.

65. Official Gazette, No. 7981 of 13 Dec. 1951.
66. See Official Gazette, No. 18210 of 3 Nov 1983; Official Gazette, No. 22311 of 12 Jun. 1995; Official Gazette, No. 24335 Mük. of 3 Mar. 2001, pp. 29–40. During the last decade, FSEK has also been amended by the Act, No. 5101 of 3 Mar. 2004 (Official Gazette, No. 25400 of 12 Mar. 2004), Act, No. 5571 of 28 Dec. 2006, Act, No. 5728 of 23 Jan. 2008, and Act, No. 6279 of 22 Feb. 2012. See Official Gazette, No. 28219 of 29 Feb. 2012.
67. Cf. Directive 2009/24/EC of the European Parliament and of the Council of 23 Apr. 2009 on the legal protection of computer programs.

- Council Directive 92/100/EEC of 19 November 1992 on rental rights and lending right and on certain rights related to copyright in the field of intellectual property (EC Rental and Related Rights Directive);
- Council Directive 93/83/EEC of 27 September 1993 on the coordination of certain rules concerning copyright and rights related to copyright applicable to satellite broadcasting and cable retransmission (EC Satellite/Cable Directive)
- Council Directive 93/98/EEC of 29 October 1993 on harmonizing the term protection of copyright and certain related rights.
- Commission Directive Proposal on the legal protection of databases and its amended proposal; Directive 96/9/EC of the European Parliament and of the Council of 11 March 1996 on the legal protection of databases (EC Database Directive).[68]
- Directive 2006/115/EC of the European Parliament and of the Council of 12 December 2006 on rental rights and lending rights and on certain rights related to copyright in the field of intellectual property.

160. In 1995, amendments of several provisions of the '*Rome Convention for the Protection of Performers, Producers of Phonograms and Broadcasting Organizations'* of 1961 and of the EC Council Directive 91/250 of 14 May 1991 on the legal protection of computer programs were adopted and new solutions were introduced to *FSEK*.[69]

II. Aim of *FSEK*

161. The aim of *FSEK* is the protection of intellectual and artistic works and the rights of authors (creators).[70]

162. The copyright protection begins with the creation of the work and does not require any fixation in material form.[71]

163. Under *FSEK*, a work made available to the *public with the consent of its author* (right holder) is deemed to have become public (Article 7(1)).

164. However, a work is considered as *published*, provided its copies obtained through the reproduction of the original are made available to the public by the consent of its right holder through putting the work up for sale or distributing or placing it in commercial circulation by any other means (Article 7(2)).

---

68. Cf. Directive 2009/24/EC of the European Parliament and of the Council of 23 Apr. 2009 on the legal protection of computer programs.
69. Cf. Directive 2009/24/EC of the European Parliament and of the Council of 23 Apr. 2009 on the legal protection of computer programs (implementing regulation) on Neighbouring Rights to Author's Rights (Official Gazette, No. 23172 of 16 Nov. 1997).
70. *See* Art. 1 as amended by the Act, No. 4630, and Art. 1(A) and 1(B) as added by the same Act and Art. 1(B) as amended By the Act, No. 5101.
71. *See* Art. 8 as amended by the Act, No. 4630.

III. International Aspects

165. Türkiye has *ratified* several *international conventions* in the field of copyright law.

166. Türkiye is a *party* to the following conventions:

- the Berne Convention for the Protection of Literary and Artistic Works (Paris Revision 1971) (Act No. 4117).
- the Stockholm Convention establishing the WIPO (1968).
- the Rome Convention for the Protection of Performers, Producers of Phonograms and Broadcasting Organizations (1961).
- Agreement Establishing the World Trade Organization, Annex 1/C: Agreement on TRIPS.

167. Türkiye is *not a party* to the following conventions: The Universal Copyright Convention (its amended Paris version of 1971); Geneva Convention for the Protection of Producers of Phonograms against Unauthorized Duplication of Their Programs (1971); Brussels Convention Relating to the Distribution of Programme-Carrying Signals Transmitted by Satellite (1974); Treaty on the International Registration of Audiovisual Works; European Agreement on the Protection of Television Broadcasts (Strasbourg Television Agreement) (1960); WIPO Copyright Treaty (1996).

§2. Kinds of Works Protected

168. Under Turkish Copyright Law, the protected works are the works which are any kind of intellectual and artistic creations carrying the *characteristics of their authors* (Article 1 as amended in 2001 by Act, No. 4630).

169. *FSEK* has distinguished the following categories of intellectual and artistic works.

I. Scientific and Literary Works

170. Under *FSEK* scientific and literary works are as follows (Article 2. Cf. Berne Convention, Article 2(1):

(1) all works expressed in speech or writing, in any mode or form of expression;
(2) computer programs: The 1995 Amendment introduced computer programs into the list of protected works, classifying them specifically as 'literary works'. The term 'computer programs' includes their preparatory design material. Protection shall apply to the expression in any form of a computer program.

However, ideas and principles which underlie any element of a computer program, including those which underlie its interfaces, are not protected by copyright;[72]

(3) all kinds of dances, written choreographic works, pantomimes and analogous theatrical works without any words (1983 Amendment);
(4) all types of photographic works of technical and scientific nature, all kinds of maps, plans, projects, sketches, drawings, three-dimensional works relative to geography and topography, all kinds of architectural and city planning designs and projects, architectural models, industrial, environmental designs and projects, stage designs and projects irrespective of aesthetic character (1995 Amendment).

II. Musical Works

171. Musical works are all kinds of *musical compositions with or without words* (*FSEK*, Article 3).

III. Artistic Works

172. Artistic works having *aesthetic value* are (Article 4):

(1) oil paintings and watercolours, all kinds of drawings, designs, pastels, engravings, scripts and gildings, etchings, lithographs, woodcuts or other articles by engraving, carving, ornamental inlaying or other analogous methods, calligraphy, silk screen printing;
(2) sculptures, reliefs and carvings;
(3) works of architecture;
(4) handicrafts and secondary works of art, miniatures and products of the art of ornamentation, textile and fashion designs;
(5) photographic works and slides;
(6) graphic works;
(7) caricatures;
(8) all kinds of type-castings.

173. The exploitation of sketches, drawings, models, designs and the like as design and model does not affect their nature as intellectual and artistic work.

174. Works of applied art are protected in Türkiye by *SMK*, No. 6769 (Articles 55–81) on Designs. However, they can also be protected by *FSEK* as long as they are creative and have the character of individuality (*SMK*, Article 58(3)).

72. Cf. EC Directive 91/250, Art. 1(1)(2); TRIPS Agreement, Art. 10(1).

IV. Cinematographic Works

175. Under *FSEK*, cinematographic films (motion picture), motion pictures having an educational or technical purpose or portraying current events (newsreel), and dispositive of all kinds of scientific, technical, or aesthetic characteristics are understood as 'cinematographic works'.[73]

176. The above-mentioned works are considered cinematographic work, provided that they are shown by projection, irrespective of whether these are fixed on a substance other than film or glass.

177. The evaluation, classification and support of cinema films are subject to Act, No. 5224 of 14 July 2004.[74]

V. Adaptations and Compilations

178. Adaptations (*islenme*) are the intellectual and artistic works created by benefiting from another work and are not independent in regard to this work.

179. Under *FSEK* adaptation bearing the characteristics of the person who has made the adaptation is considered as 'work' (Article 6(2)).

180. *FSEK* defines the following as adaptation (Article 6(1)):

(1) translations;
(2) converting a novel, story, poem and play into one of them;
(3) making motion pictures from musical, scientific or literary works or transformation thereof for broadcasting on radio or television;
(4) musical arrangements and transcriptions;
(5) converting artistic works from one form to another;
(6) making a compilation of all works or of the works of the same kind of an author;
(7) arrangement of selected works in accordance with a special plan and for a specific purpose;[75]
(8) preparation of an unpublished work so as to make it available for publication by scientific research and study;[76]
(9) explanation, commentary or abridgement of a work belonging to someone else;

---

73. *See* Art. 5 as amended by the Act, No. 4630. Cf. Berne Convention (1971 Paris Version), Art. 14 bis.
74. *See* Official Gazette, No. 25529 of 21 Jul. 2004. This Act repealed the Act, No. 3257 of 23 Jan. 1986 on Cinema, Video and Musical Works Official Gazette, No. 19012 of 7 Feb. 1986.
75. Cf. Berne Convention, Art. 2(5).
76. Ordinary transcriptions or facsimiles that are not products of scientific research and study are excluded (*FSEK*, Art. 6(1), No. 8).

(10) adaptation, editing or any modification of a computer program (1995 Amendment);
(11) databases obtained as a result of the selection and completion of data and materials according to a specific purpose and within the framework of a special plan.[77]

§3. AUTHORSHIP

I. Concept

181. Under Turkish law, the *author* is the *creator of the work* (*FSEK* Article 8(1)) as amended by the Act, No. 4630). It follows from the nature of 'work' as a personal intellectual creation, the copyright can only originate from a natural person and not a legal person.

182. Legal capacity is not a pre-condition. Therefore, even a *child* or a *legally incapacitated person* may qualify as an author.

II. Categories of Authorship

A. Literary and Artistic Works

1. Individually Created Works

183. The owner of a work created individually is the person who created it.

2. Collective Works

184. Regarding jointly created works, the following distinction is made:

– If a work created by several persons can be *separated* into parts, *each of these persons* is considered the author of the part created by him/her (Article 9(1)).

185. In such a case, each author who contributed to the creation of the collective work may request the cooperation of others in the modification or publication of the work unless otherwise agreed. If a co-author does not give his/her consent without a just ground, the permission is granted by the court (Article 9(2)).

186. Regarding economic rights, the same rules apply (Article 9(2)).

– If the work created by several persons constitutes an *indivisible whole*, the author of the work is the *co-authorship of the creators* (Article 10).

77. *See* 1995 Amendment by the Act, No. 4110 and 2001 Amendment by the Act, No. 4630.

187. The *co-authorship* is subject to the provisions of ordinary partnership (Turkish Code of Obligations, Articles 620 et seq.). In such a case, if one of the creators does not give his/her consent without a just ground to any transaction to be done together, the permission can be requested from the court (Article 10(2)).

188. In case of infringement on the rights of co-authorship, each co-author is entitled to act independently (Article 10(2)).

B. Employee's Works

189. The owner of the economic rights of works created by *civil servants, public employees, and employees* in the normal course of the execution of their duties is the *employer* unless otherwise agreed in the employment agreement or is construed from the nature of the respective employment. The owner of a work created by an *organ* is the legal entity. (Article 18).

C. Adaptations and Compilations

190. The author of an adaptation or compilation is the *person who made it* (Article 8(1)). However, the rights of the author of the original work are duly protected (Article 8(2)).

D. Cinematographic Works

191. In cinematographic works, the director; the original music composer, the author of the screenplay and the author of dialogues are joint authors of the work (Article 8(3)).

E. Computer Programs

192. Under *FSEK*, *computer programs* take place in the group of *'literary and scientific works'* (Article 2(1) No. 1). Therefore, the author of a computer program is the *person who created the work* (Article 8(1)).

193. In case of *adaptation, editing or modification of a computer program*, the author is the person who has done such works (Article 6(1) No. 10 and Article 9(2)).

F. Databases

194. Under *FSEK*, *databases* are protected as adaptations (*FSEK*, Article 6(1) No. 11). Therefore, the author of a database is the person who created this work (Article 8(1)).

G. *Neighbouring Rights (Komsu Haklar)*

195. Performers, producers of phonograms and broadcasting organizations are the owners of the neighbouring rights (Article 80).[78]

196. Regarding these rights, the holders of such rights are not just limited to *natural persons*. The rights and duties of *radio-TV organizations* are regulated by Article 80(C) (as amended in 2004 by Act, No. 5101).

III. Presumption of Authorship

A. *In Works on Which the Name of the Author Is Revealed*

197. A person who uses his/her name or his/her known pseudonym as the author's name in the published copies of the work or in the original of an artistic work is regarded as the owner of such work until it is proved otherwise (Article 11(1)).

198. According to *FSEK*, a *person introduced as the author* in the usual manner during lectures or performances conducted on public premises or broadcast by radio or television is considered the author of such work, unless any other person is deemed to be the author of such work through the presumption prescribed by Article 11(1) (Article 11(2)).

B. *In Anonymous Works*

199. Unless the *author of a published work* is not revealed (Article 11), the *publisher* (yayimlayan), and if he/she is not revealed either, the *reproducer* (çogaltan) may exercise in his/her own name the rights and privileges belonging to the author (Article 12(1)).

200. Where the author is deemed to be unknown (Article 11(2)), such rights belong to the *person delivering the lecture or causing the performance* (temsili icra ettiren) to be given (Article 12(2)).

201. The provisions on an *ordinary mandate* (adi vekalet, German: Auftrag) apply to the relations between the persons with such rights (Turkish Code of Obligations, Articles 502 et seq.) as described here and the true owners of the right unless otherwise stipulated (Article 12(3)).

78. *See* other amendments by the Act, No. 5101 of 3 Mar. 2004 and 5728 of 23 Jan. 2008.

§4. CONTENTS OF THE AUTHOR RIGHTS

202. Author rights extend to the *whole and parts of the work* (Article 13(2))[79]

203. FSEK distinguishes the author's rights into two categories: *moral rights* and *economic rights.*

I. Moral Rights

A. *Kinds of Moral Rights*

204. Under *FSEK*, the author's moral rights cover the following rights: the right to publication, the right to request to mention the author's name, and the right to prohibit modification to the work.

1. Right of Publication

205. The *author* has the exclusive right to decide whether by whom and how his/her work will be made accessible to the public (right of publication) (Article 14(1)).

206. The *author* alone may supply information on the work, the whole or an essential part of which has not become public (Article 14(2)).

207. In spite of his/her authorization, the *author* may prohibit the presentation of his/her work to the public or its publication, if the manner of the work's communication to the public or its publication can potentially violate his/her honour and dignity. The renunciation of this right by contract is null and void (Article 14(3)).

208. Co-authors enjoy the right of public dissemination *jointly*. Nevertheless, a co-author may not without just reason refuse to give the other co-authors his/her consent to the dissemination of the work. If the consent is refused without any sound reason or in bad faith, the other co-authors may obtain the consent by a court judgment (Article 9(2)).

2. Right of Recognition of Authorship

209. The right to decide whether to communicate the work to the public or to have it published under his/her own name or pseudonym or anonymously is reserved exclusively to the *author* (Article 15(1)).

---

79. Article 13(3) as amended by the Act, No. 5101 deals with records and registrations to be made by film and phonogram producers for the purpose of proving of their rights on cinema and musical works.

210. The *name or mark of the author* must be indicated clearly, as agreed or in the usual manner, on:

- the copies obtained by reproduction of a work of art; or
- the original or copies of an adaptation.

211. Moreover, it must clearly be indicated whether the work produced is a copy or adaptation (Article 15(2)).

212. In case of a dispute regarding the identity of the person who has created the work, or if some other person claims to be the author of the work, the *actual author* may initiate proceedings to have his/her rights recognized (Article 15(3)).

213. In case of *works of architecture*, the name of the author (architect) upon his/her written request is inscribed indelibly on a visible place of the work using a material found suitable by the author (Article 15(4) as added by Act, No. 4110).

3. Right to Prohibit the Modification of the Work

214. The *right of modification* of the work is an exclusive right of the *author*. This right pertains to the right of respect for the integrity of one's work. Therefore, no abbreviation or addition or other modification of the work or of the name of the author can be made without his/her consent (Article 16(1)).

215. Anyone who authorized by law or with permission of the author, adapts, communicates to the public, reproduces, publishes or presents a work in any other manner may make reasonable modifications for technical reasons even without the special permission of the author (Article 16(2)).

216. If the author has given his/her unconditional written authorization, he/she may still object to all kinds of modifications that harm the characteristics of his/her work or infringe on his/her honour and reputation. To renounce this right by contract is null and void (Article 16(3) as amended by the Act, No. 4630).

B. Exercise of Moral Rights

1. In General

217. The moral rights on work can be exercised by the natural person author *during his/her lifetime. Persons with limited capacity to act* (minors and persons under guardianship) may personally enjoy moral rights without authorization of their legal representatives (Article 19(1)).

218. Legal entities may use moral rights as far as they exist (Article 18).

2. Other Persons Entitled to Exercise Moral Rights

219. If the author has not determined the mode of exercising the moral rights or entrusted this issue to any person, these rights are exercised after his/her death by his/her *executor* (vasiyeti yerine getirme görevlisi) (*see* Turkish Civil Code, Articles 550 et seq.).

220. If no executor has been appointed, the moral rights of the author can successively be exercised by his/her surviving spouse, children, appointed heirs, parents or brothers and sisters (Article 19(1)).

221. After the death of the author, the person mentioned above may exercise the moral rights in their own name for the duration of economic rights and in any case for *a period of seventy years after the death of the author* (Article 19(2) as amended by the Act, No. 4630).

222. Where there are several right holders and they cannot agree with respect to intervention, the court shall settle the dispute taking into account the *presumed wish of the author* (Article 19(4)):

(a) If the persons cited above do not exercise the moral rights, the person who acquires from the author or his/her successor an economic right may exercise these rights in his/her own name provided that he/she proves the existence of a legitimate interest (Article 19(3)).
(b) If the author of the work and the other persons mentioned above do not exist or do not exercise moral rights, the *Ministry of Culture* and Tourism (Kültür ve Turizm Bakanligi) may exercise these rights:
   - after the expiry of the periods of time specified for other right holders (Article 19(5)); and
   - if it considers exercising moral rights for the cultural interest of the country (Article 19(5))

C. Rights of the Author Against the Possessor and Owner of the Work

223.

(a) Under *FSEK*, the owner of the rights of reproduction or adaptation may claim from the possessor of the work the right to benefit from the work within the limits required for the exercise of these rights (Article 17(1) as amended by the Act, No. 4630).
(b) The possessor of the original of the work may dispose of it as agreed with the author, provided he/she does not mutilate or destroy the work or harm the lawful interests of the author (Article 17(2)).

(c) Where a work is unique and original, the author may ask for such work for the purpose of display in a retrospective exhibition covering all his/her productive phases if he/she takes all precautions for its protection and return (Article 17(3)).

II. Economic Rights

A. *Nature of Economic Rights*

224. FSEK protects the author in his/her rights to *exploit the work*. These rights include the right of an author to exploit his/her work in material form, comprising, in particular, the right of reproduction; the right of distribution; the right of exhibition, as well as the exclusive right to communicate his/her work to the public in non-material form, comprising, in particular, the right of performance and presentation; the broadcasting right; the right of communicating the work by means of sound or visual recordings; the right of communicating broadcast.

1. Work That Has Not Yet Become Public

225. The *right to benefit* from a *work that has not yet become public* belongs exclusively to the author (Article 20(1)).

2. Work That Has Become Public

226. The right to benefit from *a work that has become public* also belongs to the *author*. The author benefits only from the rights indicated by *FSEK* as economic rights (Article 20(1)).

227. Economic rights are not bound to each other. They need not be exercised together. The exercise of any one does not affect others (Article 20(1)).

B. *Persons Entitled to Use Economic Rights*

1. Author

228. Economic rights belong, in principle, to the *author of the work* (Article 20(1)).

2. Producer and Publisher

229. The *producer* (yapimci) or *publisher* (yayimlayici) of a work may only exercise the economic rights under an agreement to be made with the author of the work (Article 18(3) as amended by Act No. 4630).

3. Owner of Adaptation

230. The *owner of an adaptation* (islemenin sahibi) can only exercise the economic rights conferred upon him/her in such capacity and to the extent permitted by the author of the original work. This rule does not apply in the case where the adaptation is free (Article 20(4)).

4. Professional Associations

231. Previously if the author was a member of a professional association, the monitoring of economic rights indicated in the written authorization certificate and collection and distribution of royalty payments were conducted by the association (Article 20(2). This paragraph has been repealed by Act, No. 5101 Article 28(2)).[80]

C. *Kinds of Economic Rights*

1. Right of Adaptation

232. The right to benefit from a work by *adaptation* (isleme hakki) belongs exclusively to the author (Article 21).

2. Right of Reproduction

233. The *right to reproduce* (çogaltma hakki) the original or adaptation of a work belongs exclusively to the *author* (Article 22(1)).

234. Under *FSEK*, the following acts are deemed as *reproduction* (Article 22(2)):

- reproduction of a second copy of an original work;
- recording of works on devices or on various other means enabling the transmission and reproduction of signs, sounds and images;
- all kinds of recordings of sounds and music;
- application of the plans, projects and sketches of architectural works.

235. Right of reproduction also covers loading, displaying, running, transmission and storage of the computer program, in so far as these acts necessitate the temporary reproduction of the computer program (Article 22(3)).

---

80. The rules related to the authorization certificate to be granted by authors of intellectual and artistic works have been specified by an implementing regulation issued by the Ministry of Culture and Tourism. *See* Implementing Regulation on the Document for Authorization to be Given by Authors of Intellectual and Artistic Works *(Fikir ve Sanat Eserleri Sahiplerinin Verecekleri Yetki Belgesi Hakkinda Yönetmelik)* in Official Gazette, No. 19211 of 4 Sep. 1986.

3. Right of Distribution

236. *FSEK* Article 23 deals with the *distribution rights* (yayma hakki) of the author.

237. The right of distribution covers the right to benefit from a work by distributing, renting out or putting up for sale, or to make the subject of commerce the copies obtained by reproducing the original or its adaptation.

238. Right of distribution is enjoyed exclusively by the *author* (Article 23(1)).

239. In case of importing the copies reproduced abroad, the right to disseminate and benefit from the work may exclusively be used by the *author* (Article 23(2)).

240. Moreover, the right to prohibit the importation of infringing copies reproduced without his/her authorization belongs exclusively to the *author* (Article 23(2)).

241. In copyright law, the distribution rights are exhausted, usually, by the first sale made by or with the consent of the copyright holder. However, even after the exhaustion of his/her distribution rights, the author retains a claim to royalties, if copies of the work such as books or records are rented or lent commercially or are available via a public institution.

242. *'Rental'* (kiralama) means making it available for use for a limited period of time and for direct or indirect economic or commercial advantage. *'Lending'* (ödünç verme) means making available for use for a limited period of time not for direct or indirect economic or commercial advantage when it is made through establishments which are accessible to the public.[81]

243. The exclusive right to authorize or prohibit rental and lending belongs to the author in respect of the original and copies of his/her work; to the performer in respect of fixations of his/her performance; to the phonogram producer in respect of his/her phonograms, and to the producer of the first fixation of a film in respect of the original and copies of his/her film.[82]

244. Under *FSEK*, where the first sale or distribution of specific copies of the work are placed into commercial circulation as a result of the right of the owner's use of his/her right of distribution within its territory by means of the transfer of property, further distribution of them by resale or rental, provided that the right of renting and public lending are reserved, does not infringe the distribution rights conferred on the author (Article 23(3)).

---

81. Cf. Council Directive 92/100 on rental and lending right and on certain rights related to copyright in the field of intellectual property, Art. 1(2) and (3).
82. Cf. Council Directive 92/100, Art. 2(1).

4. Right of Performance

245. The *'right of performance'* (temsil hakki) belongs exclusively to the author (Article 24(1) as amended by Act No. 4630).

246. Under performance right it is understood the right of benefiting from work through performance by reciting, playing, dancing and displaying in public premises either directly or by means of devices enabling the transmission of signs, sounds or images (Article 24(1)).

247. Moreover, the right of transmission of the performance from the premises where the presentation occurs to another location by means of any technical device also belongs to the *author* (Article 24(2)).

248. Right of performance may not be exercised by other (natural) persons or legal entities without the written permission of the author. If the author is a member of a professional association, permission is given by the association within the framework of authorization granted to it by the author (Article 24(3)).

5. Right of Broadcasting by Analogous Technical Instruments Enabling Transmissions of Signs, Sounds or Images

249. Right of broadcasting a work (eseri yayinlama hakki) belongs exclusively to the *author*. The following acts are defined under the *right of broadcasting*:

- benefiting from work by broadcasting the original or its adaptations by radio-television or by analogous technical instruments enabling transmission of signs, sounds or images; or
- re-broadcasting of such broadcasted works either by wire or on the air or diffusion from another radio establishment; or
- the performance of such works in public premises by means of loudspeakers or other analogous technical instruments enabling the transmission of signs, sounds or images (Article 25).

6. *'Droit de Suite'*

250. Under the *Berne Convention* (1971 Paris Revision), the author or after his/her death, the persons or institutions authorized by national legislation shall with respect to original works of art and original manuscripts of writers and composers enjoy the inalienable right to an interest in any sale of the work subsequent to the first transfer by the author of the work (Berne Convention, Article 14ter).

251. In accordance with the *Berne Convention, FSEK* has granted the *'droit de suite'* (the right of request for payment on resale of artistic works; *pay ve takip hakki*) to the authors of some intellectual and artistic works (e.g., oil paintings, watercolours, all kinds of drawings, sculptures, reliefs, carvings, literary works or musical compositions).

252. Under *FSEK*, after the first sale of the original work of art by the author or his/her heirs, if it is resold at an exhibition or at public auction or at a shop engaged in such articles during the term of protection and if there is an obvious disproportionate difference between the price of such subsequent sale and the price of the original sale, the vendor may be made to pay for every sale an adequate royalty on the difference resulting from the resale. Normally the payment shall be made to the author. After the death of the author, the payment shall be made to his/her legal heirs to the second degree (including) and to the spouse, and in their absence to the professional association, in accordance with the rules and procedures to be laid down by a decree to be issued by a Decision of the President (Article 45(1)).[83]

253. The decision shall contain a payment tariff to be determined in proportion to the difference in price, provided it does not exceed 10 percent of such difference (Article 45(2)).

254. The '*droit de suite*' can be directed toward the *owner of the establishment where the sale has taken place* and the *vendor*. They are jointly responsible for payment (Article 45(3)).

255. In case of *attachment*, the payment is made only after all other debts have been settled in full (Article 45(4)).

256. Statute of limitation for '*droit de suite*' is *five years* from the sale which gave rise to such right (Article 45(5)).

§5. Term of Protection

I. Term of Economic Rights

A. In General

257. Exclusive rights of the author are limited in time. After the term of protection, *anyone* may benefit from the economic rights of the work (Article 26(1)).

258. The terms of protection for the original and adaptations of a work are in principle independent from each other (Articles 26(2); (46) and (47)).

259. This rule also applies to the works created by several authors (Articles 9(1) and 26(3)).

83. *See* the Decree having the Power of Law (*KHK*), No. 700 of 2 Jul. 2018, Art. 24.

B. *Work That Has Become Public*

260. The term of protection does not begin until the work becomes *public* (Articles 7 and 26(3)):

(a) For *works of serial publication*, the publication date of the last publication in the series is deemed to be the date on which the work becomes public (Article 26(4)).
(b) In *works consisting of consecutive volumes published at intervals*, for each volume the date on which the work becomes public is the publication date of each publication (Article 26(4)).
(c) The same rule also applies to works such as *bulletins, pamphlets, periodicals and yearbooks* (Article 26(4)).

C. *Calculation of Terms*

261.

(a) Terms of protection that start from the *date on which the work becomes public* are calculated from the first day of the year following the year in which the work becomes public for the first time (Article 26(5)).
(b) In calculating terms for protection starting from the *death of the author*, the first day of the year of the author's death is deemed to be the starting date (Article 26(6)).

262. In case of several authors, the term of protection starts after the death of the last surviving co-author (Article 26(6)).

II. Length of Terms

A. *Literary, Musical and Artistic Works*

263. Literary, musical and artistic works are protected for *a term of seventy years* after the end of the year of the *author's death*. Where a work has been created by several authors jointly, copyright lapses seventy years after the end of the year of the death of the *last co-author* (Article 27(1)).

264. In works which have first become public after the death of the author, the term of protection is seventy years from the date of death (Article 27(2)).

265. In the cases of the use of one's name or his/her known pseudonym as the author's name in the published copies of a work or in the original of an artistic work

(Articles 11 and 12(1)), the term of protection is seventy years from the date the *work has become public,* unless the author reveals his/her name before the expiry of this term (Article 27(3)).

266. If the owner of the original work is *a legal entity*, the term of protection is seventy years from the date on which the *work has become public* (Article 27(4)).

B. Cinematographic and Photographic Works

267. Under *FSEK*, *cinematographic and photographic works* are protected for a term of seventy years from the date the *work has become public* (Article 27).

C. Handicraft and Secondary Works of Art

268. Previously under Article 29 as amended in 1995, *handicrafts and secondary works of art* also enjoyed a seventy-year term of protection. This Article was repealed by the Act, No. 4630, Art. 36(c)).

D. Neighbouring Rights

269. Under *FSEK*, neighbouring rights are protected for *seventy years* (Article 82(4)–(7)).

1. Performers

270. The term of protection for the rights of *performing artists* is seventy years commencing with the date of the first publication of the fixation of performance. If a performance has not yet been published, the term of protection commences with the date of the performance first becoming public (Article 82(5)).

2. Phonogram Producers

271. The term of protection for the rights of *phonogram producers* is seventy years commencing with the date of the first broadcasting of sound carriers (Article 82(6)).

3. Broadcasting Organizations

272. The rights of *broadcasting organizations* are protected for a term of seventy years commencing with the date of the first broadcasting of the programme (Article 82(7)).

273. Under the *Rome Convention,* neighbouring rights enjoy relatively more limited protection. In particular, the protection periods are shorter. The minimum term for protection under the Rome Convention is a period of twenty years to be computed from the end of the year in which (i) the fixation was made as far as phonograms and performances incorporated therein are concerned, or (ii) the performance took place as regards performances not incorporated in phonograms, or (iii) broadcast took place for broadcasts (Article 14).[84]

E. Databases

274. Copyright protection for a database is the same as that for any protected collection of *literary works*. This term is seventy years after the death of the *author* (Article 27).

III. Terms of Protection Concerning Translations into Turkish

275. Previously, if a scientific or literary work, first published in a foreign language had not been translated and published in Turkish either by the author or by a person authorized by him/her within a period of seventy years from the date of publication of the original, it might be translated into Turkish upon the lapse of seventy years (*FSEK* Article 28 as amended by the 1995 Amendment). This Article was repealed by Act, No. 4630 Article 36(b).[85]

§6. Protection of Computer Programs and Databases

I. Computer Programs (Software)

276. Under *FSEK*, *computer programs* expressed under any form and the *preparatory designs thereof* provided that programs can result from these designs at a later stage are protected as *'literary work'* (Article 2 No. 1 as amended by Act No. 4110 and Article 1(B) added by Act No. 4630).[86]

---

84. In some national laws, the protection periods for several kinds of neighbouring rights are different. They are shorter than protection period under *FSEK*. For instance under the Dutch Act on Neighbouring Rights of 18 Mar. 1993, the protection terms of neighbouring rights are as follows: (i) for recitations and performances: fifty years after the end of the year in which the work was performed or recited; (ii) for phonograms: fifty years after the end of the year in which they were recorded or, respectively, published; (iii) for broadcasts: thirty years from the end of the year of the broadcast. Under the Swiss Act on Copyright and Neighbouring Rights, these rights expire fifty years from the end of the calendar year in which the performance took place, the recording or film was made, or the broadcast was initially aired.
85. Cf. Berne Convention, Art. 8 (Paris Revision 1971).
86. Cf. TRIPS Agreement Art. 10(1) states that computer programs shall be protected as 'literary works' under the Berne Convention (1971). *See* Council Directive 91/250 [EC Software Directive] (14 May

277. Moreover, adaptation, editing or any modification of a computer program is protected as *adaptation* by *FSEK* (Article 6 No. 10 as amended by the 1995 Amendment).

A. *Object of Protection*

278. Under *FSEK*, a computer program is protected if it is original in the sense that it is the author's own intellectual creation.[87]

B. *Authorship of Computer Programs*

279. The author of a computer program is the natural person or group of natural persons who has created the programme (*FSEK* Article 8).[88]

280. Where a computer program is created by a group of natural persons jointly the exclusive rights shall be owned *jointly* (*FSEK* Articles 9 and 10).

281. Where a computer program is created by an employee in the execution of his/her duties or following the instructions given by his/her employer, the employer shall be exclusively entitled to exercise all economic rights to the programme so created, unless otherwise provided by contract (*FSEK*, Article 18(2)).

C. *The Author's Rights on Computer Programs*

282. *FSEK* has cited several *author's rights* on computer programs. Although it is permitted to reproduce all intellectual and artistic works for personal use without pursuing profit, this may not prejudice the legitimate interests of rightsholders without good reason or conflict with the normal exploitation of the work. (Cf. *FSEK* Article 38(1)). The provisions of *FSEK* related to the protection of computer programs were adopted from the EC Software Directive 91/250.[89]

283. The exclusive rights of the holder of the right on computer programs include the right to do or authorize:

- the permanent or temporary reproduction of a computer program by any means and in any form, in part or in whole;

1991) on the legal protection of computer programs (Cf. Directive 2009/24/EC of the European Parliament and of the Council of 23 Apr. 2009 on the legal protection of computer programs); WIPO Treaty, Art. 4.

87. Cf. EC Software Directive 91/250, Art. 1; Directive 2009/24/EC of the European Parliament and of the Council of 23 Apr. 2009 on the legal protection of computer programs.
88. Cf. EC Software Directive 91/250 Art. 2.
89. Cf. Directive 2009/24/EC of the European Parliament and of the Council of 23 Apr. 2009 on the legal protection of computer programs.

- the translation, adaptation, arrangement and any other alteration of a computer program and reproduction of the results thereof, without prejudice to the rights of the person who alters the program;
- any form of distribution to the public, including rental, of the original computer program or of copies thereof.[90]

284. Authorization by the holder is also required for loading, displaying, running, transmission or storage of the computer program in so far as these acts necessitate reproduction.

D. *Exceptionally Free (Non-Restricted) Acts*

285.

(a) The following acts -in short- do not require the author's authorization (*FSEK*, Article 38(3)-(8)):[91]
  - unless otherwise agreed, reproductions, translations, adaptation and arrangements by the rightful acquirer in accordance with the intended purpose of the computer program including for error correction (Article 38(3));
  - the making of a back-up copy by a rightful user (Article 38(4));
  - within certain specified limits, the observation, study or testing of the program by a rightful user (Article 38(5)).

(b) Where *reproduction of the code and the translation of its form* (decompilation), within the meaning of reproduction and adaptation of the computer programs are indispensable to obtain the information necessary to achieve the interoperability of an independently created computer program with other programs, the performing of such acts is permitted, provided the following conditions are met:
  - these acts are performed by the licensee or by another person entitled to use the copy of a computer program, or any person authorized to do so (rightful user);
  - the information necessary to achieve interoperability has not been made available to the persons mentioned above;
  - these acts are confined to the parts of the programmes which are necessary to achieve interoperability (Article 38(6)).[92]

286. The information obtained cannot be used, however, for goals other than to achieve the interoperability of the independently created computer program; to give this information to others, except when necessary for the interoperability of the independently created computer program; to use it for the development, production

90. Cf. EC Software Directive 91/250, Art. 4. Cf. further Directive 2009/24/EC of the European Parliament and of the Council of 23 Apr. 2009 on the legal protection of computer programs.
91. Cf. EC Software Directive, Art. 5.
92. Cf. EC Software Directive, Art. 6.

or marketing of a computer program substantially similar in its expression, or for any act which infringes on copyright (Article 38(7)).[93]

287. These exceptions may not be interpreted in a way that conflicts with the normal exploitation of the program or that unreasonably prejudices the rightholder's legitimate interests (Article 38(8)). [94]

II. Protection of Database

A. *Nature of the Right on Database*

288. Database is defined as 'a collection of independent works, data, or other materials arranged in a systematic or methodical way and individually accessible by electronic or other means'.[95]

289. The *EC Database Directive* aims to harmonize copyright protection of databases and introduces a parallel, sui generis form of protection that would be automatically available for all databases but would be more limited than copyright protection. Likewise, under the TRIPS Agreement, compilations of data or other material, whether in machine-readable or other form, which by reason of the selection or arrangement of their contents constitute intellectual creations are protected as such. Such protection shall not extend to the data or material itself (Article 10(2)). The WIPO Treaty has protected databases (compilations of data). This protection does not extend to the data or the material itself and is without prejudice to any copyright subsisting in the data or material contained in the compilation (Article 5).

290. The *EC Database Directive* has introduced a sui generis right. The scope of the sui generis right is limited compared to copyright but it has the advantage that it shall exist automatically, irrespective of the 'originality' of the database. The sui generis right consists of the right to prevent the unauthorized extraction or re-utilization of the contents of a database, in whole or in substantial parts for commercial purposes. This right belongs to the owner of the rights in the database and applies irrespective of the eligibility of a database for copyright protection.[96]

291. The 1995 *FSEK* Amendment relating to the protection of databases benefited from the solutions of the Database Directive. Therefore, the solutions of the *EC Database Directive* can be transferred to Turkish copyright law with regard to explaining and solving several issues related to databases.[97]

93. Cf. EC Software Directive, Art. 6(2).
94. Cf. EC Software Directive, Art. 6(3).
95. Cf. EC Database Directive, Art. 1.
96. Cf. EC Database Directive, Art. 7.
97. For details *see* Tekinalp, Ünal, pp. 131 et seq.

B. Object of Protection

292. In order to be protected by copyright, a database must be *original* in the sense that it is a collection of works or materials which, by reason of their selection or their arrangements, constitutes the author's own intellectual creation.

C. Authorship

293. The author of a database is the *natural person or group of persons* who created the database.

294. The economic rights on a database created by an *employee* in the course of his/her duty belong to his/her *employer* unless otherwise provided by contract.

D. Contents of Right

295. The *owner of copyright in a database* has, in respect of the selection or arrangement of the contents of the database, as well as its thesaurus, index or system for obtaining or presenting information the following exclusive rights:

- reproduction right;
- the right to translate, adapt, arrange or otherwise alter the database;
- the right to reproduce the results of any of the previous acts;
- the right of distribution to the public in any form, including rental;
- the right to communicate, display or perform the database to the public.

E. Term of Protection

296. The duration of copyright protection of databases will be the same as that provided for 'literary works'. Under the *EC Database Directive,* the sui generis right runs from the date of creation of the database and expires at the end of a period of fifteen years from the date when the database was first lawfully made available to the public (Additional Article 8).

§7. PROTECTION OF NEIGHBOURING RIGHTS

I. Nature of Neighbouring Rights

297. The rights accorded to persons who present creative works to the public but are not regarded as creators in their own right are generally known as *'neighbouring'* or *'related rights'.*

298. Neighbouring rights mean without prejudice to the protection of copyright in literary and artistic works, the *rights of performers* (actors, singers, musicians, dancers who act, sing, deliver, declaim, play in, or otherwise perform literary or artistic works), *producers of phonograms* (natural or legal person who first fixes the sounds of performance or other sounds), and *broadcasting organizations* (radio and television organizations engaged in transmission by wireless means for public reception of sounds or of images and sounds).[98]

299. Neighbouring rights under the *TRIPS Agreement* receive fairly extensive protection. *Performers* have the right to prohibit the unauthorized fixation and broadcast 'by wireless means' and 'communication to the public' of their live performances (Article 14).

300. In the 1995 *FSEK* amendments, several provisions of the Rome Convention for the Protection of Performers, Producers of Phonograms and Broadcasting Organizations (1961) were introduced to *FSEK* as Article 80.[99]

301. Under *FSEK*, regarding economic rights, the protection of neighbouring rights is less extensive than copyright protection. Likewise, the 'moral rights' of the owners of neighbouring rights are far less comprehensive than those of copyright owners. They mainly consist of their right to demand a mention of their name on the work to which their neighbouring right relates.

II. Protection of Neighbouring Rights

302. Under *FSEK*, the neighbouring rights are protected for seventy years (Article 82(5)–(7) as amended by Act, No 4630).

A. Protection of Performers' Rights

303. Performers may prevent:

- the broadcasting and the communication to the public, without their consent, of their performance;
- the fixation, without their consent, of their unfixed performance;
- the reproduction, without their consent, of a fixation of their performance if the reproduction is made for purposes different from those for which the performers gave their consent, etc.[100]

98. Cf. Rome Convention for the Protection of Performers, Producers of Phonograms and Broadcasting Organizations (1961), Art. 3.
99. This Article has been amended in February 2001 by Act No. 4630.
100. *FSEK* Art. 80. Cf. Rome Convention, Art. 7.

304. Protection of neighbouring rights is also less extensive in other respects. For instance, videograms or phonograms which have been produced and disseminated with the consent of the performing artist (and, as the case may be, the organizer) may be used for broadcasts without his/her consent.

305. Performance rights can be transferred to a producer by contract in return for reasonable remuneration. Where the performance is carried out by an orchestra, chorus or theatrical group, the permission of the conductor is sufficient. If an individual performing artist or ensemble has been engaged under a contract for recital, performance or presentation by an entrepreneur, the permission of the entrepreneur is also required.

B. Protection of Phonogram Producers' Rights

306. Producers of phonograms enjoy the right to authorize or prohibit the direct or indirect reproduction of their phonograms.[101]

C. Protection of Broadcasters' Rights

307. Broadcasting organizations enjoy the right to authorize or prohibit re-broadcasting of their broadcasts, fixation of their broadcasts, reproduction of fixations, made without their consent, of their broadcasts; the communication to the public of their television broadcasts if such communication is made in places accessible to the public against payment of an entrance fee.[102]

III. Exceptions

308. In the following cases, written permission is *not required* (Article 80):

- use solely for the purpose of teaching or scientific research;
- private use;
- use of short excerpts in connection with the reporting of current events;
- ephemeral fixation by a broadcasting organization by means of its own facilities and for its own broadcast.[103]

§8. Restrictions

309. FSEK sets out numerous exceptions to the *author's exclusive rights*. Under *FSEK*, the restrictions of the author's rights can be distinguished into four categories.

---

101. Cf. Rome Convention, Art. 9.
102. Cf. Rome Convention, Art. 13.
103. Cf. Rome Convention, Art. 15.

I. Private Use

A. *Reproduction*

310. Under *FSEK*, reproduction of all intellectual and artistic works is permitted for *private use* where there is no intent to exploit the work for profit. Such reproduction may not unreasonably prejudice the lawful interests of the rights owner or conflict with the normal exploitation of the work (Article 38(1)).

B. *Adaptations*

311. Previously, under *FSEK*, any person could have made or authorized the making of adaptations of musical, scientific, and literary works (Article 38(2)). This provision was repealed by Act, No. 4630, Article 36(d)).

C. *Computer Programs*

312.

(a) Under *FSEK*, the reproduction and adaptation of a computer program by a lawful purchaser are permitted where these are necessary for the use of the computer program in accordance with its intended purpose including for error correction (Article 38(3)).
(b) A person acquiring a computer program through legal means is entitled to the loading, running and error correction of the program.[104]
(c) A person having the right to use the computer program may make a back-up copy in so far as it is necessary for the use of the program. This right may not be prevented by contract.[105]
(d) The person has a right to use a copy of a computer program and is entitled to observe, study, or test the functioning of the program in order to determine the ideas and principles which underlie any element of the program in the course of performing any of the acts of loading, displaying, running, transmitting or storing the program which he/she is entitled to do.[106]

D. *Composer Rights*

313. Before 2001, composer rights were distinguished and regulated by a specific Article in *FSEK*. According to Article 39, a literary work could have been

104. Article 38(IV.) Cf. EC Software Directive, Art. 5(1). Further Directive 2009/24/EC of the European Parliament and of the Council of 23 Apr. 2009 on the legal protection of computer programs.
105. Article 38(4). Cf. EC Software Directive, Art. 5(2). Further Directive 2009/24/EC of the European Parliament and of the Council of 23 Apr. 2009 on the legal protection of computer programs.
106. Article 38(5). Cf. EC Software Directive, Art. 5(3). Cf. Directive 2009/24/EC of the European Parliament and of the Council of 23 Apr. 2009 on the legal protection of computer programs.

used in a musical work only with the written permission of the author. This provision was repealed by Act, No. 4630, Article 36(e).

314. If lyrics, librettos and analogous works used in any musical work were composed, permission must have been documented before the joint work was recorded, registered and placed into commercial circulation. These works could be inspected at each stage by the right owner as well as other persons concerned. This provision of Article 39 was repealed also by Act, No. 4630, Article 36(e).

315. Before Article 39 was repealed in 2001, it was possible to reproduce and distribute the lyrics free of charge by including these on sound-carrying devices and in print to be supplied together. Where such lyrics were reproduced and distributed, the title of the literary work and the name of the author would have to be mentioned.

E. Copy and Exhibition

316.

(a) Under *FSEK,* it is permitted to reproduce artistic works placed in a permanent manner on public roads and squares by means of drawings, graphics, photographs and otherwise (Article 40(1)). It is also allowed to display such works by projection in public premises or to broadcast by radio or analogous means (Article 40(1)). In respect of architecture, this permission extends only to the external form (Article 40(1)).
(b) Artistic works may be exhibited in public places by their owners or with their permission by other persons as long as there is no specific restriction placed on them by the author (Article 40(2)).
(c) Works to be sold at auction may be exhibited to the public. It is permitted to reproduce and diffuse works exhibited on public premises and put up for auction by means of catalogues, guides and analogous printed matter by the persons who have organized the exhibition or auction (Article 40(3)).

317. In such cases, the name of the author can be omitted provided there is no established custom to the contrary (Article 40(4)).

F. Use of Audio or Video Reproductions on Public Premises

318. Under *FSEK,* it is possible with the permission of the author to perform by means of playing and displaying on public premises whose entrances in return for a fee or not musical, scientific and literary works specially marked for performance on public premises and which have been recorded on devices enabling the reproduction of sound and/or vision. For this purpose, an agreement has to be made with the author or his/her professional association in accordance with Article 52 (Article 41(1)).

II. Public Order

319. The rights of the author may not prevent the work from being used as *evidence* in court or in other official departments.

320. *Photographs* may be reproduced and diffused in any form by the authorities for purposes of public order or for judicial purposes without the consent of the author (Article 30(1)).

III. Public Interest

321. Several restrictions have been laid down by *FSEK* for considerations of public interest.

A. Speeches

322. *FSEK* permits the reproduction or broadcasting by radio or by other means of diffusion of speeches delivered in the Turkish Grand National Assembly and in other official meetings and congresses, in courts and in public meetings for purposes of reporting news and giving information (Article 32(1)). In such cases, the name of the person who made a speech cannot be mentioned if the nature of the event does not necessitate doing so (Article 32(2)).

323. It should be noted that the right to reproduce and diffuse such speeches for purposes other than reporting belongs to the author (Article 32(3)).

B. Legislation and Court Decisions

324. Under *FSEK*, it is free to reproduce and diffuse the Presidential decrees (*Cumhurbaskanligi kararnamesi*), *regulations, communiqués, circulations and judicial decisions* announced or published officially (Article 31).

C. Freedom of Performance

325. *Performance of a published work on public premises*, exclusively for purposes of education and instruction is permitted. It is required, however, to mention in the usual manner, the name of the author and the title of the work. The same rule applies to performances the total net profits of which are entirely allocated to charity (Article 33).

D. Selections and Compilations for Purposes of Education

326. It is permitted to quote, for *scholarly use of protected works*, from published musical, scientific and literary works and publicly exhibited art works, in order to create selections and compilations, bringing together contributions from different authors (Article 34(1)).

327. These rules apply also to the school broadcasts prepared exclusively for schools and approved by the Ministry of Education (Article 34(2)).

328. In all cases, the title of the work and the name of the author must be cited in the usual manner.

E. Freedom of Quotation and Borrowing

329. FSEK permits, in principle, to make quotations from a work which has already been made available to the public:

(a) Under *FSEK*, *some sentences and paragraphs of a work that has become public* can be quoted and borrowed into an independent scientific and literary work.
(b) *Artistic works* which have become public and other works which have been published can be reproduced in scientific work in proportions justified by its purpose of clarifying the text.
(c) Moreover, *artistic works which have become public* can be shown by projection or by similar means during lectures for the purposes of clarifying the subject (Article 35(1)).

330. It must be noted that the quotation or borrowing must be made openly. In scientific works, the title of the work, the name of the author and the source of quotation or borrowing must be mentioned in the usual manner (Article 35(2)).

F. Quotations from Newspapers

331. Under *FSEK*, daily news and information diffused by the press or by radio may be freely quoted (Article 36):[107]

(a) If the right to quote from newspaper or periodical articles concerning *current social, political or economic problems* has not been expressly reserved, they may be freely borrowed as they are or in an adapted form by other newspapers or periodicals and broadcast by radio (Article 36(2)).[108]

107. Cf. Berne Convention, Paris Revision, 1971, Art. 10.
108. Cf. Berne Convention, Paris Revision, 1971, Art. 10 bis (1).

(b) If the right is reserved it is permitted to reproduce such an article in the form of press *summaries*, broadcast or diffuse it in any manner (Article 36(2)).

In all these cases, the name, the issue and date of the newspaper, review, press agency, and all other sources from which such borrowing has occurred, as well as the name, pseudonym or the mark of the author of the article must be mentioned (Article 36(3)).

G. News

332. Under *FSEK*, it is permitted to record certain passages of intellectual and artistic works related to current events as *interview* on devices enabling the transmission of signs, sounds and images. The reproduction, performance and broadcast by radio-television of such passages borrowed in this manner are permitted (Article 37).

333. Broadcast by radio-television of certain passages of scientific and literary works which have become public is permitted, provided that they are in the nature of news and do not exceed the limits of providing information (Article 36).

IV. Government Authority

A. Royalty in Broadcasting

334. Under *FSEK*, *royalty payments* must be made for intellectual and artistic works used in broadcasts on the radio or television (Article 43).

B. Identification of Intellectual and Artistic Works

335. *FSEK* provides for several protective measures for the author's rights:

(a) The owners of economic rights and the manufacturers and printers of devices enabling the reproduction by signs, sounds or images of intellectual and artistic work are *jointly responsible* (müstereken sorumlu) for placing an *identification sign and serial number* on all copies of a work to be reproduced, offer for sale, distributed or put into commercial circulation in any manner within the meaning of *FSEK* (Article 44(1)).
(b) Natural persons and legal entities producing or importing for commercial purposes empty video cassettes, sound cassettes, compact discs, and computer discs must deposit to a special account opened in a national bank in the name of the Ministry of Culture and Tourism, an amount not exceeding 3 of the production cost or importation cost to be fixed by a Presidential decree within the first half of the following month (Article 44(2)).

(c) Under *FSEK* the Ministry of Culture and Tourism shall use the money deposited at the special account to strengthen the intellectual property rights and to protect cultural heritage in Türkiye and abroad (Article 44(3)).

336. The details based on the principles and rules laid down in Article 44 have been arranged by an implementing regulation issued by the Ministry of Culture and Tourism (Article 44(4)).

C. *Authority to Enjoy the Work by the State*

337. Under *FSEK,* works as yet unpublished or not made public whose author has not expressly prohibited the reproduction and publication thereof and which are preserved in public libraries or museums or other similar establishments shall belong to the public institution or establishment in which they are situated, provided the term of protection in connection with economic rights has expired. The details are regulated by an implementing regulation to be issued by a presidential decree (Article 46).

D. *Expropriation*

338. Under *FSEK,* if a work is of importance to the country's culture, the power to enjoy the economic rights may be *expropriated* in return for an appropriate remuneration to the owner of the rights (Article 47(1)).[109]

339. A Presidential decree is required for expropriation.

340. In order to take a *decision of expropriation,* the work must be published in Türkiye or by Turkish nationals abroad (Article 47).

341. The expropriation decree must contain (i) the title of the work and the name of the author; (ii) the name of the institution or establishment which will enjoy the rights, and (iii) the amount of remuneration to be paid to the author upon request and which institution responsible for payment of remuneration; (iv) The purposes for which the net profit to be obtained after the redemption of the remuneration will be used (Article 47(2)).

§9. Transferability

342. Under *FSEK,* copyrights are *transferable* and can be *inherited.*

---

109. *See* Expropriation Act, No. 2942 of 4 Nov. 1983 (as amended).

I. Transactions Between Living Persons

A. *Original Acquisition*

1. Transfer

343. Under *FSEK*, the *author* or *his/her heirs* may *transfer* to third parties their economic rights for a limited or unlimited term (Article 48(1)).

2. Licensing

344. Only the use of economic rights can be *licensed* to others (Article 48(2)).

345. If a licence does not prohibit the owner of economic rights from assigning such licence to others, it is a *non-exclusive licence*. If a licence is granted to a certain person, it is an *exclusive licence* (Article 56(1)).

346. As a rule, a licence is considered *non-exclusive* (Article 56(2)).

347. Articles 357 et seq. of the Turkish Code of Obligations (TCO) on *usufructuary leases* (ürün kirasi) apply to non-exclusive (basit) licenses. Exclusive (tam) licences are governed by Turkish Civil Code (TCC) Articles 794 et seq. on *usufruct* (intifa hakki) (*FSEK*, Article 56(3)).

B. *Acquisition by Assignment*

348. Any party who has acquired from the author or his/her heir an *economic right* or *licence* to exploit this right may only *assign* (transfer) or *licence* (ruhsat) such right with his/her written consent (Article 49(1)).

349. In regard to the *assignment of the right of adaptation,* the consent of the author or his/her heirs is required (Article 49(2)).

C. *Agreements*

1. Agreements Related to Works to Be Produced

350. The assignment or licence related to a work which is not yet produced or which has still to be completed is null and void (Article 48(3)). However, commitments related to such agreements are valid (Article 50(1)). Commitments are transactions from which the obligation to make an assignment or to conclude an agreement result.

351. Such commitments concerning either all or a certain kind of works to be produced by the author in the future may be *cancelled* by either party on one year's notice (Article 50(2)).

352. On the other hand, if the author dies before the completion of the work, or becomes unable to complete it, the *commitment* (obligation) becomes *ipso iure* null and void.

353. The same rule applies to cases where the other party is declared *bankrupt* or becomes unable to benefit from the economic rights assigned to him/her (Article 50(3)).

2. Agreements Related to Future Possible Benefit

354. Agreements for the assignment or licence of economic rights which may accrue to the author in accordance with *future legislation* are null and void (Article 51(1)).

355. Likewise, agreements concerning the renunciation of powers resulting from the extension of the scope of economic rights by virtue of future legislation are invalid (Article 51(2)).

D. Form

356. Agreements concerning economic rights as well as *licence agreements* are subject to *written form.* In the agreement, the rights as the subject matter of the agreement must be specified (Article 52).

E. Guarantee

1. Existence of Right

357. The person assigning an economic right or granting a licence for its use is under the obligation to guarantee the existence of the right under the 2011 Turkish Code of Obligations, No. 6098 (Articles 191 and 193) to the person acquiring such right (*FSEK*, Article 53(1)).

358. The rights deriving from tort and unjust enrichment are reserved (Article 53(2)).

2. Non-existence of Power of Disposition

359. Under *FSEK*, any person acquiring an economic right or licence for use from a person who has no power to make such dispositions is not protected even if he/she acted in good faith (Article 54(1)).

360. In such a case, the person who assigned an economic right or granted the use thereof without the power of disposition is liable for compensation for damages caused by the nullity of the transaction. However, he/she may be exonerated from liability if he/she proves that the other party was aware or ought to have been aware that he/she had no power of disposition. In case of negligence, the court may award additional compensation if equity so requires (Article 54(2)).

361. The rights deriving from tort and unjust enrichment are reserved (Article 54(3)).

F. Rules of Interpretation

362. FSEK provides for several rules of interpretation related to the assignment or licensing of economic rights.

1. Scope

363. As a rule, the assignment of an economic right or the granting of a licence, unless agreed to the contrary does not extend to the translation or other adaptations of the work (Article 55).

2. Transfer of Ownership

364. Under *FSEK*, unless agreed to the contrary, the transfer of ownership of the original work or its reproductions does not entail the transfer of intellectual property rights (Article 57(1)).

365. Anyone who acquires from the owner a right of reproduction of an artistic work or the ownership of moulds and other devices of reproduction is considered to have acquired the right of reproduction unless agreed to the contrary (Article 57(2)).

G. Right of Renouncement

366. FSEK has granted the author the *right of renouncement* (cayma hakki).

367. If the assignee of an economic right or a licensee does not exercise his/her rights within the period of time agreed upon by the parties or within a reasonable time and if the author's interests are seriously affected thereby, the author may renounce the agreement (Article 58(1)).

368. In order to exercise this right, the author must notify *through a notary,* the assignee or the licensee to exercise his/her rights under the agreement (Article 58(2)).

369. If the assignee or licensee does not exercise his/her rights within the notified period of time, the renunciation becomes complete upon sending a notice through a notary (Article 58(3)).

370. No action for objection may be brought against the renunciation after the expiration of four weeks from the date of service of notice of renunciation (Article 58(3)).

371. If the assignee is not negligent for failure to exercise economic rights or if greater negligence is found on the part of the author, the assignee may claim compensation where equity so requires (Article 58(4)).

372. The right of renunciation may not be forfeited in advance. Likewise, any restrictions on claims to such right for a period exceeding two years are null and void (Article 58(5)).

H. Return of the Right to the Owner

1. Transfer of Economic Rights

373. If an author or his/her heirs assign economic rights for *a specific purpose* or for a *designated term*, such rights return to the owner on the elimination of the purpose or expiration of the term (Article 59(1))

374. This provision does not apply in the *event of death or bankruptcy assignee* of an economic right who is not allowed by agreement to assign it to a third party unless the nature of the matter requires the use of the right by the assignee him/herself (Article 59(1)).

2. Licence

375. Licences granted for a specific purpose or a specific term terminate upon elimination of the purpose or expiration of the term (Article 59(2)).

II. Right of Waiver

376. Under *FSEK*, an author or his/her heirs may waive their legal economic rights conferred by law by an *official deed* and *publication of the matter in the Official Gazette*. The waiver does not prejudice the dispositions made previously (Article 60(1)).

377. The waiver is effective from the date of its publication. It produces the same legal results as the expiration of the term of protection (Article 60(2)).

III. Succession

A. *In General*

378. Economic rights may be *inherited* by succession. They may be subject to dispositions dependent on death *mortis causa* (Article 63).

379. If economic rights are inherited by the heirs of the deceased author, a *representative* is appointed to dispose of these rights under the Turkish Civil Code (Article 640). Such a representative must obtain the heirs' decision on any transaction related to economic rights (*FSEK*, Article 65).

B. *Death of One of the Joint Authors of a Work*

1. Death Before the Work Has Become Public

380. If a *co-author* dies *before the work is completed or has become public*, his/her share is distributed among the other authors. The surviving authors must pay proper remuneration to the heirs of the deceased author. In case of disagreement, the amount of remuneration is determined by the court (Article 64(1)).

2. Death after the Work Has Become Public

381. If a co-author dies *after the work has become public*, the other authors are free to continue or discontinue the joint ownership with his/her heirs (Article 64(2)):

- If they decide to *continue the joint-authorship*, the surviving authors may request the heirs to appoint a *representative* to exercise their rights in the joint-authorship (Articles 64(3) and 65).
- If it is decided to *discontinue the joint-authorship*, the share of the deceased author is distributed between the surviving authors in return for *proper remuneration* to the heirs of the deceased (Article 64(4)).

IV. Seizure and Pledge

A. *Permitted Cases*

382.

(a) Under *FSEK*, the following may *constitute* the *subject of a legal or contractual pledge*, or a *forced execution* or *retention*:
  - draft or original work made public;
  - reproduced copies of a published work;

- economic rights of the author over a work that has become public (provided the author's moral rights are not effected prejudicially);
- money debts due to the author as a result of legal transactions concerning economic rights (Article 62(1)).

(b) *Pledge agreements* concerning intellectual and artistic works or economic rights thereof must be *in writing* and the *subjects of the pledge* must be specified in the agreement (Article 62(2)).

(c) Under *FSEK*, moulds and other devices used to *reproduce artistic works* may be *temporarily seized from their holders* (possessors) if they are considered necessary for the execution of enforcement of collection of a debt relating to economic rights (Article 62(3)).

(d) Likewise, excepting architectural works, *originals of artistic works* and *drafts of musical, scientific and literary works* belonging to the author or his/her heirs may be *temporarily seized from their holders* (possessors) thereof as deemed necessary for the execution of enforcement of collection of a debt relating to economic rights (Article 62(4)).

B. Prohibited Cases

383. Under *FSEK*, the following may *not constitute* the subject of a legal or contractual pledge or a forced execution or retention:

- *drafts or originals of a work not yet made public*, which are the property of the author or one of his/her heirs;
- *economic rights of such works*, except cinematographic works;
- *debts due to the author other than money* resulting from legal transactions concerning economic rights (Article 61(1)).

384. It should be noted that in the cases mentioned above, Articles 24 and 30 of the Code of Enforcement and Bankruptcy (*Icra ve Iflas Kanunu*) No. 2004 (as amended) are reserved.

§10. Civil Remedies

I. In General

385. In cases of infringement on an author's rights, *FSEK* has a number of civil remedies which provide *comprehensive protection* to an author.

386. The *civil remedies* provided for by *FSEK* are harmonious with the solutions of other national laws.[110]

110. Regarding civil remedies Swiss law can be cited as an example. The Swiss Act on Copyright and Neighbouring Rights of 9 Oct. 1992 (BG über das Urheberrecht und verwandte Schutzrechte [Urheberrechtsgesetz, URG]) has enumerated the civil remedies in Arts 61 et seq. These remedies

II. Remedies Provided for by Civil Actions

A. Action for Cease-and-Desist of Infringement

387. In case of danger of infringement on his/her moral or economic rights, the author may initiate *an action for cease-and-desist of infringement* (Tecavüzün men'i davasi). In cases where there is a likelihood of continuation or repetition of an infringement that has occurred the same action can be initiated (Article 69).

388. This action is directed against the *infringer* or against the *owner of an undertaking* (isletme), if the infringement has been committed by a representative or employee of the undertaking during the course of the execution of their work (Articles 66(1) and (2) and 69(2)).

389. Neighbouring rights holders may initiate the action for cease-and-desist (Article 80(1)(a)).

B. Action for Prevention of Infringement

1. In General

390. Any person whose moral and economic rights have been infringed may initiate an *action for the prevention of infringement* (tecavüzün ref'i davasi).[111]

391. This action is directed against the *infringer* or the *owner of the undertaking* (isletme) if the infringement has been committed by its representative or employees during the performance of their duties (Article 66(1)–(2)).

392. The *negligence* on the part of the infringer is not required for such action (Article 66(3)).

393. The court may render its decision on the *measures* necessary to prevent the infringement, taking into account the author's moral and economic rights, the scope of the infringement, the existence or non-existence and gravity of negligence and the damage likely to be suffered by the infringer in the event of elimination of the infringement (Article 66(4)).

---

include, a declaratory judgment that the given act or situation is against the law (Feststellungsklage); an order to compel the infringing person to state from where the infringing copies come (Leistungsklagen); monetary awards of damages for actual losses and for the claim of the defendant's profits; awards of damages for pain and suffering; seizure, sale, confiscation, or distraction of infringing goods, and publication of the judgment (Veröffentlichung des Urteils). A temporary restraining order (injunction; provisionary measures) may be obtained, but it must be followed by a formal claim.

111. For an example, *see* Oguz / Yilmaztekin / Üner, FMHUArb, pp. 141–149.

394. Like authors, *neighbouring right holders* may also initiate the action for the prevention of infringement (Article 80).

395. The author may initiate the action for the prevention of infringement *at the place where he/she is domiciled* (Article 66(5)).

2. Infringement on Moral Rights

396. *FSEK* has provided for extensive protection with regard to infringements on the moral rights of the author:

(a) If *a work which has not yet become public* is communicated to the public without the author's consent or against his/her will, *action for prevention of infringement* may only be commenced if communication to the public by the *publication of the reproduced copies* is affected.
(b) The same rule also applies if the *author's name is placed on the work against his/her will.*
(c) If the author's name:
   - is not placed on the work at all; or
   - is placed erroneously; or
   - the name placed is of a nature likely to give rise to confusion; and
   - the author has, in addition to the *action for mentioning his/her name* (Article 15), requested the *prevention of infringement*, the infringer must insert the author's name on the original as well as on the reproduced copies in circulation (Article 67(2)).

   In the action for prevention of infringement, the announcement of the judgment in no more than three newspapers at the cost of the infringer may be demanded (Article 67(2)).
(d) If *a wrong or insufficient source* or *no source at all has been indicated* in cases related to speeches (Article 32), presentation of a published work (Article 33), selection and compilations for purposes of education (Article 34), quotations or borrowing from scientific, literary or musical works (Article 35), quotations of articles on social, political or economic issues from newspapers (Article 36), exhibition of artistic works in public places (Article 40), the *action for prevention of infringement* may be initiated. In such cases, the court orders the infringer to *insert the author's name* (Article 67(3)).
(e) If a work has been *wrongly modified*, the holder of the right may direct against the infringer the following claims (Article 67(4)):
   - The author may request that *reproduction, publication and performance of the work* in its modified form and its *broadcast by radio* must be stopped and that the infringer rectifies the modifications made by him/her contained in the copies in circulation or that he/she restore the work to its previous form.
   - If the modification has been made on the diffusion of the work by *newspapers, magazines or radio broadcasts*, the author may request all newspapers, magazines and radio broadcast administrations (undertakings) which

have diffused the work in the modified form to rectify the modification by way of publication at the cost of the infringer (Article 67(4)(1)).

- Regarding *artistic works*, the author may demand that it be made known that modification of the original work was not made by him/her, or that his/her name on the work be removed or altered (Article 67(4)(2)).

397. If it is possible to restore the work to its original form and if the elimination of the modification does not prejudice the interests of the public or of the owner in any fundamental way, the author may restore the work to its original form (Article 67(4)(2)).

3. Infringement on Economic Rights

398. In cases of infringement of economic rights, the author may demand the *prevention of infringement and compensation* (Article 68).

399. Like authors, neighbouring rights holders are also entitled to initiate the action for the prevention of infringement (Article 80).

C. Action for Compensation

1. In General

400. If the infringer is *negligent*, the person whose economic rights have been infringed may claim damages (Article 70(2); TCO Article 49). *Neighbouring rights holders* may claim compensation like authors (*FSEK*, Article 80).

2. Compensation for Infringement on Economic Rights

401.

(a) If the *work* has been:
- translated without the author's consent; or
- published outside the scope of the contract, or in excess of the number indicated in the contract; or
- adapted in some other way; or
- broadcast by radio or television; or
- performed without the consent of the author, the author may claim as compensation up to three times the amount of damages sustained thereby according to the current value (Article 68(1)).[112]

112. Article 68(1) as amended by the Act, No. 4630 and by Act, No. 5728 of 23 Jan. 2008, Art. 137. Turkish Constitutional Court has rejected a request for annulment of the remedy for 'compensation

(b) If the *benefit is being derived from a work through unauthorized reproduction* and the reproduced copies *have not been put into commercial circulation*, the owner of the work may demand:
   - the destruction of the reproduced copies, as well as;
   - devices such as films, moulds, etc. enabling reproduction be handed over to him/her in return for a reasonable remuneration not to exceed the cost price; or
   - three times the amount he/she would have claimed where a contract had existed. This does not eliminate the legal liability of the person carrying out unauthorized reproduction (Article 68(2)).

(c) If *copies of a work reproduced without the consent of the author have been put up for sale* or if the nature of the sale constitutes unfair practice, the author may choose one of the above-mentioned alternatives in respect of the copies in possession of the infringer (Article 68(3)).

(d) The person making a monetary claim may bring forward against an infringer all rights he/she would have had if there had been an agreement between them (Article 68(6)).

402. In action for compensation, the author whose economic rights have been infringed may request, not only *compensation* but also the *transfer of profit*. In such a case, the amount claimed in accordance with Article 68 is deducted (Article 70(3)).

3. Compensation for Infringement on Moral Rights

403. If the author's moral rights have been infringed, he/she may demand *compensation for 'moral damages'* (damage moral) (Article 70(1)).

404. Compensation is usually a monetary award. However, the court may award other kinds of compensation in lieu of, or in addition to, money (Article 70(2)).

405. In cases of moral damages, in addition to compensation, the author whose moral rights have been infringed may request the *transfer of profit* (Article 70(3)).

D. Action for Security (Recording) of Evidence

406. In cases of infringements on the author's rights, the author may initiate the action for the security of evidence. This action is subject to the Code of Civil Procedure, No. 6100 (CCP, *HMK*, Articles 400 et seq.).

up to three times' emphasizing that it is not contrary to the Constitution. *See* Decision of the Constitutional Court of 28 Feb. 2013 (E 2012/133; K 2013/33).

E. Action for Provisionary (Interim) Measures (Injunction)

407. In case of serious damage, the author whose rights have been infringed may initiate the *action for provisionary*[113] *measures*. Such measures can be requested under the Code of Civil Procedure (CCP, *HMK* Articles 389–399). However, *FSEK* has provided some special provisions on provisionary measures for the protection of the author's rights (Article 77).

408. Under *FSEK*, the court may, in order to prevent serious damage, sudden danger or a 'fait accompli' order the defendant to do or refrain from doing certain acts.

409. The court may order the temporary seizure of reproduced copies of a work or of the moulds and other devices for reproduction. The decision specifies that the penalties set out in Article 343 of the Code of Enforcement and Bankruptcy, No. 2004 (as amended) would apply in case of failure to comply with the order.

410. The provisionary measures can be requested in the actions for prevention of infringement, cease-and-desist, and compensation. These measures can also be requested before the initiation of such actions.

411. When the court orders *provisionary measures*, the main action (for cease-and-desist, prevention, compensation) must be initiated within two weeks (CCP, *HMK*, Article 397).

F. Announcement of the Judgment

412. Under *FSEK*, if the successful party has a justified ground or interest, he/she may demand that the *full text* or *a summary of the final judgment* be announced in newspapers or analogous means at the cost of the defendant. The form and contents of the announcement are specified in the decision. The right of announcement must be used within three months from the date when the judgment has become *final* (res judicata) (Article 78).

III. Specialized Courts and Mediation

A. Subject-Matter Jurisdiction (Görev)

413. The civil actions relating to copyright must be initiated before '*specialized*' courts of first instance. Under *FSEK* Article 76, these courts are specified by direct reference to the relevant procedural provisions of *SMK*, No. 6769 (Industrial Property Law, Article 156). For further explanations, *see* below paragraph in Chapter 2 – Patents and Utility Models – 'Specialized Courts and Mediation'.

---

113. It should be noted that the terms 'interim, interlocutory, precautionary, preliminary and provisional' are used in various legal texts with the same meaning.

B. Territorial Jurisdiction (Venue, Forum, Yetki)

414. The territorial jurisdiction of the above-mentioned specialized civil courts is covered in the Code of Civil Procedure (CCP, *HMK*, Article 6). The court at the place of domicile (yerlesim yeri) of the respondent (natural or legal person) at the time the action is brought shall have jurisdiction. In case of prevention or cease-and-desist of infringement, the author may also initiate the action before the court of the place where he/she is domiciled (*FSEK*, Article 66(5)).

C. Mandatory Mediation Attempt and 'The Singapore Convention on Mediation'

415. In recent years, the parties to private law disputes are encouraged to mediate before initiating litigation.[114] An increasing number of specific private law disputes are mandatorily subject to mediation before being tried before courts. The types of suits (actions) which require a mandatory mediation attempt (dava sarti, Prozessvoraussetzungen) as a pre-condition for court litigation are not specifically listed. The prospective litigants are expected to follow the relevant general principles laid out primarily in the Act on Mediation in Civil Law Disputes (AMedC, *Hukuk Uyusmazliklarinda Arabuluculuk Kanunu, HUAK)*, No. 6325 (Official Gazette of 22 June 2012, as amended). Moreover, certain disputes regarding intellectual property are subject to pre-conditional commercial mediation (dava sarti ticari arabuluculuk) under Articles 4(1) and 5(A) of the Turkish Commercial Code (TComC), No. 6102.

416. Türkiye is a State Party to the United Nations Convention on International Settlement Agreements Resulting from Mediation, also known as the Singapore Convention on Mediation ('Convention'). On 11 April 2022, the Convention entered into force, in accordance with the Article 14 of the Convention and the Presidential Decree no. 5235, 6 months after the deposit of the instrument of ratification to the United Nations (UN). Settlement agreements made in accordance with the Convention can easily be recognised and enforced internationally, i.e., in other State Parties.

§11. Penal Sanctions for Offenses

I. Infringement of Moral, Economic or Related Rights

417. Any person who, by infringing the moral, economic and related rights regarding intellectual and artistic works protected under *FSEK*; adapts, performs,

114. For a summary of arbitration and mediation regarding patents and utility models within a monography on Patents, *see* Çolak, Ugur, *Türk Patent Hukuku*, Ankara, 2022, Part Nineteen, pp. 1213–1244.

reproduces, changes, distributes, communicates to the public by technical devices or publishes a work, performance, phonogram or production without written permission of right holders or puts up for sale, sells, distributes by renting or lending or in any other way, buys for commercial purposes, imports or exports, possesses or stores for non-personal use any works adapted or reproduced unlawfully (Article 71(1)(No. 1)); gives a title to the work of another person as his/her own (Article 71(1)(No. 2)); cites from a work without referring to the source (Article 71(1)(No. 3)); makes a declaration to the public without permission of the right holders concerning the content of a work which has not yet been made public (Article 71(1)(No. 4)); gives a reference regarding a work in a wrong, incomplete or misleading way (Article 71(1)(No. 5)); reproduces, distributes, publishes or broadcasts a work, performance, phonogram or a production by using the name of a well-known other person (Article 71(1)(No. 6)) shall be sentenced to various terms of imprisonment or a judicial fine.

418. Persons who commit the further particular offences in *FSEK*, and content providers who continue to infringe the rights recognised under *FSEK* shall be sentenced to various imprisonment penalties (Article 71(2)).

419. Where any person who puts up for sale, sells or buys any kind of illegally produced work, provides information as to his/her sources and enables them to be captured before the prosecution process, the penalty to be imposed may be omitted or reduced (Article 71(3)).

II. Circumventing Technological Protections

420. It is possible to control the use of works, performances, phonograms, productions and broadcasts with various effective technological measures such as access control or encryptions in order to protect the rights granted in *FSEK*. Persons who supply or keep products and tools for various commercial purposes with the aim of rendering these protective measures ineffective[115] are punished by imprisonment.[116]

115. The solutions of *FSEK* regarding offences related to computer programs comply with EU legislation. As known under EC Software Directive 91/250, the following acts are punished by penal sanctions (Art. 7): any act putting into circulation a copy of a computer program knowing, or having reason to believe, that it is an infringing copy; the possession, for commercial purposes, a copy of a computer program knowing, or having reason to believe, that it is an infringing copy; any act of putting into circulation, or the possessing for commercial purposes of, any means the sole intended purpose of which is to facilitate the unauthorized removal or circumvention of any technical device which may have been applied to protect a computer program. Cf. Directive 2009/24/EC of the European Parliament and of the Council of 23 Apr. 2009 on the legal protection of computer programs.
116. *FSEK* Articles 73 and 74 were revoked in 2008.

III. Seizure, Sequestration and Destruction

421. Under *FSEK* Article 77(2) seizure, sequestration and destruction are subject to the Law on Customs *(Gümrük Kanunu)*, No. 4458, Article 57.

IV. Prosecution

A. *Complaint of the Infringed Person*

422. Criminal prosecution takes place, as a rule, upon complaint of the *copyright holder* (infringed party) (Article 75(1)).

B. *Duty to Inform the Right Holder of Infringements*

423. The Ministry of National Education and the Ministry of Culture and Tourism, as well as concerned natural and legal persons are under a duty to inform the right holders of any such infringements (Article 75(2)).

V. Jurisdiction and Competent Court

424. Criminal cases are handled by the specialized courts established under Article 156 of *SMK* (*FSEK*, Article 76(1)).

§12. Other Protective Measures

425. Besides civil remedies and penal sanctions, 1995, 2001 and 2008 Amendments to *FSEK* have provided for some other measures for the protection of authors' rights and neighbouring rights.

I. Duty to Affix a Banderole (*bandrol*) on Non-serial Publications

A. *Duty to Affix Banderole*

426. It is obligatory to affix on non-serial publications a *banderole* to be secured from the Ministry of Culture and Tourism (Article 81(1)–(3)).

B. *Sanction*

427. In cases of unauthorized exercise of economic and neighbouring rights (Article 80) in intellectual and artistic works and violations relating to the duty to affix banderole, the infringers are punished (Articles 81(4) et seq.).

II. Unfair Competition

A. *Unauthorized Use of Names and Marks*

1. Infringement

428. Under *FSEK, the title and marks of a work* and *the forms of its reproduced copies* may not be used in another work or its reproduced copies in any manner which may give rise to confusion (Article 83(1)).

429. This provision does not apply to titles, marks and external forms used publicly and having no distinctive character (Article 83(2)). Moreover, the provisions of the Press Law (PL) (Article 14) relating to names of periodicals are reserved (Article 83(4)).

2. Sanction

430. Even if an infringer is *not a merchant*, the provisions of the Turkish Commercial Code No. 6102 of 13 January 2011 on unfair competition (Articles 54 et seq.) are applicable to any person acting in violation of Article 83(1) (unauthorized use of names and marks of work by causing confusion) (Article 83(5)).

B. *Unauthorized Use of Signs, Images and Sounds*

1. Infringement

431. Any person who fixes a sign, image or sound on a device enabling the transmission of the same or reproduces or diffuses thereof rightfully for commercial purposes may prevent a third party from reproducing or diffusing the same sign, image or sound by benefiting from the same devices (Article 84(1)).

432. This provision is also applicable to *any photographs* which do not qualify as works, images fixed by analogous means and cinematographic productions (Article 84(3)).

2. Sanction

433. The provisions of the Turkish Commercial Code (TComC, *TTK*) on *unfair competition* (Articles 54 et seq.) apply in such cases, even if the infringer is *not a merchant* (*FSEK* Article 84(2)).

C. *Letters*

1. Rule

434.

(a) Even *if they do not have the character of a work, letters, memoirs and analogous writings* may not be published without the consent of their writers (Article 85(1)).

If the writer is dead, the consent of the persons cited in Article 19(1) must be obtained. If an *executor* has been appointed by the deceased, the consent can be given by his/her executor. If no executor has been appointed, the consent successively of the *surviving spouse and his/her children, his/her appointed heirs, his/her parents, his/her brothers and sisters* is required, unless a period of *ten years* has elapsed since the death of the writer (Article 85(2)).

(b) In addition to the conditions of the above paragraph, letters may not be published without the *consent of the addressee*, or if he/she is dead of the persons cited above unless a period of *ten years* has elapsed (Article 85(2)).

2. Sanction

435. Publication of letters without consent is an *offence* under *FSEK*, Article 85(3), Turkish Penal Code (TPC), No. 5237, Articles 132, 134, 139 and 140.

436. Moreover, *civil remedies* provided for by the 2011 Turkish Code of Obligations, No. 6098 (Article 58) are applicable in such violations (*FSEK*, Article 85(3)).

437. In cases where diffusion is permitted, civil remedies for the protection of '*personality rights*' under the Turkish Civil Code, No. 4721 (Article 24) are reserved (*FSEK*, Article 85(4)).

D. *Pictures and Portraits*

1. In General

438. Rule: Even *if they do not have the character of a work, pictures and portraits* may not be exhibited or communicated to the public in any other way without the consent of the person portrayed (Article 86(1)).

439. If he/she is dead, the consent of the persons cited in Article 19(1) is required unless a period of *ten years* has elapsed since the death of the person portrayed (Article 86(I)).

440. On the other hand, unless agreed to the contrary, *photographs* may be taken of any pictures and portraits executed *on order* by the person who has placed the order or by the person portrayed or by their heirs (Article 87(1)).

441. This rule does not apply to *portraits and pictures from prints*. However, if it is impossible or rather difficult for the above-mentioned persons to obtain pictures and portraits produced in this manner, their photographs may also be taken (Article 87(2)).

442. *Exceptions*: Consent is not required in the following cases (Article 86(2)):

(i) pictures of persons who have played a role in the political or social life of the nation;
(ii) pictures showing official parades or receptions or general meetings in which the persons portrayed have participated;
(iii) pictures relating to current events, together with news on the radio and on film.

2. Sanction

443. To exhibit or communicate pictures or portraits without the consent of the person portrayed is an offence (*FSEK*, Article 86(3)).

444. Article 49 of the Turkish Code of Obligations, No. 6098 applies to civil remedies (i.e., compensation for moral damages) (*FSEK*, Article 86(3)).

445. Where diffusion is permitted, the *'personality right'* is protected by *Turkish Civil Code,* No. 4721 (Article 24; *FSEK* Article 86(4)).

§13. Professional Associations: Collecting Societies

I. Foundation of Professional Associations

A. Legal Regulation of Professional Associations

446. Under *FSEK* Article 42, authors and owners of neighbouring rights may establish professional associations in accordance with the *'regulation'* (yönetmelik) and *'uniform statutes'* (tip statüler) to be issued by the President in *order to protect the mutual interests of their members, to pursue their rights and to ensure the collection of fees and distribution of fees to the right owners.*[117]

117. Although professional associations (collecting societies) have first been regulated by Art. 42 of *FSEK* in 1951, they were not established until the article was amended in 1983 by the Act No. 2936. Under the duty prescribed by this article, the Ministry of Culture and Tourism prepared the first 'Regulation on Professional Associations and Federation for Authors of Intellectual and Artistic

447. Under *FSEK*, more than one professional association (collection society) may be established in each professional field. Each collection association may open the necessary branch offices (Article 42(1)-(2)).

448. Members of professional organizations are not obliged to invest capital, participate in profits and losses, or assume legal responsibility (Article 42(3)).

449. Professional associations may establish a higher organization (federation) (Article 42(2)). Professional associations and their higher organizations (federation) are subject to private law (Article 42(3)).

B. Duties of Professional Associations

450. The professional associations are entitled to manage the economic rights of their members and to *protect their mutual interests*. They are authorized to pursue their rights, collect the fees and distribute the fees to the right owner (Article 42).

451. For further details relating to the duties and supervision of professional associations *see FSEK* Articles 42(A), 42(B) and the relevant Regulation, No. 5405

II. Existing Professional Associations

452. The following professional associations have been founded under *FSEK* Article 42.

453. MESAM (Müzik Eseri Sahipleri Meslek Birligi): for musical and cinematographic works.[118]

454. MSG (Musiki Eseri Sahipleri Grubu Meslek Birligi): professional association for the group of owners of musical works.

455. MÜYAP (Baglantili Hak Sahibi Müzik Yapimcilari Meslek Birligi): professional union for musical works producers who are owners of related rights.

456. MÜYORBIR (Müzik Yorumculari Meslek Birligi): professional union of music interpreters (performers).

Works' (approved by the Decree, No. 86/10534 of the Council of Ministers) and 'Uniform Statute for Professional Associations' (approved by Decree No. 86/10835 of the Council of Ministers). Art. 42 was further amended by Act No. 4110 in 1995; Act No. 4630 in 2001, and Act No. 5101 in 2004. The current 'Regulation on Professional Associations [collecting societies] in the Field of Copyrights' (*Telif Haklari Alaninda Meslek Birlikleri Yönetmeligi*; Presidential Decree of 6 April 2022, No. 5405, Official Gazette of 7 April 2022, No. 31802) replaced the previous Regulation (Tüzük) of 1999 (as amended) covering similar issues.)

118. MESAM is the counterpart of GEMA in Germany and SUISA in Switzerland.

457. *RATEM* (Radyo Televizyon Yayincilari Meslek Birligi): professional union for radio-TV broadcasters.

458. *ILESAM* (Ilim ve Edebiyat Eseri Sahipleri Meslek Birligi): professional union for owners of scientific and literary works.[119]

459. *YAYBIR* (Yayincilar Meslek Birligi): professional union for publishers.

460. SESAM (Sinema Eseri Sahipleri Meslek Birligi): professional association of the owners of cinematographic works (cinematographers, art directors, costume designers, sound engineers, picture authors, including visual artists, photographers and film authors).[120]

461. SETEM (Sinema ve Televizyon Eseri Sahipleri Meslek Birligi): professional association of film directors, writers and composers, established in 2003.

462. GESAM (Güzel Sanat Eseri Sahipleri Meslek Birligi): professional association for the rights of authors of fine arts.

§14. CONFLICT OF LAWS

463. At present under the *Act on Private International Law and Procedural Law*, No. 5718 of 27 November 2007 'intellectual property rights are subject to the *law of the country under which the protection is requested*' (Article 23(1)).

464. The parties may agree on the application of the law of the court regarding the claims arising out of the infringement of intellectual property rights *after the infringement has been committed* (Article 23(2)).[121]

119. ILESAM is the counterpart of PROLITTERIS in Switzerland.

120. SESAM is the counterpart of BILD/KUNST in Germany.

121. Previously the provisions of *FSEK* were applicable to (i) all works communicated to the public for the first time in Türkiye; (ii) all works existing in Türkiye but not yet communicated to the public; (iii) all letters and pictures existing in Türkiye, irrespective of the nationality of the author (Art. 88). As regards works not yet communicated to the public outside Türkiye, previously *FSEK* also applied to (i) all works of foreigners which have not yet been communicated to the public outside Türkiye; or (ii) all works of foreigners which have been communicated to the public outside Türkiye provided that there are appropriate provisions in an international convention to which Türkiye is a party (Art. 88).This Article has been repealed by Act, No. 5718 of 27 Nov. 2007, Art. 64(3). *FSEK* had regulated also works of Turkish nationals communicated or not yet communicated to the public abroad. Previously, *FSEK* also applied to (i) all works of Turkish nationals which had not yet been communicated to the public for the first time outside Türkiye; or (ii) all works of Turkish nationals which had been communicated to the public for the first time outside Türkiye (Art. 88(I) No. 2. This Article has been repealed by the Act on Private International Law and Procedural Law, No. 5718. At present the provisions of the Act, No. 5718 apply to such cases (Art. 23).

Chapter 2. Patents and Utility Models

§1. Legal Sources

I. National Sources

A. *Overview*

465. The previous Turkish patent law was regulated by 'Decree Having the Power of Law on the Protection of Patent Rights, *KHK*/551' *(Patent Haklarinin Korunmasi Hakkinda Kanun Hükmünde Kararname, KHK*/551) of 27 June 1995. At present, this *KHK* is abolished and replaced by 'Industrial Property Law', No. 6769 (*Sinai Mülkiyet Kanunu*) of 22 December 2016 (for patents and utility models *see* Articles 82–141; 142–145; regarding the common provisions of all industrial property *see* Articles 146 et seq.).[122]

B. *The Structure of* SMK, *No. 6769 Book Four on Patents and Utility Models*

466. Book Four in *SMK* deals with 'Patent and Utility Models' (Articles 82–145).

467. Part One is dedicated to 'Patent Right' (Articles 82 et seq.). Chapter One in this Part regulates the 'Requirements of Patentability' (Articles 82–84). Chapter Two handles 'Scope of Patent Right' (Articles 85–89).[123]

468. Second Part lays down the rules relating to 'Application, Grant of Patent and Objection' (Articles 90 et seq.). Chapter One regulates the requirements of 'Application and Priority Right' (Articles 90–94); Chapter Two is devoted to the issues relating to 'Grant of Patent' (Articles 95–98). Chapter Three lays down the provisions on 'Objection and Examination of Objection' (Articles 99–100). Chapter Four deals with the 'Term of Protection and Annual Fees' (Article 101).

469. Part Three regulates 'Transactions regarding Patent Process' (Articles 102–108).

---

122. Official Gazette, No. 29944 of 10 Jan. 2017. On this occasion we would like to mention some significant points which were introduced to the Turkish patent law by *KHK*/551: (i) regulation of utility models; (ii) introduction of a patent system based on examination and non-examination; (iii) criteria for patentability (novelty, inventive step, susceptibility of industrial applicability); (iv) publication of applications; (v) opposition by third parties; (vi) protection terms (seven years for non-examined patents; ten years for utility models, and twenty years for patents granted upon examination); (vii) employee inventions; (viii) compulsory licensing which is compatible to the TRIPS Agreement; (ix) a system of satisfactory protection against infringements; (x) specialized court for patent infringements.

123. For a comprehensive examination of patent law in Türkiye in a monography, *see* Çolak, Ugur, *Türk Patent Hukuku*, Ankara, 2022.

470. Part Four concerns 'Right Ownership and Usurpation' (Articles 109–112).

471. Part Five deals with the issues relating to 'Employees' Inventions' (Articles 113–122).

472. Part Six lays down the rules on 'Supplementary and Confidential Patent' (Articles 123–124).

473. Part Seven regulates patent 'License' (Articles 125 et seq.). Chapter One lays down rules on 'License based on a Contract' (Articles 125–128). Chapter Two regulates 'Compulsory License' (Articles 129–137).

474. Part Eight deals with the situations relating to 'Termination of Right' (Articles 138 et seq.). Chapter One handles the situations concerning 'Invalidity' of patent (Articles 138–139); Chapter Two lays down provisions on 'Other Grounds of Termination and Their Effects' (Article 140).

475. Part Nine regulates the cases of 'Infringement on Patent Right' (Article. 141).

476. Part Ten is dedicated to the issues relating to 'Utility Models' (Articles 142–145).

477. The Implementing Regulation issued by the Turkish Patent and Trademark Office [or Authority, i.e. TürkPatent] in 2017 lays down details regarding the implementation of patents and utility models as well as other industrial property rights.[124]

II. International Sources

478. Türkiye is a party to the *Paris Convention for Protection of Industrial Property Rights (Paris Convention)* (for Articles 13–30 of the Paris Convention: *Act of Stockholm* of 1967 since 1976; for Articles 11–12: *Act of Stockholm* since 1 February 1995) and also to the WIPO Treaty.[125]

479. Türkiye signed and ratified the Agreement Establishing the WTO Agreement of 15 April 1994. Annex 1C deals with the Agreement on Trade-Related Aspects of Intellectual Property Rights (TRIPS).[126]

124. Official Gazette, No. 30047 of 24 Apr. 2017. On patents and utility models *see* Arts 71–118; utility models *see* Arts 119–123.
125. For the Turkish text of the Stockholm Treaty signed on 14 Jul. 1967 *see* Official Gazette, No. 15417 of 19 Nov. 1975.
126. *See* Ratification Act, No. 4067 of 26 Jan. 1995 in Official Gazette, No. 22186 of 26 Jan. 1995 and the Decision of the Council of Ministers, No. 95/6525 in Official Gazette, No. 22213 *Mük.* of 25 Feb. 1995. For the Turkish text of the Agreement and its Annexes *see* the same Official Gazette.

480. Other international agreements to which Türkiye is a party are: *Patent Cooperation Agreement* of 1970 (since 1 January 1996 by Act No. 4115 of 7 July 1995); *Strasbourg Agreement on International Classification of Patents* of 24 March 1971 (since 1 October 1996 by Governmental Decree No. 95/7094 of 12 July 1995).[127]

481. *European Patent Agreement* of 5 October 1973 (as amended on 21 December 1978, 17 December 1991, 13 December 1994, 20 October 1995 and 5 December 1996).[128]

§2. Aim of *Sinai Mülkiyet Kanunu (SMK)* No. 6769 Regarding Patents and Utility Models and Persons Benefiting from Patent Rights

I. Aim of *SMK*, No. 6769 Regarding Patents and Utility Models

482. The aim of *SMK* is to protect the rights relating to patents and utility models as well as other industrial property rights (trademarks, geographical indications and traditional product names, designs) and thus to promote innovation and contribute to technical, economic and social development (Article 1).

II. Persons Benefiting from Protection

483. The following category of persons may benefit from the protection of *SMK* regarding patents and utility models (Article 3):

(1) citizens of the Republic of Türkiye;
(2) natural persons and legal entities having a domicile or engaging in industrial or commercial activities within the territory of the Republic of Türkiye;
(3) persons entitled to file an application under the Paris Convention or Agreement Establishing the WTO dated 15 April 1994;
(4) Moreover, persons and legal entities of the States that provide Turkish citizens with the protection of industrial property rights in accordance with the principle of 'reciprocity' may benefit from the protection.

III. Priority of International Conventions

484. Before the enactment of *SMK*, persons benefiting from *KHK*/551 were entitled to enjoy the provisions of international conventions that are more favourable than the provisions of *KHK*/551 (Article 4). *SMK* does not contain any provisions parallel to the provisions of Article 4 of *KHK*. Nevertheless, we are of the

127. Official Gazette, No. 22373 of 13 Aug. 1995. For the Turkish texts of these agreements *see* Kaya/Varol/Okutan, *Fikri Mülkiyet Hukuku ve Radyo Televizyon Hukuku Mevzuati* (Intellectual Property Law and Radio Television Legislation), Beta, Istanbul, 1998.
128. *See* Act, No. 4504 of 27 Jan. 2000 in Official Gazette, No. 23948 of 29 Jan. 2000.

opinion that in accordance with the Turkish Constitution international conventions have priority over domestic legislation (Constitution, Article 90).

485. On this occasion, we would like to emphasize once again that Türkiye is a party to the *'Paris Convention for the Protection of Industrial Property'* of 1883 (Stockholm Revision of 1967) and to the *'Convention Establishing the World Intellectual Property Organization'* (WIPO Convention) of 1967.

§3. Requirements of Patentability

I. Patentable Inventions

486. Under *SMK*, No. 6769 inventions that are *novel*, involved in an *inventive step* and *industrially applicable* may be patented (Article 82(1)).

A. Innovation

487. An invention which is not known in the *'state of art'* (teknigin bilinen durumu) is new (Article 83(1)). The state of art covers everything accessible by the public that was presented in any location of the world through written or oral introduction or explained through usage or in any manner before the application date (Article 83(2)). The contents of national patent and utility model applications that were published or after the application date and that are dated prior to the application date are considered 'the state of the art' (Article 83(3)).

B. Inventive step

488. An invention that is not obvious according to an expert in the relevant field when considering the state of the art is assumed to include an inventive step (Article 83(4)).

C. Applicability to Industry

489. An invention is deemed applicable to the industry if it is producible or usable in any field of industry including agriculture (Article 83(6)).

II. Non-patentable Inventions and Matters

490.

(1) The following matters are not regarded as *inventions* and accordingly are outside the scope of *SMK*, Article 82(2):

(a) discoveries, scientific theories and mathematical methods;
(b) schemes, rules and methods for performing mental acts, playing games and doing business;
(c) computer programs;
(d) literary and artistic works, scientific works, aesthetic creations;
(e) presentation and transmission of information.

(2) No Patent is granted to the following inventions (Article 82(3)):
(a) inventions contrary to public policy or good morals;
(b) plant and animal varieties or biological processes mainly for the production thereof except microbiological procedures or productions derived from these procedures;
(c) all methods for treatment of human or animal body by surgery or therapy and diagnostic methods practiced on human and animal body;[129]
(d) discovering only one of the parts of the human body including human body and a gene sequence or a partial gene sequence in the various phases of their formation and evolution;
(e) the human cloning processes, the processes of genetic identity of the human germ line, the use of human embryos for industrial and commercial purposes, procedures regarding the change of genetic identity that may inflict pain on animals without providing important medical benefits for humans or animals and animals derived from such operations.

III. Statements Which Do Not Affect the Grant of a Patent or Utility Model to the Invention

491. Under Article 84(1), statements made within twelve months before the application date or twelve months before the priority right date, if priority right is requested, under the conditions below, do not affect the grant of patent or utility model to the invention, even if they are effective on the invention to be granted a patent or utility model:

(a) The statement is made by the inventor;
(b) The statement is made by an authority to which the application for a patent was made and the information released by this authority (i) is mentioned in the inventor's other application and the mentioned application is revealed by the relevant authority even though it was required not to be revealed; (ii) is mentioned in the application that was filed by a third party who obtained the information directly or indirectly from the inventor without the inventor's permission;
(c) The statement regarding the invention is made by a third party who obtained the information directly or indirectly from the inventor (Article 84(1)(a)–(c)).

129. This provision does not apply, however, to products, in particular, substances or compositions for use in any of these methods (Art. 82(6)).

§4. Granting of Patent

I. Right to Claim a Patent

A. *Applicant*

492. The right to apply for a patent belongs to the inventor or his/her successors (Article 109(1)). If the invention was made by two or more persons, they may jointly apply for a patent (Article 109(2)).

493. If the same invention was made independently by multiple persons, the right to claim a patent belongs to the person who applies first, provided that the application with the previous date has been published (Article 109(3)).

494. The first applicant for a patent has the right to claim a patent until proven otherwise (Article 109(4)).

B. *Issues Regarding Right Ownership in Patent Applications*

495. It cannot be alleged before the Turkish Patent and Trademark Office [or Authority, i.e. TürkPatent] that the right to claim a patent does not belong to the applicant. Until proven otherwise it is assumed that the applicant has the right to claim a patent (Article 110(1)).

496. Nevertheless, during the process of granting the patent the person who claims the real owner of the right to claim the patent may file a lawsuit against the applicant and notifies TürkPatent of this lawsuit. The process for granting the patent may be suspended by the court until the date of the finalization of the decision (Article 110(2)).

497. In case the decision made as the result of the lawsuit regarding the right ownership is finalized in favour of the plaintiff, he/she can within three months following the finalization of the decision (a) request that the patent application is considered and processed as his/her own; or (b) make a new patent application for the same invention benefiting from the same priority right, if any; or (c) request TürkPatent to reject the application (Article 110(3)).

498. Moreover, a person who alleges that he/she made the invention together with the applicant and he/she has a partial right, can file a lawsuit with the request that joint ownership is granted (Article 110(6), cf. Article 110(2)).

II. Filing

A. *Application*

499. Persons seeking a patent should file an application with TürkPatent. Persons domiciled abroad (foreign nationals and nationals not living in Türkiye) may file through a registered patent attorney (patent vekili) domiciled in Türkiye (Articles 3 and 160). The following documents should be attached to the application (Article 90(1)):

- application form;
- description (tarifname) of the subject matter of invention;
- claims (istemler);
- drawings (resimler) referred to in the description and claims;
- summary;
- evidence of payment of application fee.

500. Description and *claims* can also be submitted in one of the official languages of the States that are parties to the *Paris Convention* or to the *Agreement establishing the WTO* (e.g., English, French, etc.).

B. *Date of Filing*

501. The date of filing is effective as of the date, hour and minute in which the applicant submits the following documents to TürkPatent: (i) request for grant of a patent; (ii) information on the identity and contact details of the applicant; (iii) the description (Article 90(3)).

502. The inventor is normally stated in the application. Nevertheless, the inventor may request that his/her name is kept confidential (Article 90(5)). The inventor is entitled to request the applicant or owner of the patent that he/she is recognized as an inventor and his/her name is stated (Article 90(6)).[130]

C. *Integrity of the Invention and Divided Applications*

503. Usually, the patent or utility model application contains *a single invention* or a *group of inventions* which are gathered to form a single general inventive idea. *Divided applications* can be made for any application upon the applicant's request regardless of the integrity of the invention (Article 91(1)–(2); *SMK-Yön*, Article 83).

---

130. For details on the *documents, application form, description, claims, drawings and summary see SMK-Yön*, Arts 71–78, 82.

D. Explanation of the Invention, Description, Claims and Summary

504. The invention should be explained in the patent application through the description, claims and drawings in a very clear and complete way. The explanation should enable the application of the invention by a person who is an expert in the technical field related to the subject matter of the invention (Article 92(1)).[131]

E. Priority Right and Its Effect

505. Any person or his/her successor who has filed an application for a patent or utility model in any country including Türkiye which are party to the Paris Convention or Agreement establishing the WTO benefits from the priority right within twelve months following the date of the first application for the purpose of making an application in Türkiye for the same invention (Article 93(1)).

506. Further, natural persons or legal entities who exhibit a product that includes the subject of a patent or utility model in national or international exhibitions held in Türkiye or in international exhibitions in the countries party to the Paris Convention that are officially recognized benefits from a priority right regarding the application in Türkiye for obtaining patent or utility model within twelve months following the date of the display in the exhibition (Article 93(6)).

507. The request for the priority right is made with the application or within two months following the application by paying the fee and the documents concerning this request are submitted to TürkPatent within three months following the application date. Failing this the request for priority right is deemed as not made (Article 94(1)).

III. Examination of Application

A. Rejection of Application

508. If the application does not meet the requirements prescribed by Article 90 (i.e., description, claims, drawings, summary, paying of the application fee) it is rejected by TürkPatent. In such a case, the application shall not be processed (Article 95(1)).

131. Regarding the inventions related to biological materials and gene technology *see* Art. 92(2) and (3); *SMK-Yön*, Arts 80–81. Cf. *Budapest Treaty on the International Recognition of the Deposit of Microorganisms for the Purposes of Patent Procedure* (Decree of the Council of Ministers No. 97/9731 of 5 Aug. 1997).

B. Examination of the Application as to Formal Requirements

509. TürkPatent examines, first, the patent application as to formal requirements. If TürkPatent finds any deficiencies it notifies the applicant who is given an opportunity to clarify or modify his/her application. The applicant should remedy the deficit within two months following the date of notification (Article 95(1)–(4); *SMK-Yön*, Article 96(2)). Once TürkPatent accepts the application, a research report *(arastirma raporu)* is issued in accordance with *SMK* Article 96.

C. Request for Research and Issuance of the Research Report

510. The applicant makes a request for research along with the application or within twelve months following the application date by paying the fee. Otherwise, the application is deemed withdrawn (Article 96(1)).

D. Publishing of Application and Its Effect

511. Eighteen months after the date of filing the application or the date of priority claimed, after the formal examination and the initiation of a search on the 'state of art', the application is published in the Bulletin and submitted to examination by the public. However, the application may also be published earlier upon the request of the applicant, provided that these requirements are met (Article 97, *SMK-Yön*, Article 101).

E. Request for Examination and Issuance of the Examination Report

512. Within three months following the *notification date of the research report*, the applicant requests an examination from TürkPatent by paying the relevant fee. Otherwise, his/her application is deemed to have been withdrawn (Article 98(1)).

513. After the examination, if it is stated in the examination report that the application and the invention are in conformity with the provisions of *SMK*, it is decided to grant a patent and this is reported to the applicant. The decision of granting the patent and the patent is published in the Bulletin (Article 98(5)).

IV. Granting Patent

514. After the publishing of the patent, upon request and payment of the documentation fee, the issued document is given to the patent owner (Article 98(7)).

515. The grant of a patent does not mean that its validity and utility are guaranteed by TürkPatent. TürkPatent is not liable for these respects (Article 98(9)).

§5. OBJECTION AND EXAMINATION OF OBJECTION

I. Objection and Examination of Objection

A. *Requirements for Objection*

516. Within six months following the publishing of the decision on the grant of the patent, *third persons* can raise an objection to the patent by paying the fee and depending on at least one of the following grounds (Article 99(1)):

(a) the subject of the patent does not meet the conditions of patentability (Cf. Articles 82–83);
(b) the invention is not explained adequately (Cf. Article 92);
(c) the subject of the patent exceeds the scope of the first state of the application or, the subject of the patent exceeds the first state of the previous application in case the patent is based on a divided application made according to Article 91 or an application made according to Article 110(3)(b) (cf. Article 91).

517. If the fee for objection has not been paid or the objection is not made according to the requirements stated in the *SMK-Yön* (Article 105), the objection is deemed not to have been made (Article 99(2)).

518. In case no objection is made or an objection is considered as not made, the decision regarding the grant on the patent becomes final. The final decision is published in the Bulletin (Article 99(3)).

B. *Information about Objection to the Patent Owner*

519. The objection is notified to the patent owner by the Turkish Patent and Trademark Office [or Authority, i.e. TürkPatent]. The patent owner is entitled to present his/her *opinions* within three months following this notification. He/she can also make *amendments* to the patent (Article 99(4)).

C. *Examination of the Objection by TürkPatent*

520. The objection is examined by TürkPatent in light of the patent owner's opinion. TürkPatent takes into account also the request for amendment (Article 99(4)).

521. If TürkPatent is of the opinion that the patent or its amendment complies with the requirements laid by law, it decides the continuation of the patent.

522. If TürkPatent reaches the conclusion that the patent does not comply with the legal requirements, it decides the invalidity of the patent. The decision of invalidity is published in the Bulletin (Article 99(5)). Further, TürkPatent's final decision made as the result of the objection is published in Bulletin (Article 99(7)).

II. Objection to the Decisions of TürkPatent

523. The patent applicant, the patent owner or the third persons concerned are entitled to raise an objection to the decision of TürkPatent within two months following the notification of the decision. Such objections are examined by the Board within the Department of Re-examination and Evaluation (Article 100).

§6. Transactions Relating to the Patent Process

I. Patent Application and Examination of the Patent by Third Persons

524. Patent applications that were not published yet cannot be examined by the third persons without written permission of the applicant (Article 102(1)). Nevertheless, third persons who can prove that the applicant intends to direct the rights granted to him/her with the application against them may examine the unpublished application without this permission of the applicant (Article 102(2)).

II. Amendments and Corrections to Be Made on the Patent Application and the Patent

A. *Amendments*

525. The patent application can be changed by the applicant during the process before the Turkish Patent and Trademark Office [or Authority, i.e. TürkPatent] provided that it does not exceed the scope of the first stage of application (Article 103(1)).

526. If an objection is raised to the patent, the patent can be changed by the patent owner until the final decision by TürkPatent regarding the objection provided that it does not exceed the scope of the protection provided by the patent (Article 103(2)).

B. *Corrections*

527. Spelling errors and obvious errors of facts in the patent application can be corrected upon request (Article 103(3)).

III. Conversion of the Application

A. *Conversion of the Patent Application into a Utility Model Application*

528. The patent applicant may request his/her pending application is converted into a utility model application. In such a case, TürkPatent notifies the applicant that he/she must submit the necessary documents and request for research by also paying the research fee within one month after the date of notification (Article 104(1)). If these requirements are met within this term the provisions of Article 143 on utility model apply (*SMK-Yön*, Article 112).

B. *Conversion of a Utility Model Application to the Patent Application*

529. The utility model applicant can request for the conversion of his/her utility model application to a patent application at the latest until the expiry of the three-month term following the notification of the research report. In such a case, TürkPatent notifies the applicant that he/she must submit the necessary documents and request for research by also paying the research fee within one month after the date of notification (Article 104(1)). If these requirements are met within this term the provisions on the grant of a patent apply (Article 104(2); *SMK-Yön*, Article 113).

C. *Common Provisions on Conversion*

530.

(a) If the application is published the decision of TürkPatent regarding the acceptance of conversion is published in the Bulletin (Article 104(3)).
(b) In case of conversion, if a priority right is requested for the converted application, the same priority right is granted also for the application that has been converted (Article 104(4)).
(c) *SMK*, No. 6769 does not allow any reconversion request. Such requests are not processed (Article 104(5)).

IV. Withdrawal of the Patent Application

A. *Published Patent Applications*

531. The patent application can be withdrawn at any time by the applicant before the announcement that the patent is granted. The withdrawal of a published patent application is also published in the Bulletin. This request cannot be renounced after the publishing of the withdrawal of an application (Article 105(1)).

532. The application cannot be withdrawn without the consent of third persons who established rights on the patent application in the registry (Article 105(2)). In case a published application is withdrawn, no new application can be made for the same invention (Article 105(4)).

B. Unpublished Patent Applications

533. If a patent application that is not published yet is withdrawn or rejected, a new patent application for the same invention subject can be made (Article 105(3)).

V. Entry at the Registry and Its Effects

534. Patent applications and patents are entered in the registry of TürkPatent. The registry is public. An approved copy of the patent is given upon request provided that the fee is paid (Article 106(1); *SMK-Yön*, Article 111).

535. The rights provided by the patent application and the patent cannot be brought against third persons in good faith unless they are entered in the registry properly (Article 106(3)).

536. Transfers and licenses regarding patent applications or the patents and voluntary or mandatory dispositions affecting the patent applications or the patents become effective against third persons in good faith as of the entry date (Article 106(2)).

537. The person who brings forward the rights provided by a patent application or patent should inform the number of the patent application or the patent to the parties against whom these rights are directed (Article 106(4)).

538. In case there are statements on the product or its label or its announcements, advertisements or printed documents of any kind that give the impression that the protection provided by the patent application, or the patent is present, the person who puts these statements must state the number of the patent application or the patent (Article 106(5)).

VI. Continuation of the Processes and Re-establishment of Rights

A. Continuation of the Process

539. If the applicant does not comply with the time periods regarding the processes of the patent application, he/she can request the continuation of the processes by paying its fee within two months following the date of notification of the outcome of failure to comply with the time period. In case the request is accepted, the legal consequences of non-compliance with the time period are deemed as not occurred (Article 107(1); *SMK–Yön*, Article 114).

540. Even the failure to comply with a mandatory time period caused the rejection of a patent application, the patent to be withdrawn, the invalidity of the patent application or the loss of any other right despite the fact that the due diligence is exercised by the patent applicant or the patent owner, the re-establishment of the rights can be requested by paying its fee within two months following the notification of the consequences of the failure to comply with the time period (Article 107(2)). In case the request is accepted, the legal consequences of non-compliance with the time period shall be considered as not occurred (Article 107(2); *SMK-Yön*, Article 114).

B. *Consequences of Re-establishment of Rights*

541. In case the rights are reestablished, this situation is published in the Bulletin (*SMK-Yön*, Article 115). Persons who use the invention in Türkiye in good faith during the term starting from the loss of rights to the publishing of the decision regarding the re-establishment of these rights can continue to use the invention free of charge (Article 107(3)).

VII. Erroneous Processes

542. Excluding the grounds for invalidity (Cf. Articles 138, 144), in case the processes of the application or its documents erroneously continue, the erroneous process and the following processes are cancelled and the process restarts from the stage at which the error was made (Article 108).

§7. Ownership of Right on Patent

I. Patent Right Owner

A. *Sole Inventor*

543. The right to claim a patent belongs to the inventor or his/her successors in title. It may be transferred to third persons (Article 109(1)).

B. *Joint Inventors*

544. If the patent application or the patent belongs to more than one person, the ownership of the right is determined according to the agreement of the parties (Article 112(1)). If there is no such agreement, the provisions of the Turkish Civil Code, No. 4721 on *'joint ownership'* (payli mülkiyet) apply (Articles 688 et seq.).

Each joint owner can dispose of his/her own share; he/she can use the investion after he/she notifies the other joint owners. Further, he/she can take the necessary measures for the protection of the patent. When the patent right is infringed by a third person, he/she can initiate a lawsuit against the infringer (Article 112(1); Turkish Civil Code, Articles 689 et seq.).

545. Regarding licensing of the patent, the principle of unanimity applies. If unanimity cannot be achieved, the court may, taking into consideration the circumstances, authorize one or some of the right holders to grant a license of the patent (Article 112(2); Turkish Civil Code, Article 692).

II. Usurpation of the Patent

546. If a patent has been granted to a person not entitled to obtain it, the person entitled to the patent may claim the transfer of the patent without prejudice to any other rights and claims deriving out of the patent (Article 111(1)).

547. This right can be used within two years following the publishing of the grant of the patent. Nevertheless, in case of bad faith, it can be used until the expiry of the term of the protection (Article 111(3)). The lawsuit initiated for this purpose and the decision rendered by the court are entered in the registry of the Turkish Patent and Trademark Office [or Authority, i.e. TürkPatent] and published in the Bulletin. The decision becomes effective as of the registration date towards third persons in good faith (Article 111(4)). Under these circumstances if the right ownership on the patent changes, the license and other rights of third persons on the patent come to an end (Article 111(5)).[132]

§8. Employee Inventions

I. Concepts of Service (Employment) and Independent Inventions

A. *Concepts Relating to Employees' Inventions*

548. Under *SMK*, No. 6769 employee inventions are distinguished as *service (employment) inventions and independent inventions* (Article 113).

549. Inventions that are made as the result of an employee's professional activity in a public or private enterprise are *service (employment) inventions*. These inventions are based on the experience and researches of employees in public corporations or private enterprises (Article 113(1)).

550. The provisions regarding employee inventions apply to *students* and *interns* who work unpaid with no time limitation (Article 113(3)).

---

132. For details *see* Art. 111(6)–(9).

551. As regards the inventions made by employees of public institutions and organizations, the provisions of employment inventions apply without prejudice to other legal regulations and agreements that are made between the parties (Article 113(4)).[133]

552. Inventions that do not belong to the category of employment inventions are *independent inventions* (Article 113(2)).

B. Mandatory Nature of Provisions on Employees' Inventions

553. Under *SMK*, the provisions on employees' inventions are in mandatory nature. No regulations and applications can be made by employers in a manner contrary to these provisions (Article 117(1)).

554. Under these rules, the freedom of contract regarding employees' inventions starts after the application for the grant of a patent for service inventions and after the obligation of the employee to inform the employer of the independent invention (Article 117(1)).

555. Agreements between the employer and the employee regarding the service inventions and independent inventions are deemed *invalid* when they are significantly not compatible with *'equity'* even if they are not contrary to the mandatory provisions relating to employees' inventions. The same rule is valid for the fee determined by the parties (Article 117(2)).

556. Nevertheless, objections regarding the agreement and the determined fee not 'equitable' can be made in writing within at the latest of six months of the end of the employment contract (Article 117(3)).

II. Service (Employment) Invention

A. Notification Obligation for Service Invention

557. Under *SMK*, an employee who makes a service (employment) invention is obliged to inform his/her employer in writing without delay (Article 114(1)). The employee should explain the technical problem, its solution and how he/she made the service invention in his/her notification. (Article 114(2)). Moreover, the employee should explain the experience and works of the undertaking and if any, the contributions of other employees (Article 114(3)). The employee is obliged to keep his/her service invention confidential unless it acquires the qualification of independent invention (Article 114(6)).

133. The fee that will be paid to the employees of public institutions and organizations for their inventions cannot be less than one-third of the income obtained from the invention (Art. 113(5)).

558. The employer should inform the employee within two months following the date on which the notification reached him/her in what aspects the notification needs to be amended. The employer should provide assistance with regard to the notification (Articles 114(4)–(5)).

B. Employer's Right on the Invention

1. Request for Full Ownership

559. In case of employment invention, the employer may claim in written full or partial right on the invention within four months following the date on which the notification of the employee reached him/her. In case no notification to the employee is made within this period of time the service invention acquires the qualification of independent invention (*SMK*, Article 115(1)). If the employer claims full ownership of the invention, all rights pass to the employer (Article 115(2)). When the service invention becomes an independent invention, the employee can freely dispose of it (Article 115(12)).

560. In such a case, the employee is entitled to claim an appropriate remuneration for the invention (Article 115(6)). The remuneration is fixed according to the economic appraisal of the invention, the employee's function in the enterprise and the contribution of the enterprise in the invention (Article 115(7)). The payment is determined by an agreement between the parties.

561. If the employer has claimed the right of full ownership of an employment invention, he/she may apply for a foreign patent in any country (Article 116(5)).

2. Request for a Patent on Invention

562. In case of service invention, the employer has the right and obligation to apply to the Turkish Patent and Trademark Office [or Authority, i.e. TürkPatent] (first application) to obtain a patent for the invention (Article 116(1)).

563. In such a case the employee is obliged to submit the information necessary to obtain a patent, to the employer and provide the necessary assistance (Article 118(1)).[134]

564. The obligation of the employer relating to the first application to TürkPatent for the service invention is removed upon the occurrence in at least one of

134. In return, the employer is obligated the copies of the application he made to obtain a patent for the service invention and its annexes to the employee and inform him/her the developments during the application process to the employee upon his/her request (Art. 118(1)).

the cases below: (i) if the service invention acquires the qualifications of the independent invention; or (ii) the employee's consent not to file a patent application for the invention, or (iii) protecting the undertaking's secrets requiring not to apply (Article 116(2)).

565. If the employer does not file an application on the service invention on which he/she requested full rights or does not apply within the time period that is to be determined by the employee, the invention acquires the qualifications of an independent invention (Article 116(4)).

III. Independent Invention: Employee's Obligation to Inform and to Make an Offer to the Employer

566. The employee is obliged to inform the employer as soon as possible of any independent invention if it is made during his/her employment contract (independent invention) (Article 119(1)).

567. Such declaration must contain sufficient information to allow the employer to decide whether the invention is to be considered an independent invention (Article 119(1)).

568. If the employer fails to respond in writing within three months, he/she may not later claim the invention to be an independent invention (Article 119(2)).

569. If the independent invention falls within the field of the undertaking or the undertaking is engaged in serious activities in that field, the employee shall, before attempting to use his/her invention in a different way while remaining in his/her existing employment relationship, submit a written proposal to provide the employer with an opportunity to benefit from the invention under appropriate conditions without granting full rights (Article 119(4)).

570. If the employer does not respond to this proposal within three months, this means his/her waiver of such opportunity (Article 119(4)).

571. If the employer accepts the employee's proposal, but the parties cannot reach an agreement, judicial intervention can be demanded by either party. In such a case, the conditions of the agreement are determined by the court (Article 119(4)).

IV. Employee's Right of Pre-emption

572. If the employer is declared bankrupt and the bankruptcy intends to transfer the invention separate from the business, the employee has the right of pre-emption on the invention on which the employer claimed full rights (Article 120(1)).

573. The fee claim of the employee arising from his/her invention is among the privileged claims. The bankruptcy administration distributes multiple credits of this quality to the creditors proportionate to their credits. In such a case, instead of claiming a fee, the employee may request the *conversion of his/her invention* to an independent invention (Article 120(2)).

V. Inventions Made in Higher Education Institutions

A. *In General*

574. SMK, Article 121 deals with inventions made as the result of scientific works or research conducted (i) in the higher education institutions under the Law on Higher Education, No. 2547; (ii) in the higher education institutions connected to the Ministry of National Defence and (iii) Ministry of Interior. Such inventions are subject, as a rule to the provisions on 'employees' inventions' under Articles 113 et seq.

B. *Obligation of the Inventor*

575. When an invention is made in higher education institutions in this category, the inventor is obliged to notify his/her invention in writing without delay to higher education institution. If a patent application has been filed, a notification should be made to the higher education institution regarding the application (Article 121(2)).

C. *Claims of Right on the Invention by Higher Education Institution*

576. In case the higher education institution claims rights on the invention, it is obliged to make a patent application. Otherwise, the invention acquires the qualifications of an independent invention (Article 121(3)).

577. Against the claim of the higher education institution for the right ownership, the inventor can make an objection alleging that the invention is an independent invention. This objection is examined and resolved by the higher education institution. Otherwise, the invention becomes an independent invention (Article 121(5)).

D. *Renounce of the Patent Right by Higher Education Institution*

578. If the higher education institution renounces the application for patent or patent right or the invention acquires the qualification of an independent invention after a patent application, the higher education institution, first, offers the inventor to take over the application or the patent right. In case the inventor accepts the offer the rights are transferred. In such a case, the higher education institution submits to the inventor the documents necessary to obtain and protect the patent (Article 121(6)).[135]

579. In case the inventor does not accept the offer, the disposition right to the patent application or the patent belongs to the higher education institution (Article 121(6)).

E. Distribution of Income Between the Inventor and the Higher Education Institution

580. The income to be obtained using the invention is shared between the inventor and the higher education institution in a manner that at least one-third of the income is paid to the inventor. The income share of the higher education institution shall be used for the needs of the institution and particularly for scientific research (Article 121(8)).

F. Liability of Higher Education Institution

581. If the higher education institution causes termination of the application process or of patent right due to its negligence, it is obliged to compensate damages incurred by the inventor (Article 121(7)).

VI. Inventions Generated in Projects with the Support of Public Institutions or Bodies

A. Duties of the Person Benefiting from the Project Support

582.

(a) Regarding the inventions generated in projects with the support of public institutions and bodies, it is mandatory to report these inventions to the supporters. After such notification, the person who benefits from the project support should notify his/her preference within one year to the public authority whether he/she requests the right ownership of the invention (Article 122(1)).

If the preference is not notified within this period by the inventor, the right of ownership can be obtained by the supporting public authority (Article 122(1)).

135. In case of the higher education institution transferring the application or patent right to the inventor it can reserve its non-exclusive usage right for a reasonable fee. *See* Art. 121(6).

(b) The person benefiting from the project support is obliged to make an application for a patent if he/she requests patent right ownership. In this application, it is requested to state the public institution or body which supports the project (Article 122(2)).

B. Rights of the Public Institution or Body Which Supports the Project

583.

(a) The public institution or body is entitled to request information regularly from the person who has benefitted from the project support in respect of the use of the invention (Article 122(3)).
(b) In case the person benefiting from the project support requests patent right ownership, the public institution or body is entitled to a free license right regarding the use of the invention for its own needs (Article 122(4)).
(c) Further, in the following situations the public institution or body is entitled to use the invention or to request the grant of license to third persons under reasonable conditions: (i) if the person benefiting from the project support does not use the invention or does not attempt to use it; or (ii) if the product produced by the person benefited from the project support or the licensee is not able to fulfil the needs emerging due to reasons relating to public health and national security; or (iii) if the product produced by the person benefited from the project support does not fulfil the needs of the supporting public institution or body (Article 122(4)(a)–(c)).

§9. Term of Patent and Annual Fees

I. Term of Patent

584. The protection term of a patent granted is twenty years starting from the date of application. This term may not be extended (Article 101(1)).

II. Annual Fees

585. Annual fees necessary for the patent application or protection of the patent are paid on the date on which the second year following the application date expires and on the due date of each subsequent year during the protection term (Article 101(2); *SMK-Yön*, Article 106).

586. If any annual fee is not paid on the due date, it can be paid with an additional fee within six months following the due date (Article 101(3)).

587. In case an annual fee is not paid the patent right expires as of the due date of this fee. In such a case a notification is made regarding the expiry of the patent right and this situation is published in the Bulletin (Article 101(4)).

588. Nevertheless, if a compensation fee is paid within two months following the date of the above-mentioned notification the patent right regains validity as of the date on which this fee is paid and is published in the Bulletin. The notification regarding the expiry of the patent right is made, at the latest, until the end of one year time period that starts as of the date of the due date on which the patent right expires (Article 101(5)).

589. The fact that the patent regains its validity does not affect the rights of third persons who acquired such rights as the result of the expiry of the patent right. The rights of third persons and their scope are determined by the court (Article 101(5)).

§10. Scope and Effects of Patent Right

I. Right of Exclusive Use by the Patent Owner

590. The patent confers on its owner the right to use the subject matter of the patent (Article 85(1)).

II. Right of Prevention of Third Person's Uses

591. The patent owner has the right to claim prevention of the below acts if they are committed without his/her permission:

(a) production, sale, use or import of the patented products or keeping those at hand for a reason other than personal need;
(b) the use of process that is subject to a patent;
(c) offering others to use a process patent which is known or should be known to be forbidden to use;
(d) sale, use, import of products which are directly obtained through the process subject to patent and keeping them for a reason other than personal need (Article 85(2)(a)–(ç)).

III. The Acts Outside of the Scope of Patent Right

592. The following acts are outside the scope of the right provided by the patent (Article 85(3)):

(a) acts which do not involve industrial or commercial purposes and are limited to private purposes;
(b) experimental acts involving the invention subject to a patent;

(c) licensing of drugs and experiments and tests necessary for it;
(d) the use of drugs made in pharmacies only for the formation of a prescription without mass production;
(e) using the invention subject to a patent in manufacturing and operating ships, space crafts, airplanes or land transport vehicles of the States party to the Paris Convention or in meeting the needs of such vehicles, provided that these vehicles are temporarily or coincidentally within the borders of Türkiye;
(f) acts regarding an aircraft of a State in accordance with provisions of Article 27 of the Convention on International Civil Aviation ratified by Law No. 4749 of 5 June 1945.[136]

IV. Prevention of the Indirect Use of the Invention

593. Under *SMK*, No. 6769, the patent owner has the right to prevent third persons from giving elements or instruments of a part which constitutes the basis of the invention and enables the application of the invention to persons who are not authorized the use of the invention subject to patent. This right against third persons can only be raised where they have knowledge that these are sufficient to apply the invention and would be used for this purpose, or this situation is sufficiently clear (Article 86).

V. Rights Arising from the Previous Use

594. The applicant for the patent or the owner of the patent is not entitled to prevent persons who have been using the invention as of or before the application date domestically in good faith from continuing to use the invention. However, the continuation of their use is limited to the reasonable needs of the undertakings they own. The right arising from the previous use cannot be expanded through licensing. This right can only be transferred together with the undertaking (Article 87).

VI. Legal Monopoly

595. If a patent is granted for an invention in the field of activity of public economic enterprises whose entire capital is owned by the State and that are established to produce and market goods or services for the benefit of the public and has the right of monopoly regarding those goods and services, the use of the invention by the monopoly right holder is dependent on the permission of the patent owner (Article 88(1)).

---

136. For exceptions relating to small farmers under *the* Protection of the Rights of Plant Breeders regarding New Plant Species Law, No. 5042 (*Yeni Bitki Çesitlerine Ait Islahçi Haklarinin Korunmasi Hakkinda Kanun*) of 8 Jan. 2004. *SMK*, No. 6769, Art. 85(4)–(5).

596. The monopoly right holder is obliged to use the invention which can provide considerable economic benefits and significant technical progress in the industrial field in which it is operating by obtaining the right of use (Article 88(1)).

597. The monopoly right holder is entitled to request permission from the patent right owner to obtain the use of the patented invention. In case the monopoly right holder makes such a request, the patent owner can request it to take over the patent. (Article 88(2)).

598. The fee to be paid for the use of the invention is determined by the parties. If they cannot reach an agreement on the fee, it is determined by the court (Article 88(2)).

§11. Dispositions of Patent Application and Patent Right

I. Transfer of Patent Right

599. Patent application and patent right may be transferred. It may pass by inheritance or the right of use may be the subject of a license. Patents can be the subject of security transactions. They can be attached (Article 148(1)).

600. Transactions between living persons relating to a patent or patent application should be in writing (Article 148(4)).

II. Obligation to Use

601. A patent owner or a party authorized by the patentee should use the patented invention (Article 130(1)). The patent should be used within three years from the publication of the patent in the relevant Bulletin or four years following the patent application (*SMK*, Article 130(2)), taking into account the conditions of the relevant market.

III. Licensing

A. Proposal for Licensing

602. If an exclusive license has not been registered, a patent applicant or owner may submit a written request to the Turkish Patent and Trademark Office [or Authority, i.e. TürkPatent] to the effect that he/she will grant a license to anyone who wishes to use his/her invention. Accordingly, the offer of licensing is published in the Bulletin. The offer may be withdrawn at anytime (Article 128).

B. License Agreements

603. The right to use a patent application or patent may be the subject of an exclusive or non-exclusive license agreement (Article 125(1)).

604. In case of an exclusive license, the licensor may not grant licenses to third persons (Article 125(2)).

605. Unless otherwise agreed, a license shall not be exclusive. In such a case, a licensor may use the patented invention or may grant licenses to third persons (Article 125(2)).

606. Unless otherwise agreed, a licensee may not transfer his/her rights to third persons (Article 125(3)).

C. Obligation to Provide Information

607. Unless provided otherwise in the agreement, the patent right owner who grants a license on his/her patent is under the obligation to provide information to the licensee with the technical information necessary for the normal use of the patented invention. (Article 126(1)).

608. As regards the licensee, he/she is obligated to take measures for the prevention of the disclosure of the classified information provided to him/her (Article 126(2)).

D. Liability Relating to Licensing

609. In case it is subsequently understood that the person who granted a licence for the patent is not authorized to grant it, he/she becomes liable to the interested persons (Article 127(1)).

610. In case the licensor acts in bad faith, he/she is *always* liable for his/her actions. If the licensor did not submit the reports and decisions in Turkish or in a foreign language regarding the preservability of the invention with a patent or the facts he/she knows regarding this to the licensee and did not include documents with statements regarding this in the agreement the malice is deemed present (Article 127(3)).

E. Compulsory Licence

611. A compulsory licence may be granted for a patent for which no proposal to grant a licence has been made and if any one of the following conditions exists (Article 129(1)):

(a) failure to use the patented invention (Article 130);
(b) in the case of dependence on the patent (Article 131);
(c) in the case of public interest (Article 132);
(d) in the case of the conditions specified in the Protocol Amending the Agreement on Trade-Related Aspects of Intellectual Property Rights (Cf. Law, No. 6471 of 30 April 2013) for the export of pharmaceutical products due to problems concerning health in foreign countries;
(e) if the breeder fails to develop a new plant variety without infringing a previous patent;
(f) if the patent owner carries out activities distorting or limiting competition while the patent is used.

612. The patent owner or the person authorized by him/her should use the invention protected by the patent. In case of failure to use the patent, all related persons can request a compulsory licence on the ground that the patent is not used (Article 130).

613. In case of *public interest*, the compulsory licence is determined by the President of the Republic (Article 132).

614. Compulsory licence is *not exclusive* except when it is granted on the *ground of public interest* (Article 133).

615. A compulsory licence should be transferred together with the *undertaking* (Article 135). When a compulsory licence is granted, the licensee has no right to sublicense and import the subject of the patent. Nevertheless, if the compulsory licensee is granted on the ground of public interest, the licensee can import the subject of the patent if he/she is explicitly authorized due to the public interest (Article 133(2)).

616. In case of compulsory licence, the patent owner is entitled to *a reasonable remuneration* (Article 133). When the court determines the amount of remuneration, the economic value of the patent is taken into account.

617. The provisions of licence agreements apply to compulsory licensee, provided that they are not contrary to provisions in Articles 129 to 136 (Article 137).

§12. Supplementary Patents and Secret Patents

I. Supplementary Patents

618. Supplementary patent is a patent to protect an invention which improves upon the original patent and which constitutes an integrated whole with the original patent (Articles 123 et seq.). The supplementary patent application can be made until the publishing of the decision regarding the presentation of documents for the main patent application. The term of the supplementary patent starts as of the date of the supplementary patent application and continues until the expiry of the term of the main patent (Article 123(5)).

619. In case the main patent is annulled or the main patent owner gives up his/her patent, the supplemental patent is converted into an independent patent (Article 123(8)).

620. Unless provided explicitly otherwise and it does not contradict the nature of the patent, the *SMK* provisions on the main patent also apply to supplementary patents (Article 123(13)).

II. Secret Patents

621. If a patent is important to national defence, the Turkish Patent and Trademark Office [or Authority, i.e. TürkPatent] should notify the Ministry of National Defence of the patent application in order to obtain its opinion. The applicant is also informed of this situation by TürkPatent (Article 124(1)). In case the Ministry is of the opinion that the application procedures should be carried out in secret, it notifies its decision to TürkPatent within three months following TürkPatent's notification. In such a case, the applicant is informed of the confidentiality and the application is entered in the registry of TürkPatent as a secret patent application (Article 124(3)).

622. If the patent application or patent is subject to secrecy, the applicant or the patent owner should avoid becoming involved in acts which would cause unauthorized parties to obtain information on the contents of the invention (Article 124(4)).

623. Upon request of the patent owner, the Ministry may allow the use of the invention (Article 124(5)).

§13. Invalidity of Patents and Other Grounds of Termination

I. Invalidity of Patents

A. Grounds of Invalidity

624. Under *SMK*, No. 6769, the Turkish Patent and Trademark Office [or Authority, i.e. TürkPatent] is not entitled to nullify a patent on its own initiative. An *action for nullification* is required for the nullity of a registered patent.

625. After the final decision of TürkPatent, a patent may be nullified, i.e., ruled invalid by the relevant court in case of one of the following grounds (Article 138):

(a) the invention has failed to meet conditions of patentability;
(b) the invention has not been sufficiently described to enable an expert in the field to put it into the application;
(c) the invention (patent subject) extends beyond the scope of the application;
(d) the patent owner is not entitled to apply for a patent;
(e) the scope of protection is exceeded.

626. The action for nullity may be brought by parties who have suffered damage or by the competent authorities or public prosecutors (Article 138(5)–(6)).

627. Such actions may be initiated at any time during the term of the patent or within five years following termination of the patent rights (Article 138(5)).

B. *Effect of Invalidity of the Patent*

628. Effect of nullification is *retroactive*. Therefore, the patent or application is deemed not to have existed (Article 139(1) and (4)). The final decision related to the invalidity of the patent is sent to TürkPatent by the court ex officio. Thereupon the nullified patent is deleted from the registry by TürkPatent ty and this is published in the Bulletin (Article 139(4)).

629. Compensation claims resulting from the nullification and certain exceptions are also covered in Article 139(2).

II. Other Grounds for Termination of Patent

A. *Grounds for Termination of Patent*

630. Patent rights terminate in the following cases (Article 140(1)):

(a) expiration of term of patent;
(b) renouncement of the patent right by the patent owner;
(c) non-payment of annual and additional fees (Cf. Article 101).

631. Under *SMK*, the patent owner may renounce the entire patent or one or more patent claims (*SMK*, Article 140(3)). However, the patent cannot be renounced without the permission of the owners of registered rights and licensees. Likewise, in case a right ownership has been alleged on the patent by a third person and the decision of injunction related to this matter has been entered at registry of Türk-Patent the rights arising from the patent cannot be renounced without the permission of this person (Article 140(5)–(6)).

632. In case of renouncement, the Authority should be notified in writing. The renouncement becomes effective as of the date of recording to the registry (Article 140(4)).

B. Effect of Termination of Patent

633. The Authority publishes in the Bulletin that the patent right terminates. When a patent right terminates, the subject of the patent belongs to the public as of the moment on which the ground for invalidity occurred (Article 140(2)).

§14. Infringements of the Patent Right

I. Cases of Infringement

634. Under *SMK*, No. 6769 Article 141, the following situations are regarded as patent right or utility model infringement:

(a) to produce without authorization a full or partial imitation of the invented product;
(b) to sell, distribute or introduce in commerce by other means or import for said purpose or hold for commercial purpose or use products which are known to be produced by such imitation;
(c) to use a process constituting the subject matter of an invention or to sell or distribute or use products produced directly by means of such process;
(d) to usurp the patent right;
(e) to expand the rights granted by the patent owner through a licence agreement without permission or to transfer these rights to third persons.

II. Burden of Proof

635. In case the subject of the patent is a procedure regarding the obtaining of a product or a material, the court may demand the defendant to prove that the procedure to obtain the same product or material is different from the procedure subject to the patent (Article 141(2)).

§15. Civil Remedies in Cases of Patent Infringements

I. Civil Remedies

636. Under *SMK*, No. 6769, the patent right owner whose patent right has been infringed can initiate several actions before the civil court with the following claims:

A. *Declaratory Action*

637. With regard to the infringement of a patent right, the patent owner may initiate an action for ascertainment of the infringement (tespit talebi) if he/she needs a judicial decree on the existence of an infringement of a patent (Article 149(1)(a). Cf. Code of Civil Procedure (CCP, *HMK*), No. 6100, Article 106).

B. *Action for Cease-and-Desist and Prevention of Infringement*

638. Where there are existing and probable infringements of a patent right, the patent owner may initiate an action for prevention, and cease-and-desist of infringement (Article 149(1)(a)–(g)).

C. *Action for Removal of Infringement and Compensation for Damages*

639. If the infringement has been committed by negligence on the part of the infringer material damage incurred by the patent owner may be claimed (Article 149(1)(ç)). As regards compensation for damage, the owner of the patent right may claim actual damage (damnum emergens) and loss of profit (lucrum cessans) (Article 151).

640. The loss of profit can be calculated in accordance with the following evaluation methods specified in Article 151(2);

(a) the probable profit that would have been obtained by the patent right owner if the competition by the person infringing the patent right had not existed;
(b) the net profit obtained by the person infringing the patent right;
(c) the license fee that the infringer of the patent right would have been obligated to pay if he/she would have used this right through a licence agreement.

D. *Action for Compensation for Non-material (Moral) Damage*

641. The infringer must also compensate for non-material damages suffered by the owner of the patent right (Article 149(1)(ç); 150(2)).

E. *Action for Security (Recording) of Evidence*

642. Action for the security of evidence (*delil tespiti*) can be initiated under provisions of the Code of Civil Procedure (CCP, *HMK* Articles 400 et seq.). In this action, the patent owner seeks by expert opinion to secure evidence that will be used in a future action for cease-and-desist, prevention, or compensation.

F. Provisionary (Interim) Measures (Injunction)

643. Action for provisionary[137] measures (*ihtiyati tedbir talebi*) has been regulated by the Code of Civil Procedure (Articles 389–399) and *SMK* (Article 159).

644. In this action, the court may grant several provisionary measures such as seizure or safekeeping of products which are the subject matter of patent infringement; prevention of the acts infringing the patent right; giving guarantee with regard to the compensation of damage etc. (Article 159).

G. Announcement of Court's Judgment

645. Under *SMK*, the owner of a patent may demand from the court the announcement of its judgment in daily newspapers when it becomes final (res judicata) at the expense of the infringer (Article 149(1)(g)).

H. Other Remedies

646. Further, the owner of a patent right may, in addition to damages, request:

(a) confiscation of products that have been produced or imported by infringing on patent rights (Article 149(1)(d));
(b) ownership of the confiscated products in return for payment of their values (Article 149(1)(e));
(c) destruction of the confiscated products and means under some conditions (Article 149(1)(f)).

II. Parties in Actions for Civil Remedies

A. Claimant

1. Owner of Patent Right

647. Actions relating to patent right infringements are, normally, initiated by the owner of patent rights.

2. Licensees

a. Holder of an Exclusive License

648. Unless otherwise provided, the holder of an exclusive license may initiate in his/her own name all actions available to the patent owner (Article 158(1)).

---

137. It should be noted that the terms 'interim, interlocutory, precautionary, preliminary and provisional' are used in various legal texts having the same meaning.

b. Holder of Non-exclusive License

649. Holders of non-exclusive licenses are not entitled to initiate actions against the infringer. In the event of infringement, the licensee may give notice through a notary public to the owner of the patent and request him/her to initiate proceedings against the infringer. If the patent owner refuses this request or fails to initiate action within three months after the receipt of the notice, the licensee may start proceedings (Article 158(2)).

B. Respondent

650. The actions mentioned above are directed against the *infringer on patent rights* (Articles 149 et seq.).

651. Under *SMK*, actions for civil remedies cannot be directed against a category of persons specified by Article 153.

652. First of all, the patent right owner cannot file proceedings against the persons who keep or use the products that were introduced to the market by the infringer. Likewise, patent right owner may not file proceedings against persons who use commercial purposes the products put on the market due to the right owner's failure of confiscation by the person who pays compensation of damages to the right owner (Article 153).

III. Specialized Courts and Mediation

A. Subject-Matter Jurisdiction (Görev)

653. The procedural rules of *SMK* (Article 156) below, commonly apply to various disputes regarding patents, utility models, trademarks, designs, and geographical indications as well as those regulated under *FSEK*, No. 5846 (Article 76). Under *SMK*, actions in the first instance relating to legal remedies or penal sanctions are in principle heard by *'specialized civil and criminal courts for intellectual and industrial rights'* established by the Ministry of Justice (Article 156(1)). However, as with most civil law cases before other civil courts, cases usually end up at the relevant Chambers (Daire) of the Court of Cassation (Yargitay) (C.Cass.)[138] in the Capital, i.e., in Ankara. For actions to be initiated against the decisions taken by the Turkish Patent and Trademark Office [or Authority, i.e. TürkPatent] and actions to

138. For various decisions of Yargitay regarding patent disputes, *see*, *inter alia*, Yargitay 11 HD, T. 21.05.2014, E. 2014/2278, K. 2014/9411, Yargitay 11 HD, T. 12.04.2017, E. 2016/8523, K. 2017/2088, Yargitay 11. HD, T. 23.12.2014, E. 2014/12097, K. 2014/20282, Yargitay 11. HD, T. 22.09.2014, E. 2014/7840, K. 2014/14248; regarding utility models (faydali model), *see*, *inter alia*, Yargitay 11. HD, T.26.04.2016, E. 2015/10460, K.2016/4679, Yargitay 11 HD, T.03.05.2010, E.2008/13429, K.2010/4754, Yargitay 11 HD, T.21.05.2014, E. 2014/2278, K. 2014/9411, Yargitay 11 HD, T. 16.01.2013, E. 2012/93, K. 2013/828, Yargitay 11 HD, T. 04.07.2014, E. 2014/5778, K. 2014/12927, Yargitay 11 HD, T. 04.07.2017, E. 2014/6383, K. 2014/12884.

be initiated against TürkPatent by third parties who incurred damages due to the decisions of TürkPatent, Ankara Civil Courts for Intellectual and Industrial Property Rights shall have jurisdiction (Article 156(2)).

B. *Territorial Jurisdiction (Venue, Forum, Yetki)*

654. Under the Code of Civil Procedure, No. 6100 (CCP, *HMK*), the competent court for civil actions is in principle the court of the domicile of the respondent, i.e., the infringer (CCP, Article 6). However, civil actions under *SMK* may also be initiated at the court of the domicile of the claimant (i.e., holder of the relevant right) or at the place where the infringement has been committed or at the place where the infringement had its effects (*SMK*, Article 156(3)).

655. Where the claimant does not have domicile in Türkiye, the competent court is the court of the domicile of the patent or trademark attorney recorded at the registry of TürkPatent and if the attorney's record has been deleted, the court of the place where TürkPatent is located (Article 156(4)), i.e., Ankara, the Capital.

656. As for civil actions initiated by third parties against the holder of the relevant right, the competent court is the court where the defendant is domiciled. If the defendant is not domiciled in Türkiye, the provisions of Article 156(4) as above apply (Article 156(5)).

657. If no such specialized civil courts or criminal courts have yet been established at the place to be determined as above, local civil courts of general jurisdiction (asliye hukuk mahkemesi) or local criminal courts of general jurisdiction (asliye ceza mahkemesi) shall have jurisdiction.

C. *Mandatory Mediation Attempt and 'The Singapore Convention on Mediation'*

658. In recent years, the parties to private law disputes are encouraged to mediate before initiating litigation.[139] An increasing number of specific private law disputes are mandatorily subject to mediation before being tried before courts. The types of suits (actions) which require a mandatory mediation attempt (dava sarti, Prozessvoraussetzungen) as a pre-condition for litigation are not listed by their names. The litigants are expected to follow the relevant general principles laid out primarily in the Act on Mediation in Civil Law Disputes (AMedC, *Hukuk Uyusmazliklarinda Arabuluculuk Kanunu*), No. 6325 (Official Gazette of 22 June 2012, as amended). Moreover, certain disputes regarding intellectual property are subject to pre-conditional commercial mediation (dava sarti ticari arabuluculuk) under Articles 4(1) and 5(A) of the Turkish Commercial Code (TComC), No. 6102.

139. For a summary of arbitration and mediation regarding patents and utility models within a monography on Patents, *see* Çolak, Ugur, *Türk Patent Hukuku*, Ankara, 2022, Part Nineteen, pp. 1213–1244.

659. Türkiye is a State Party to the United Nations Convention on International Settlement Agreements Resulting from Mediation, also known as the Singapore Convention on Mediation ('Convention'). On 11 April 2022, the Convention entered into force, in accordance with the Article 14 of the Convention and the Presidential Decree No. 5235, 6 months after the deposit of the instrument of ratification to the United Nations (UN). Settlement agreements made in accordance with the Convention can easily be recognised and enforced internationally, i.e., in other State Parties.

§16. Utility Model

I. Utility Model Concept

660. An invention considered *new* and *capable of industrial application* may be protected by granting a utility model (Article 142(1)).[140]

661. The following inventions are not protected by a utility model: (i) inventions regarding chemical and biological substances or procedures or products derived from such procedures; (ii) inventions relevant to substances regarding pharmacy or procedures or products derived from such procedures; (iii) biotechnological inventions; (iv) inventions regarding procedures or products derived from such procedures (Article 142(3)).

II. Owner of Utility Model

662. The right to apply for a utility model belongs to the inventor or his/her successor.

III. Transactions on Utility Models

663. This right can be transferred to other persons (Article 109(1)). The right to utility model can be *inherited, subject to license, attached and subject to security transactions* (Article 148).

IV. Term of Protection

664. The protection granted to the owner of a patent has also been granted to the holder of a utility model (Article 101(1)). The *protection term of the utility models* is ten years starting from the date of application. This term cannot be extended (Article 101(1)).

140. For the summary of utility models within a monography on Patents, *see* Çolak, Ugur, *Türk Patent Hukuku*, Ankara, 2022, Part Sixteen, pp. 1171–1189.

V. Invalidity of Utility Model

665. With regard to the *invalidity of utility models*, Article 144 and compatible *SMK* provisions on the nullity of patents apply (Article 138).

VI. Actions for Civil Remedies in Infringements of Utility Model

666. The *actions* that can be initiated by the patent right owner in cases of patent infringements can also be initiated by the utility model owner (Articles 149 et seq.). The provisions relating to *court of jurisdiction, competent court* and mandatory mediation stage in patent infringements apply also in cases of infringements on utility model (Article 156).

VII. Applicability of Provisions Relating to Patents and Double Protection

667. In case there is no explicit provision regarding utility models and it does not contradict its nature, the *provisions on patents* apply to utility models (Article 145).

Chapter 3. Trademarks

§1. Legal Sources of Turkish Trademark Law

I. National Sources

A. Historical Development of Turkish Trademark Law

668. Previously the Turkish trademark law was regulated by the 'Decree Having the Power of Law for Protection of Trademarks' (*Markalarin Korunmasi Hakkinda Kanun Hükmünde Kararname, KHK*/556) of 24 June 1995.[141]

669. At present, this *KHK* was abolished and replaced by 'Industrial Property Law', No. 6769 (*Sinai Mülkiyet Kanunu: SMK*) of 22 December 2016 (for trademarks *see* Articles 4–32 and 146 et seq.).[142]

670. According to the European Commission Turkey 2018 Report, *SMK* ensures greater alignment with the IPR 'acquis' in relation to trademarks and designs and updates the Turkish IPR system in line with international agreements and practices. Simplified registration procedures were introduced. An IPR Academy was set up in July 2017 which will be responsible for all IPR training for civil servants. The first meeting of the Academy's Executive Board was held on 19 July 2017. Further, the 'Regulation on the Code of Conduct and Disciplinary Measures for Patent and Trademark Attorneys' *(Türk Patent ve Marka Kurumu Patent Vekilleri ve Marka Vekilleri Disiplin Yönetmeligi)* entered into force on 10 January 2017. This Regulation addresses a legal gap with regard to the liability of patent and trademark attorneys registered in the Turkish Patent and Trademark Office [or Authority, i.e.

---

141. The *KHK*/556 came into force on its date of publication in the Official Gazette, No. 22326 of 27 Jun. 1995. The first Implementing Regulation (*yönetmelik*) on details of several provisions of the *KHK*/556 was issued on 5 Nov. 1995. This Implementing Regulation was replaced by the Implementing Regulation of 30 Mar. 2013. Regarding the drafting of *KHK*/556 the Draft Law Commission had benefited from several foreign laws, EU trademark law and several international conventions. Among the foreign laws that were examined by the Draft Law Commission, the Swiss Federal Law on the Protection of Trademarks and Indications of Service dated 28 Aug. 1992; the Austrian Trademark Protection Law of 1970 as amended in 1984; the Italian Executive Order, No. 480 dated 16 Dec. 1992, the Spanish Trademarks Act, No. 32 dated 10 Nov. 1988 must be mentioned. Furthermore, the Paris Convention for the Protection of Industrial Property revised in 1967 in Stockholm, the EC Directive on the Harmonization of the Laws on Trademarks of the Member States adopted by the Council on 21 Dec. 1988 and the Regulation on the Community Trademark adopted 20 Dec. 1993, Trademark Law Treaty adopted at Geneva on 27 Oct. 1994 and Final Act Embodying The Results of The Uruguay Round of Multilateral Trade Negotiations of 15 Apr. 1994: Agreement Establishing The World Trade Organization, Annex 1C: Agreement on Trade-Related Aspects of Intellectual Property Rights (TRIPS Agreement) had been taken into account. For a comprehensive examination of trademark law in Türkiye in a monography, *see*, Çolak, Ugur, *Türk Marka Hukuku*, Istanbul, 2023.
142. Official Gazette, No. 29944 of 10 Jan. 2017. This law entered into force on the date of its promulgation in the Official Gazette with exceptions relating to the provisions of its Art. 23(2); Art. 69(4), and Art. 26 (seven years later). Further 'the Implementing Regulation of Industrial Property Law' (*SMK-Yön*) was promulgated in the Official Gazette on 24 Apr. 2017 (No. 30047).

TürkPatent]. TürkPatent improved its consultation on trademark registration services with IPR owners and their representatives. On judicial enforcement, *SMK* aims to ensure a higher level of legal alignment with the EU Enforcement Directive. Nevertheless, according to the Türkiye 2018 Report 'the implementation of the accelerated destruction procedure and the functioning of IPR criminal courts need to be improved' (European Commission, Turkey 2018 Report, Chapter 7 (5.7), p. 69).

B. Aim and Content of *SMK* on Trademarks

671. The aim of the provisions of *SMK*'s relating to trademarks is to protect rights and thus to contribute to technological, economic, and social progress (*SMK* Article 1(1)).

672. Book One of *SMK* deals with trademarks. Articles 4–30 lay down the principles, rules, and requirements for the protection of trademarks.

C. Structure of Book One of *SMK* on Trademarks

673. Book One of *SMK* is composed of six Parts.

674. Part One deals with 'trademark right and its scope'. In this Part, Article 4 specifies 'signs that can be trademark'. 'Grounds for absolute and relative rejection in trademark registration' are dealt with in provisions of Articles 5 and 6. Article 7 regulates 'scope of rights arising from registration of trademark and its exceptions'. Article 8 is devoted to 'use of the trademark in reference works'. Article 9 handles the issues relating to 'use of trademark'. 'Requests relating to trademarks registered in the name of commercial agents or representatives' are regulated by Article 10.

675. Part Two of Book One deals has the title 'application and objection'. Chapter One in this Part regulates 'application, priority right and examination'. Articles 11 deals with 'requirements for application, classification and division'. Provisions of Articles 12 and 13 are related to 'priority right'. Article 12 is devoted to 'priority right and its effect' while Article 13 handles 'request for priority right and its effect'. Under SMS, an 'international trademark application within the scope of Madrid Protocol' can be filed (Article 14). Article 15 deals with 'formal (procedural) examination, remedy of formality deficiencies and application date'. Issues related to 'examination of application regarding absolute grounds for refusal and publication' are handled in Article 16.

676. Chapter Two is devoted to 'opinions of third parties, oppositions and examination of oppositions': Article 17: 'opinions of third parties'; Article 18: 'opposition against publication', and Article 19: 'examination of opposition against publication'. Article 20 and 21 deal with the issue relating to 'objection to the decision', and 'examination of objection'.

677. The heading of Part Three is 'registration, term of protection and renewal'. This Part has two Article 22 ('registration'), and Article 23 ('term for protection and renewal').

678. Part Four is devoted to trademark 'license' (Article 24).

679. Part Five deals with issues relating to 'termination of right'. Part Five has been divided into two Chapters. Chapter One handles issues related to 'invalidity and cancellation' (Article 25: 'grounds for invalidity and request for invalidity'; Article 26: 'grounds for cancellation and request for cancellation', and Article 27: 'effect of invalidity and cancellation'. Chapter Two in this Part is devoted to 'other grounds for termination and their consequences' (Article 28).

680. Part Six deals with issues relating to 'infringement of trademark right'. Article 29 handles the 'actions considered as infringement of trademark right'; Article 30 lays down 'penal provisions relating to trademark right infringements'.

II. International Sources

681. Türkiye is a member of the Paris Convention for the Protection of Industrial Property (hereinafter 'Paris Convention'). Articles 1–12 of the Act of Stockholm, 1967 have been adopted and ratified by the Decree of the Council of Ministers, No. 94/5903 of 29 July 1994.[143]

682. Previously, Articles 12 et seq. of the Act of Stockholm had already been adopted and ratified by the Decree of the Council of Ministers, No. 7/10464 of 8 August 1975.[144]

683. Moreover, The Nice Agreement concerning the International Classification of Goods and Services for the Purposes of the Registration of Marks of 15 June 1957 and revised at Stockholm on 14 July 1967 and at Geneva on 13 May 1977 and as amended at Geneva on 2 October 1979 was adopted and ratified by the Decree of the Council of Ministers, No. 95/7094 of 12 July 1995.[145]

684. Türkiye adopted and also ratified the Vienna Agreement Establishing an International Classification of the Figurative Elements of Marks (done at Vienna on 12 June 1973 and amended on 1 October 1985) by the same Decree of the Council of Ministers, No. 95/7094 of 12 July 1995.

143. Official Gazette, No. 22060 of 23 Sep.1994.
144. Official Gazette, No. 15418 of 20 Nov. 1975.
145. Official Gazette, No. 22373 of 13 Aug. 1995.

685. Türkiye has also signed and ratified the Madrid Trademark Treaty by Act, 5118 of 7 April 2004. The Madrid Protocol concerning the Madrid Treaty on the International Registration of Trademark was also adopted by the Council of Ministers on 5 August 1997.[146]

§2. Definition and Kinds of Trademarks

I. Definition

686. The concept of trademark has not been clearly defined by *SMK* Article 2 on 'definitions'. Under this Article *'trademark'* is one of the 'industrial property rights' (Article 2(1); *SMK-Yön*, Article 3(o)). Taking into account these provisions with Article 4 concerning 'signs that can be trademark' it is possible to define the concept of *'trademark'* as a sign capable of distinguishing the goods or services of one undertaking from those of other undertakings.

II. Kinds of Trademarks

687. With regard to the types of trademarks, the following distinctions can be made in the Turkish doctrine:

A. *According to the Form of Trademark*

688. Under *SMK* Article 4, *a trademark* may consist of all kinds of signs being represented graphically such as words including personal names, designs, letters, numbers, sounds, shape of goods and their packaging capable of being displayed in the registry in a manner to determine the clear and precise subject-matter of the protection afforded to its owner.

689. Word trademarks are represented by words or combinations of letters in word form.

690. Letter trademarks consist of individual letters. Numerical marks are marks that consist of numbers. Combination of letters or initials may also function as trademarks.

691. Design trademarks may be represented by concrete images of animated or unanimated objects, abstract images, symbols, compositions of ornamental nature, individually artistically transformed print units and numerals and various combinations of the above-mentioned elements.

---

146. Official Gazette, No. 23088 of 22 Aug. 1997.

692. Combinations of trademarks present a combination of different elements such as design, word, three-dimensional and other elements.

B. According to the Function of Trademark

1. Trademark for Goods

693. Trademark for goods is a word, symbol, or other signifier used to distinguish a good by one undertaking from the goods of other undertakings (*SMK* Article 4).

2. Service Marks

694. The term 'service mark' means any word, name, symbol, device, or any combination thereof used by a person to identify and distinguish the services of one person from the services of others and to indicate the source of the services (*SMK* Article 4).

C. According to the Entitled Person

1. Individual Trademarks

695. Individual marks are trademarks of individual persons or firms. They identify and distinguish their goods or services from the goods or services of others (In general, *SMK* Article 4).

2. Guarantee Marks

696. Under *SMK*, No. 6769, a *guarantee mark* is a sign that is used by several undertakings under the control of the owner of the mark and which serves to guarantee the quality, geographical origin, type of manufacture or other characteristics common to goods or services of such undertakings (Articles 6(7); 31(1)).

3. Collective Marks

697. Under *SMK*, a *collective mark* is a sign of an association of manufacturing, trading or service undertaking that serves to distinguish the goods and services of the members of the association from those of other enterprises (Articles 6(7); 31(3)–(4)).

§3. Principle of Protection: Registration of Trademark

698. Under *SMK*, protection of a trademark is provided by the *registration of the mark* (Article 7(1)).

§4. Persons Entitled to Protection

699. The following persons are entitled to benefit from the protection of a trademark conferred by *SMK* (Article 3(1)(a)–(ç)):

(a) citizens of the Republic of Türkiye;
(b) natural persons or legal entities that are engaged in industrial or commercial activities within the territory of the Republic of Türkiye;
(c) natural persons who have application rights within the framework of the Paris Convention or Agreement Establishing the World Trade Organization dated 15 April 1994;
(d) persons (natural persons and legal entities) that are nationals of the States which confer (the legal or actual) protection for trademarks on nationals of the Turkish Republic may enjoy trademark protection in Türkiye in accordance with the principle of reciprocity.

§5. Unregistrable and Improper Trademarks

700. Trademarks are normally accepted for registration upon complying with the formalities and requirements prescribed by *SMK*, No. 6769.

701. Nevertheless in cases set forth by *SMK* the Turkish Patent and Trademark Office [or Authority, i.e. TürkPatent] should refuse the application of registration.

702. The grounds for refusal are divided into two categories: absolute and relative grounds.

I. Absolute Grounds of Refusal

703. Under *SMK*, trademark protection shall not be available to the following signs. In other words, the *following signs* cannot be registered as trademarks (Article 5):

(a) signs which are not capable of distinguishing the goods or services of one undertaking from the goods and services of other undertakings;
(b) signs that do not have any distinguishing quality;
(c) signs consisting exclusively of signs and indications which serve in trade the kind, quality, quantity, intended purpose, value, geographical origin, or designate the

time of production of the goods or of rendering of the service or other characteristics of goods and services;

(d) signs that are identical or indistinguishably similar to a trademark that was registered or previously applied for registration for the same or similar goods or services;

(e) signs consisting exclusively of signs and names used by everyone in trade or trademarks consisting exclusively of signs and names used to distinguish persons belonging to specific groups of profession, craftsmen or tradesmen;

(f) shapes that constitute the nature of goods themselves or shapes of the goods;

(g) signs misleading the public, such as the nature, quality or geographical origin of the goods and services;

(h) signs that shall be rejected according to Article 6ter of the Paris Convention;

(i) signs containing armorial bearings, emblems or Official signs other than those covered by Article 6ter of the Paris Convention which have not been authorized to register by the competent authorities and are of particular historical and cultural value for the public;

(j) signs which contain religious symbols;

(k) signs contrary to public policy and public morality;

(l) signs which consist of a registered geographical indication or which contain a registered geographical indication.

704. Nevertheless, if a trademark has been ‘used’ for the goods or services to be registered before its registration date and has acquired a distinctive nature as the result of its use, its registration cannot be refused under (a), (c) and (d) paragraphs of Article 5(1) (Article 5(2)).

705. Moreover, a trademark application cannot be refused on the ground of subparagraph (ç) of the first paragraph if a notarized document indicating that the previous trademark owner has expressly consented to the registration of the application is submitted to TürkPatent (Article 5(3)). The details of consent are specified by *SMK-Yön*, Article 10.

II. Relative Grounds of Refusal

706. In the following cases, a trademark cannot be registered by TürkPatent upon opposition by the owner of a registered trademark or of an application for registration:

(1) An application for trademark registration shall be rejected upon opposition if there exists a possibility of confusion on the part of the public, including the likelihood of association with the earlier trademark, due to identity with, or similarity to, the earlier trademark and the identity or similarity of the goods or services rendered (Article 6(1)).

(2) If an application for registration of an identical or indistinguishably similar trademark has been made by a commercial agent or representative of the owner

of a trademark in his/her own name without the owner's consent or any just ground, the registration is refused upon objection of the owner (Article 6(2)).

(3) Moreover, upon objection of the owner of a non-registered trademark or of another sign used in the course of trade, the application for registration of the trademark is refused if the right on the sign was acquired before the date of application for registration of the trademark, or before the date of priority specified in the application (Article 6(3)).

(4) Applications which are identical or similar to the well-known trademarks within the scope of Article 6*bis* of the Paris Convention shall be refused upon opposition in respect of the identical or similar goods or services (Article 6(4)).

(5) Under *SMK*, a trademark which is identical or similar to a registered trademark may be used for different goods or services. However, in cases where a registered trademark has created a reputation in Türkiye, if the use of the identical or similar trademark for different goods or services would cause damage to the reputation of the registered trademark or harm to its distinctive characteristic or provide for an unfair advantage for the owner of the identical trademark, the application for registration shall be refused by the Authority upon the objection of the owner of the registered trademark (Article 6(5)).

(6) The application for registration is also refused if the trademark contains the name, tradenames, photograph, copyright or any industrial property right of another person upon his/her objection (Article 6(6)).

(7) Another relative ground of refusal deals with collective and guarantee marks. The application for registration of a trademark which is identical with or similar to a collective or a guarantee mark or which contains identical or similar goods or services is refused upon objection if the application is made within three years (Article 6(7)).

(8) Further, within two years following the expiration of protection of the registered trademark due to non-renewal if an application for registration of the same or similar trademark for the same or similar goods or services is made, the application is refused upon objection of the previous registered trademark owner provided that this trademark has been used during this two year period (Article 6(8)).

(9) Another relative ground of refusal is related to the application in bad faith. Trademark applications filed in bad faith shall be refused by the TürkPatent upon opposition (Article 6(9)).

§6. Use of the Trademark

I. Use of Trademark

707. Under *SMK*, No. 6769 a trademark enjoys protection if it is used in connection with the goods and services for which it is claimed.

708. The collective and guarantee marks should be used in accordance with their technical regulations (Article 32).

709. Use of a trademark can be in various forms:

(1) Use of a trademark with different elements without changing its distinguishing character (Article 9(2)(a)).
(2) Use of a trademark on goods or their packaging solely for export purposes (Article 9(2)(b)).
(3) Use of the trademark with the consent of the owner is also deemed use by the owner him/herself (Article 9(3)).

II. Consequences of Non-use

710. If, within a period of five years following the date of registration, the trademark has not been used in Türkiye by its owner without a just ground or if the use has been suspended during an uninterrupted period of five years, the trademark is cancelled (Article 9(1)).

§7. Scope of Protection of Registered Trademarks

I. Right to the Exclusive Use of Trademark

711. The owner of a registered trademark has, normally, the right to use his/her trademark exclusively. He/she may use his/her trademark within the limitations of the law to identify his/her goods and services. He/she may transfer his/her trademark to another person (Article 148(1)) or grant a license for its use (Articles 24; 148(1)). He/she may give his/her trademark as security (Article 148(1)).

II. Right to Prohibit the Use of Trademark by Third Persons

712. The right to exclusive use of a trademark confers on the owner the right to prohibit the use of the trademark by other persons. The owner may prevent interventions to be made by third parties.

713. The rights conferred by a registered trademark can be directed by the owner against third persons from the date of publication of registration of the trademark (Article 9(3)).

A. Uses of a Registered Trademark by Third Persons That Can be Prevented by the Owner of Trademark

714. In the following cases, the owner of a registered trademark is entitled to prevent the following acts (Article 7(2)(a)–(c)):

(a) use of any sign which is identical to the registered trademark in relation to goods and/or services which are identical to those for which the trademark is registered;
(b) use of any sign where, because of its identity with or similarity to the registered trademark and identity and similarity of the goods and/or services covered by the registered trademark and sign, there exists a likelihood of confusion on the part of the public including the likelihood of association between the sign and the trademark;
(c) use any sign which is identical or similar to the registered trademark in relation to goods and/or services which are not similar to those for which the trademark is registered, where the use of that sign is detrimental to the distinctive character or reputation of the registered trademark.

B. Kinds of Use to Be Prohibited by the Owner of Trademark

715. The following uses may be prohibited by the owner of the trademark in accordance with Article 7(2), if the sign is used in a trading area (Article 7(3)(a)–(f)):

(a) affixing the sign to goods or to their packaging;
(b) offering the goods, putting them on the market or stocking them for such purposes under the sign, and offering or supplying services under the sign;
(c) importing or exporting the goods under the sign;
(d) using the sign on business papers and in advertising the undertaking;
(e) using identical or similar sign on internet media as domain name, router code, keyword or in a similar manner in the course of trade provided that the person using the sign has no right or legitimate affiliation for the use of that sign;
(f) using the sign as a trade name or undertaking name;
(g) using the sign illegally in comparative advertising.

III. Right to Prohibit the Use of Trademark Registered in the Name of a Commercial Agent

716. If a trademark has been registered in the name of a commercial agent or representative of the owner of the trademark without his/her consent, the owner may oppose and prohibit the use of the trademark unless the agent or representative proves a just ground. The owner of the trademark may also request the transfer of the said registration to him/her (Article 10).

IV. Right to Request Correction in Case of Reproduction of the Trademark

717. If a trademark is published or reproduced in a dictionary, encyclopaedia or similar reference work in printed or electronic form without indications that it is registered a registered trademark and gives the impression that it constitutes the generic name of the goods or services for which the trademark is registered, the owner of the trademark may demand correction. The publisher must correct the fault immediately in case of electronic publication or in the next edition of the publication by indicating that it is a registered trademark or removing the trademark from the reference work (Article 8).

V. Exhaustion of the Rights Conferred by a Registered Trademark

718. According to Article 152(1) after the products which are subject to the protection of industrial property right have been put on the market in Türkiye by the owner or with his/her consent acts related to these products shall remain outside the scope of the right.

719. The owner of the trademark may prohibit, however, further commercialization of the goods, particularly where the condition of the goods is changed or impaired after they have been put on the market (Article 152(2)).

VI. Limitations Relating to the Effects of Registered Trademark

720. The owner of a trademark may not prevent third persons from (a) using his/her own name or address (natural persons), (b) indications concerning the kind, quality, quantity, intended purpose, value, geographic origin, etc: or (c) other characteristics of the goods or services in the course of their trading or industrial activities (particularly in accessories, spare parts or equivalent products) as long as they act in good faith (Article 7(5)).

§8. Legal Transactions Relating to Trademarks

I. In General

721. Registered trademarks may be subject to several legal transactions. The owner of a registered trademark may transfer it to another person or grant a license for its use. Trademarks may be subject to usufruct, pledge or compulsory execution. They may be inherited by the heirs of the owner (Article 148(1)). These legal transactions may be carried out independently from the undertaking (Article 148(2)).

722. Transactions between living persons relating to trademarks shall be made in written form. The validity of the transfer agreements is subject to notarization by a notary public (Article 148(4)).

723. Like registered trademarks, trademark applications may also be the subject of all legal transactions (Article 148(8)).

II. Transfer of Trademark

A. *Transfer of Trademark Only*

724. A registered trademark may be transferred in part or all of the goods and services for which it is registered (Article 148(6)).

725. Moreover, a guaranteed mark or a collective mark may also be transferred. The transfer is only valid after entry in the registry of the Turkish Patent and Trademark Office [or Authority, i.e. TürkPatent] (Article 148(7)).

726. Transfer of a trademark is valid if it is made in writing by the parties and notarized by a notary public (Article 148(4)).

727. On request of one of the parties, the transfer of the trademark is entered in the registry and published.

728. As long as the transfer has not been entered in the registry, the parties cannot invoke the rights arising from the registration of the trademark against third persons acting in good faith (Article 148(5)).

729. If the nature of the transfer is such to mislead the public concerning the nature, quality, and geographical origin of the goods and services, TürkPatent refuses to register the transfer unless the transferee agrees to limit registration of the mark to goods or services of which it is not likely to mislead (Article 16(4)).

B. *Transfer of Undertaking*

730. Unless otherwise agreed, the transfer of the whole of an undertaking with its assets and liabilities also includes rights on the trademarks of the undertaking.

III. Licensing of Trademark

A. *Right to Grant Licence*

731. The owner of a trademark may permit others to use his/her trademark for the goods or services for which it is registered, in whole or in part (Article 24(1)).

B. *Licence Agreement*

732. Licensing of a trademark is subject to written form (Article 148(4)). A licence cannot have an effect, however, against third persons acting in good faith until it is registered (Article 148(5)).

733. Licence agreements relating to guarantee or collective trademarks are also subject to written form. They become valid upon entry into the Register (Article 148(7)).

734. Licence agreements cannot contain provisions contrary to the provisions of the *SMK*, No. 6769. The clauses of licence agreements contrary to the *SMK* are null and void.

735. A licence may be exclusive or non-exclusive (Article 24(2)).

736. Under the *SMK*, the licence is, as a rule, non-exclusive unless otherwise provided in the agreement. In non-exclusive licence agreements, the licensor may use the trademark him/herself and grant other licences to third parties (Article 24(2)).

737. In case of an exclusive licence, the licensor may not grant the licence to other persons and use the trademark unless he/she explicitly reserves his/her right (Article 24(2)).

738. In trademark licensing, the licensor shall take measures to guarantee the quality of goods to be produced or services to be rendered by the licensee (Article 24(4)).

C. Legal Situation of Licensee

739. The licensee is obliged to comply with the terms of the licence agreement. Otherwise, the owner of the trademark may claim his/her rights arising from the registered trademark against the licensee (Article 24(4)).

740. The holder of an exclusive licence has exclusive rights with respect to the use of the trademark during the term of protection. However, the licensee is not entitled to transfer the rights arising from the licence or grant a sublicence to other persons (Article 24(3)).

741. In case of an infringement on the trademark, the holder of an exclusive licence may initiate proceedings in his/her own name which are available to the owner of the trademark (Article 158(1)).

742. The holder of a non-exclusive licence is not entitled to apply for legal remedies. In case of an infringement, he/she may give notice to the licensor to initiate proceedings against the infringer. If the licensor refuses to apply for legal remedies or fails to initiate proceedings within three months after the receipt of the notice, the non-exclusive licensee may apply for legal remedies notifying the licensor (Article 158(2)). On the other hand, in the case of serious damage, the holder of a non-exclusive licence may apply to the court within the three-month period for a decision of provisionary measures (Article 158(3)).

IV. Pledge of Trademark

743. A registered trademark may be given as a pledge independently of the undertaking (*SMK*, Article 148(1)). At the request of one of the parties, the pledge on the trademark is entered in the register and published. Other issues relating to the pledge on trademark are subject to the provisions of the Turkish Civil Code (Articles 954 et seq.).

V. Compulsory Execution

744. A registered trademark can be attached independently from the undertaking (Article 148(2)). Attachment is entered at the Register and published. On other issues relating to attachment, the provisions of the Code of Enforcement and Bankruptcy, No. 2004 dated 9 June 1932 (as amended) apply.

§9. REGISTRATION OF TRADEMARK

I. Filing

A. *Requirements of Application*

1. Individual Trademarks

745. Any person may file a trademark.

746. The application filed with the Turkish Patent and Trademark Office [or Authority, i.e. TürkPatent] shall comprise (Article 11(1); *SMK-Yön*, Article 5):

(a) an application form including information identifying the applicant;
(b) a sample of the trademark (*SMK-Yön*, Article 7);
(c) a list of the goods or services for which the trademark is intended;
(d) the original receipt of the payment of the application fee;
(e) if the application has been filed for collective or guarantee trademarks, technical specification according to Article 32;
(f) if priority right is claimed, information showing that the fee of priority right claim is paid;
(g) if letters other than the Latin alphabet are used in the reproduction of a trademark, their transliteration in the Latin alphabet.

747. Each trademark is subject to a separate filing of an application (Article 11(2)).

748. Goods or services for which application is filed shall be classified in accordance with the Nice Agreement concerning the International Classification of Goods and Services for the Purpose of Registration of Marks, which was ratified pursuant to the decision of the Council of Ministers, No. 95/7094 of 12 July 1995.

749. TürkPatent may carry out the necessary amendments on the classes or class numbers under which the goods or services subject to the application fall (Article 11(3)).

750. Goods or services shall not be presumed as being similar on the ground that they are in the same class and goods or services shall not be regarded as being dissimilar on the ground that they are in different classes (Article 11(4)).

2. Guarantee or Collective Trademarks

751. As mentioned above, when filing an application for registration of a guarantee or a collective trademark (Article 31), a technical regulation specifying the ways and means of using the trademark must also be filed (Article 11(1)(d); 32). If a technical regulation does not conform to the requirements prescribed by law, TürkPatent notifies the owner of the trademark to make the necessary alterations. If the required changes will not be made, TürkPatent refuses the request for registration of the collective or guarantee trademark.

752. A trademark application may be withdrawn by the applicant before it is registered (Article 28(1)(b)).

753. Under *SMK*, No. 6769, an application made within the scope of the Protocol relating to the Madrid Agreement concerning the International Registration of Trademarks shall have the same results as an application filed directly to TürkPatent. This application is deemed to have been filed in the first hour and minute of the date of the international application. If there is more than one international application with the same date, the application with the lesser international registration number is deemed to have been filed first (Article 14(1).

754. The international application cannot be rejected on the ground of a trademark application or a registered trademark that was made after the application or if any priority date but submitted to TürkPatent before the international application. The trademark application with the later date is re-evaluated in accordance with Article 16(1) (Article 14(2)).

B. Classification

755. As explained above the goods or services relating to the trademark to be registered are classified in accordance with the international classification of goods and services (Article 11(3); *SMK-Yön*, Article 9).

756. Türkiye is a party to the Nice Convention on Classification.

C. *Right of Priority*

1. Kinds of Priority Right

a. Priority Right under International Conventions

757. Natural or legal persons or their successors

- who are nationals of any State, party to the Paris Convention or to the Agreement Establishing World Trade Organization;
- if not nationals who are domiciled or have an active business in these States may enjoy a right of priority of six months from the date of filing a valid application for registration of a trademark at the authorized bodies of these States, for the purpose of filing an application for obtaining a registration certificate in Türkiye in respect of the same trademark and same goods or services. Priority right not exercised within this period is forfeited (Article 12(1));
- moreover, if a natural or legal person who is a national of a State which is a party to the Paris Convention and to the Agreement Establishing World Trade Organization has filed a valid application in a State not party to the Convention or the WTO Agreement may enjoy the priority right in respect of that filing (Article 12(2)).

b. Exhibition Priority

758. Real or legal persons specified in Article 3 (persons eligible to the protection of trademarks under the *SMK*) who have displayed the goods or services for which the trademark is applied, at national or international exhibitions in Türkiye or at official or officially recognized national or international exhibitions in the States party to the Paris Convention or to the Agreement Establishing WTO may claim a right of priority for registration of the trademark in Türkiye if the application of priority is filed within a period of six months from the date of the first display of the goods (Article 12(3)).

2. Effect of Priority Right

759. The effects of priority rights under Article 12 arise as of the date of the application for which the priority is declared. If the goods or services for which the trademark specified in the application will be used have been displayed along with the trademark in a visible way in the exhibition before the official opening date, the period of priority right shall commence from the date when the good is put on the exhibition or services are displayed (Article 12(4)).

760. If more than one application has been filed in terms of goods or services displayed in any exhibition, the first person who displayed these goods or services benefits from the priority right; and if goods or services are displayed at the same time, the person who filed the first application benefits from the priority right (Article 12(5)).

761. If an application is filed on the basis of priority right, applications filed by third parties after the priority date and which cover identical or indistinguishably similar trademarks with identical or similar goods or services shall be refused (Article 12(6)).

762. An applicant wishing to benefit from his/her right of priority must file a declaration of priority with his/her application for registration of the trademark by depositing the fee for the request. If the document relating to the right of priority has not been submitted within three months after the date of filing, the applicant does not benefit from this right anymore. In such a case, the request for priority right is deemed not to have been made (Article 13(1)).

763. In case more than one priority right is requested for the trademark application, the priority right commences from the date of the first valid priority right (Article 13(3)).

II. Examination of Application

A. *Examination Concerning the Formal Requirements*

764.

(a) TürkPatent examines whether the application complies with the requirements specified by law (Article 15(1); Articles 3 and 11). If TürkPatent concludes that there are no deficiencies, the application is accorded the date of filing as the date, hour, and minute on which the application was originally filed at TürkPatent (*SMK*, Article 15(1)).
(b) If there are deficiencies, TürkPatent requests the applicant to remedy these deficiencies within a period of two months (Article 15(1); *SMK-Yön* Article 8).

765. Applications whose deficiencies are not remedied within the specified period shall be cancelled (Article 15(3)).

B. *Examination Concerning the Applicant*

766. If the application has not been filed by real or legal persons eligible to benefit from the protection of trademarks under the *SMK* (Article 3), the application is refused (Article 15(4)).

C. *Examination with Regard to Absolute Grounds of Refusal*

767. Upon concluding that there are no deficiencies in the requirements of filing, TürkPatent examines whether the application is eligible for registration as regards grounds of absolute refusal (Article 16).

768. When an absolute ground of refusal is found, the application is refused in whole or in part (Article 16(1)).

III. Publication of Application

769. An application for registration of a trademark which has complied with the application requirements is published in the relevant Bulletin (*SMK*, Article 16(2) and *SMK-Yön*, Article 11).

770. If the application has been refused after the publication of the application, the decision of refusal is also published (Article 16(3) and *SMK-Yön*, Article 11(3)).

IV. Opposition Procedure

A. *Remarks by Third Persons*

771. Any natural or legal person or any group representing manufacturers, producers, suppliers of services, traders or consumers may submit to TürkPatent their written remarks that the trademark does not conform to the registration requirements (e.g., unregistrable trademark, improper trademark, or one of the absolute grounds of refusal). However, they shall not be parties to the proceedings before TürkPatent (Article 17(1)).

772. The Authority evaluates these remarks and if it comes to the conclusion that they are correct, it shall refuse the trademark application partially or wholly (Article 17(2)).

B. *Opposition Against Publication*

773. Oppositions concerning a trademark application that was published in the Bulletin should not be registered in accordance with Articles 5 or 6 and shall be filed by relevant persons within two months following the publication of the trademark application (Article 18(1)).

774. Notice of opposition is lodged in writing. Opposition must contain the arguments. If the grounds for opposition are not submitted to TürkPatent within two months, the opposition shall be deemed not to have been made (Article 18(2)).

C. *Examination of Opposition*

775. The opposition is examined by the TürkPatent. During the examination, TürkPatent may request written opinions of the parties and communicate to them the opinions and remarks submitted by the parties (Article 19(1)).

776. TürkPatent may request additional documents and means of evidence (Article 19(1)). TürkPatent, if it finds it appropriate, may invite the parties to make a friendly settlement or reconciliation (Article 19(3)). Regarding reconciliation, the provisions of the Act on Mediation in Civil Law Disputes (AMedC, *Hukuk Uyusmazliklarinda Arabuluculuk Kanunu*), No. 6325 of 7 June 2012 apply (Article 19(4)).

777. If the opposition is not justified it is rejected. If it is found to be valid for some goods or services from which the trademark application has been made, the opposition is accepted in respect of those goods and services (Article 19(3)).

V. Registration of Trademark

778. If the application filed has been found valid under the *SMK* and the *SMK-Yön*, it is entered in the Trademark Register (Article 22(1)). The registered trademarks are published in the Bulletin (*SMK-Yön*, Article 13). The applicant is given a 'Trademark Certificate of Registry'.

779. In case the fee regarding registration of the trademark is not paid or the information relating to the payment of the fee is not submitted to TürkPatent within the specified period, the application is cancelled (Article 22(1); *SMK-Yön*, Article 12).

780. The registry includes the date of registration of the trademark, the application date, the list of goods and services in respect of the trademark, the classification of the goods and services, the name and nationality of the owner of the trademark (and of his/her agent/attorney), trade name and nationality of the legal entity, if the owner is a legal person changes relating to the trademark and to the rights on the trademark, etc. (*SMK-Yön*, Article 14).

781. The registry of TürkPatent is open to the public. A copy of registration can be given upon request provided that its fee is paid (Article 22(3)).

VI. Term of Registration and Renewal of Trademark

A. Term of Registration

782. The trademark is registered for a term of ten years from the date of registration (Article 23(1)).

B. Renewal of Trademark

783. Registration may be renewed for further terms of ten years (Article 23(1)). The trademark may be renewed also for a part of goods or services within the scope of the registration (Article 23(3)).

784. The request for renewal must be submitted and the renewal fee paid within a term of six months before the last day of the month in which protection expires (Article 23(2)). A period of grace of six months is allowed for the renewal of a trademark registration after its term has expired. In such a case, an extra fee is charged (Article 23(2)).

785. Renewal takes effect from the day following the date on which the existing registration expires. The renewal is entered in the registry and published in the Bulletin (Article 23(5)).

786. Trademarks that are not renewed within six months after the term of expiration of protection are deemed null and void (Article 23(5)).

§10. Termination and Invalidity of Trademark Right

I. Termination of Trademark Right

A. Expiration of the Protection Term

787. Trademark right terminates upon the expiry of the protection term and non-renewal within the prescribed period (Article 28(1)(a)).

B. Renunciation of the Right by the Owner

788. The trademark right also terminates if the owner of the trademark renounces his/her right (Article 28(1)(b)).

789. The owner of a trademark may renounce his/her rights in respect of some or all of the goods and services for which it is registered. The renunciation must be declared in writing to the Authority and termination of the trademark right is published in the Bulletin. The renunciation takes effect at the date of entry in the register (Article 28(3)).

790. The owner of a trademark may not renounce, however, his/her right without having the consent of the licensee or holder of rights registered in the Trademark Registry (Article 28(4)).

791. The termination has effect as the termination ground has occurred (Article 28(2)).

II. Invalidity and Cancellation of Trademark

A. *Invalidity of the Trademark*

1. Grounds of Invalidity

792. A registered trademark can be declared *invalid by the court* in the following cases (Articles 25):

(a) in case of existence of one of the grounds of absolute refusal (Article 5);
(b) in case of existence of one of the relative grounds for refusal (Article 6).

793. The judgment of cancellation can be total or partial (Article 26(5)).

2. Persons Entitled to Claim for Invalidity

794. Any person who has an interest (e.g., any person who has suffered damages), the public prosecutor or related official authorities are entitled to claim for cancellation of the trademark (Article 25(2)).

3. Competent Court

a. Jurisdiction

795. The action for invalidity of a trademark may be initiated before the civil court for intellectual and industrial property rights established in accordance with Article 156 of *SMK*, No. 6769. The action for invalidity is initiated against the persons who are registered as the trademark owner as of the date of the action or their legal successors. This action cannot be directed to the Authority (Article 25(3)).

b. Competent Court

796. The competent court is the court of the domicile of the trademark owner (Article 156(5)).

4. Partial Invalidity

797. If the invalidity is requested partially for some goods or services for which the trademark is registered, partial invalidity is decided only for those goods or services. The decision for invalidity which has the result of changing the sample of the trademark cannot be given (Article 25(5)).

5. Trademark That Cannot Be Invalidated

798. If a trademark has been registered contrary to subparagraphs (b), (c) and (d) of Article 5(1), but has acquired distinctive character as a result of use regarding the registered goods or services before the claim for invalidity, it cannot be invalidated (Article 25(4)).

6. Silence of the Trademark Owner

799. If the trademark owner remained silent for five years regarding the use of a trademark of a later date while being aware or should have been aware of this situation, he/she cannot allege his/her trademark as an invalidity ground unless the trademark of the later date was registered in bad faith (Article 25(6)).

B. *Cancellation of Trademark*

1. Grounds for Cancellation

800. Starting from 10 January 2024 (Article 192), in the following cases, Türk-Patent decides the *cancellation of the trademark*:

(a) non-use of the trademark within a period of five years following the registration without a justifiable reason (Articles 9 and 26(1)(a);
(b) where the trademark has become generic in respect of the goods or services by the conducts of the trademark owner (Article 26(1)(b));
(c) where, as a result of the use made by the owner or by the person authorized by him/her, there exists a likelihood of confusion on the part of the public as to the nature, quality, place of production and geographical origin in respect of the goods or services for which it is registered (Article 26(1)(c));
(d) in case of use of a collective or guarantee mark contrary to its technical regulation (Articles 32 and 26(1)(ç)).

2. Persons Entitled to Request for Cancellation of Trademark

801. Persons who have a legal interest may request the cancellation of the trademark from the Authority (Article 26(2)).

3. Persons Against Whom the Request for Cancellation Is Directed

802. Requests for cancellation of the trademark can be directed against the persons who are registered as the trademark owner as of the date of the request or their legal successors (Article 26(3)).

4. Inadmissible Requests for Cancellation

803. In case the trademark has been seriously used regarding the registered goods or services between the date of expiry of the period of five years and the date on which the cancellation request was submitted to the Authority, the requests for cancellation related to subparagraph (a) are rejected (Article 26(4); Article 9).

5. Partial Cancellation

804. If the cancellation cases are related to a part of goods or services for which the trademark is registered, a partial cancellation is decided only for those goods or services. The cancellation cannot be decided in a manner in which the sample of the trademark is changed (Article 26(5)).

6. Notification of Request for Cancellation

805. Request for cancellation of a registered trademark shall be notified to the owner of the trademark. In such a case, the trademark owner submits his/her evidence and replies to the Authority within one month regarding the request. An additional time of up to one month can be granted by the Authority.

7. Cancellation Decision

806. The Authority may demand additional information and documents related to the cancellation request. The Authority may give its decision on the file within the framework of the claims and defences as well as the submitted evidence (Article 26(7)).

C. Effects of Invalidity and Cancellation

1. Effects of Invalidity Decision of the Trademark

807. The *judgment of invalidity of the trademark* has retroactive effects (Article 27(1)). If a judgment related to invalidity of the trademark is given (Article 25(1)), it will be effective from the application date of the trademark and the trademark shall be deemed not to have had the protection provided. (Article 27(1)).

2. Effects of Cancellation Decision of the Trademark by the Authority

808. If a trademark has been *cancelled by the Authority upon a request* (Article 26), its decision is effective as of the date on which the cancellation request is submitted to the Authority. Nevertheless, if the cases for cancellation occur on a previous date, it can be decided upon request that the cancellation decision is effective as of such date (Article 27(2)).

809. The retroactive effects of cancellation, without prejudice to claims for compensation for damages caused by negligence on the part of a trademark owner, do not extend, however, to the following (Article 27(3)):

(a) any final judgment relating to infringement of the trademark that was rendered and enforced (res judicata) prior to the decision of invalidity;
(b) contracts concluded and performed prior to the decision of invalidity.

810. A *final decision (judgment) of invalidity* (res judicata) or *cancellation of a trademark by the Authority* is effective against everybody (Article 27(5)). When the judgment for invalidity of the trademark becomes final (res judicata), the court shall ex officio send the judgment to the Authority (Article 27(6)). After the *finalization of invalidity judgment* or *decision for cancellation of the Authority,* the trademark is deleted from the registry and this situation is published in the Bulletin (Article 27(7)).

§11. Infringements of Trademark and Legal Remedies

I. Infringements of Trademark

811. Under the *SMK*, No. 6769, the following are regarded as an infringement of the registered trademark (Article 29(1)(a)–(ç)):

(a) the use of any sign which is identical to the registered trademark in relation to goods and services which are identical to those for which the trademark is registered (Article 7);
(b) to counterfeit the trademark by the use of the same or confusingly similar trademark without the consent of the trademark owner;
(c) while being aware or should be aware that the trademark is counterfeited by the use of the trademark or a confusingly similar trademark, to sell, distribute, put on the market in a different form, possess for commercial purposes, import or export of goods bearing the infringed trademark or to offer to make a contract related to these goods;
(d) the transfer of rights acquired under a licence agreement to third persons or the expansion of such rights.

II. Legal Remedies

812. In case of infringement, the owner of the trademark may direct several claims against the infringer (*SMK*, Article 149).

A. *Action for Ascertainment of whether the Act is Infringement or Not (Declaratory Action)*

813. The action for ascertainment of the infringement (*SMK*, Article 149(1)(a); CCP (*HMK*), No. 6100, Article 106) can be initiated by the owner of a trademark if he/she needs a judicial decree on the existence of an infringement of a registered trademark (Article 149(1)(a)). Further, any interested person may initiate an action against the trademark owner to obtain a judgment of non-infringement. According to *SMK*, Article 154 anyone who has an interest may demand the owner of a trademark to provide his/her opinion s about whether or not commercial or industrial activities being carried out or to be carried out or serious and actual attempts carried out for these purposes in Türkiye would cause an infringement of his/her industrial property right. In such a case if no opinion is given within one month after notification of this demand or if the opinion is not accepted by the party who has an interest, he/she may initiate an action against the trademark owner for a decision on non-infringement. Notification is not a prerequisite for the initiation of the action (Article 154(1)). This action is notified to all right owners registered in the registry. Further, this action can be initiated together with an action for invalidity of the trademark (Article 154(2)–(3)).[147]

B. Action for Prevention of Probable Infringement (*SMK*, Article 149(1)(b))

814. Even in case of a probable danger of infringement, the owner may initiate an action for prevention (Article 149(1)(b)). In such actions, negligence on the part of the infringer is not a prerequisite of the action.

C. Action for Cease-and-Desist of Infringement (*SMK*, Article 149(1)(c))

815. The owner may apply to the court for an order to cease the infringing actions. (Article 149(1)(c)).

D. *Action for Removal of Infringement and Compensation for Damage and Immaterial Damage*

816. If the infringement has been committed by negligence (intention, grave or slight negligence) on the part of the infringer, damages may be claimed by the owner of the registered mark (Articles 149(1)(ç) and (150)–(151)).

817. The trademark owner may request from the infringer the documents relating to the use of the trademark without his/her consent for evaluation of damages resulting from the infringement (Article 150(3)).

---

147. However, this action cannot be initiated by a person against whom an action because of an infringement has been initiated (Art. 154(1)).

(a) In an action for compensation, the infringer must compensate the actual damages (*damnum emergens*) of the trademark owner (Article 150).
(b) Moreover, the loss of profit (*lucrum cessans*) can be claimed from the infringer (Article 151(2)).

According to Article 151, the loss of profit can be calculated in accordance with one of the following methods of evaluation on the option of the trademark owner (i.e., plaintiff):

(a) according to the probable profit that the trademark owner would have obtained as the result of the use of his/her trademark if the competition of the infringer did not exist;
(b) according to the net profit earned by the infringer as the result of the unlawful use of the trademark;
(c) according to the license fee that would be paid to the trademark owner if the infringer would have utilized the trademark under a licence agreement.

818. In the calculation of the loss of profit factors particularly as the importance of industrial property right or the number, term and type of licences related to industrial property right during the infringement and the nature and size of violation shall be taken into account (Article 151(3)).

819. As regards the compensation for the loss of profit, the *SMK* has provided for more protection: if the trademark owner has chosen one of the above-mentioned methods (a or b) of evaluation, the court may add on a reasonable extra amount to the compensation if in the court's opinion, the trademark has contributed substantially to the economic value of the goods (Article 151(4)).

E. Action for Moral Compensation

820. The infringer must also compensate non-material damages (*manevi zarar*, French: *dommage moral*) suffered by the owner of the trademark (Article 149(1)(ç)). The harm to the respectability of the trademark as the result of improper use of the infringer is the typical aspect of non-material damages.

F. Confiscation of the Products

821. This remedy enables the confiscation of products that have been produced or imported by infringing on the trademark rights. The products constituting infringement or penal sanction as well as instruments (devices and machines) which can exclusively be used in their specific production may be confiscated (Article 149(1)(d)).

G. Granting of Ownership of the Confiscated Products

822. The owner may request the granting of ownership of the confiscated products, devices and machines seized in accordance with Article 149(1)(d) (Article 149(1)(e)).

H. Changing or Destroying the Confiscated Products and Instruments

823. In order to prevent continuity of the infringement, the owner may ask the court to order to change the shape of the confiscated counterfeit products and their instruments (devices and machines), or to erase the trademarks on them, or -if this is inevitable- to destroy them. The costs of these measures shall be paid by the infringer (Article 149(1)(f)).

I. Publication or Notification of the Court's Judgment

824. If there is justified reason or interest, the court may decide to publish the final judgment (res judicata) in full or in summary, in daily newspapers or by other means at the expense of the infringer, or to notify the concerned parties (Article 149(1)(g)).

J. Action for Security (Recording) of Evidence

825. Under the provisions of the Code of Civil Procedure, No. 6100 (CCP, *HMK*), the owner of a registered trademark may seek by experts' opinion, a view of the premises or other means to secure evidence which will be used in future action for cease-and-desist, prevention or compensation (Articles 400–406).

826. In practice, before starting the action for cease-and-desist or compensation the action for securing evidence is usually initiated particularly if there is the danger of concealment or destruction of evidence by the infringer. In such a case, the petition is served usually upon the infringer after the experts' opinion was presented to the court.

K. Provisionary (Interim) Measures (Injunction)

827. Action for provisionary[148] measures is regulated by *SMK*, Article 159. According to Article 159(3), the provisions of Code of Civil Procedure (CCP,

148. It should be noted that the terms 'interim, interlocutory, precautionary, preliminary and provisional' are used in various legal texts with the same meaning.

HMK), No. 6100 (Articles 389 et seq.) apply to the matters for which there is no provision in *SMK* on provisionary measures.

1. Persons Entitled to Request Provisionary (Interim) Measures (Injunction)

828. Under *SMK*, any person entitled to initiate main actions in case of infringement on the registered trademark may request the court to order provisionary measures when he/she can prove that the actual use of the trademark constitutes an infringement on his/her registered trademark or serious preparations to use the trademark would infringe his/her rights on his/her trademark (Article 159(1)).

829. The request for provisionary measures may be filed before or with the initiation of the main action. It can also be requested during the pending main action. The request for provisionary measures is examined separately (Article 76(2)).

2. Nature of Provisionary (Interim) Measures (Injunction)

830. Provisionary measures shall be in nature to enable the enforcement of the judgment (Article 159(2)(c)).

831. For this purpose, the provisionary measures should provide:

(a) cessation of the acts of infringement on the trademark rights of the plaintiff;
(b) injunction to arrest and take custody of the goods produced or imported by infringing on the trademark rights where they are located within the borders of Türkiye, including customs, free ports or free areas;
(c) ordering to give caution for damages to be compensated;

III. Penal Sanctions (Article 30)

832. Infringements of registered trademarks constitute criminal offences. The owner of the trademark may lodge a complaint to the Office of Public Prosecutor, seeking penal sanctions.

833. According to Article 30(1)–(3), those using a mark identical or similar to a trademark registered in the name of another person or those offering for sale, selling, distributing, importing or exporting, knowingly the goods bearing the trademarks unlawfully used by a person other than the owner of the registered trademark, and those acting as accomplices in such acts are punished by imprisonment and a fine. Investigation of such offences is subject to a complaint (Article 30(6)).

IV. Persons Entitled to Initiate Civil Actions

A. *Owner of the Trademark*

834. Actions relating to infringements on trademarks are, normally, initiated by the owners of trademark rights (Article 149(1)).

B. *Holders of Exclusive Licence Right (Article 158)*

835. Unless otherwise provided for by the licence agreement, the holder of an exclusive license may, in case of an infringement of the trademark rights, initiate in his/her own name all actions available to the trademark owner (Article 158(1)).

836. Holders of non-exclusive licenses are not entitled to initiate actions against the infringer of the trademark. In the case of an infringement, the licensee may give notice through a notary public to the trademark owner and request him/her to initiate proceedings against the infringer. If the trademark owner refuses this request or fails to initiate the action within three months after the receipt of the notice, the licensee may start proceedings (Article 158(2)). In cases of serious damage, the licensee may request the court to issue an injunction for provisionary measures (Article 158(3)).

V. Defendant

A. *Infringer*

837.

(1) The defendant is normally the infringer of the registered trademark. The person who, without consent of the trademark owner, produces, sells, distributes or puts to commercial use or imports for these purposes or keeps in possession counterfeit goods is liable for damages. The action is directed at these persons (Article 149).
(2) Moreover, the person using in any form the registered trademark without the consent of its owner can be liable for damages if he/she has been informed of the infringement by the trademark owner and has been requested by him/her to cease the infringement (Article150(1)).
(3) Likewise, if the use of the trademark without consent of its owner constitutes negligence on the part of the person who uses it, he/she is liable for damages (Article 150(1)).

B. Persons Who May Not Be Sued

838. The owner of the trademark cannot direct his/her action against those who have used the products (usually consumers) put on the market by the person (infringer) who was held liable for compensation to the trademark owner (Article 153). In other words, the owner of the trademark cannot initiate the actions specified in Article 149 against the persons who retain or use for their personal needs the products put on the market by the infringer (Article 153(1)).

VI. Specialized Courts and Mediation

839. The relevant procedural provisions of *SMK*, No. 6769 (Industrial Property Law, Article 156) refer to specialized courts. For further explanations including mediation, *see* above paragraphs 653–659 in Chapter 2 – Patents and Utility Models – 'Specialized Courts and Mediation'.

VII. Prescription: Statute of Limitation

840. The claims relating to infringements on registered trademarks are subject to the provisions on the prescription of the Turkish Code of Obligations Article 146 (*SMK*, Article 157).

841. Under the Turkish Code of Obligations, the usual prescription period is ten years unless another limitation period has been provided by law (Article 146).

Chapter 4. Trade Names

§1. Trade Names and Business Names

I. Trade Names

A. Legal Sources

842. Trade name (*ticaret ünvani*) is a distinctive sign of the owner of a commercial undertaking.

843. Trade names are regulated by the Turkish Commercial Code (TComC – *TTK*), No. 6102 of 13 January 2011, Articles 39 et seq.[149]

844. Under Turkish law, trade names are subject to registration at the Trade Registry (*Ticaret Sicili,* TComC, Article 40(1)).

845. Each merchant is obliged to use his/her trade name and sign all deeds and documents relating to his/her business under his/her trade name (Article 39(1)).

846. The right of the owner on a trade name is an absolute right.

B. Principles Relating to Trade Name

847. Trade names are generally subject to the following principles:

– The trade name must be distinctive in relation to the owner of the commercial undertaking.
– Legal person may have only one trade name for all of his/her activities.
– A natural person may have more than one trade name if he/she exercises more than one independent business:
– Trade name must not be misleading (principle of truthfulness).
– The indication chosen as a trade name must not be confused with the pre-existing trade names in the same or similar business sector.
– In case of homonymous trade names, the owner of the posterior trade name is requested to add a certain indication to avoid the risk of confusion.

C. Assignment of Trade Name

848. A trade name may not be assigned without the undertaking. The owner of an undertaking may transfer, however, the undertaking by retaining his/her trade

149. *See* further Arts 42 et seq. of the Implementing Regulation of Trade Registry (*Ticaret Sicili Yönetmeligi*).

name. Unless otherwise agreed, the transfer of an undertaking also includes the trade name (TComC, Article 49).

D. *Protection of Trade Names*

1. Civil Protection

849. Under Turkish law, the exclusive use of a duly registered trade name belongs only to its owner (TComC, Article 50).

850. The owner of a trade name may request the cease-and-desist and prevention of the use of his/her trade name if it is used without his/her consent.

851. He may further demand compensation if he/she suffers damages as a result of the use of his/her trade name by an infringer in case of negligence (TComC Article 52(1)).

852. A claim for the announcement of the court's judgment can also be requested at the cost of the infringer (TComC, Article 52(2)).

853. The claim for compensation is subject to the prescription period (statute of limitation) laid down by Article 72 of the Turkish Code of Obligations. The claim for damages is barred by prescription after two years from the date when the damaged person has received the knowledge of the damage and of the identity of the person who is liable, but in any event, after ten years from the date when the act causing the damage took place.

2. Penal Protection

854. Infringement of the right on trade names constitutes an offence and is punished in accordance with TComC, Article 51.

II. Business Names (*Isletme Adi*)

855. 'Business name' distinguishes a 'business' from others. To have a 'business name' is not required by law. If a merchant chooses, however, a business name, it should be registered (TComC, Article 53).

856. A business name may be the subject matter of transactions. Unlike trade names (TComC, Article 49), business names may be transferred with or without the business.

857. The exclusive use of a duly registered business name belongs to its owner (TComC, Articles 50, 53).

858. In case of infringement on a registered business name, its owner enjoys various remedies laid down by TComC Article 52 for the protection of trade names. The statute of limitation for the claim for compensation is subject to the Turkish Code of Obligations Article 72.

§2. Distinctive Title and Other Signs

I. Distinctive Title

859. 'Distinctive title' *(ayirt edici isaret)* is an indication which characterizes the 'commercial undertaking' or the 'establishment of a commercial undertaking'.

860. The right on the distinctive title is acquired by its use in the transaction provided that it has a distinctive character.

861. If the relevant title does not possess any distinctive character, the right thereon is acquired by the establishment in the transactions.

862. The owner of a distinctive title has an absolute right upon it.

863. The right on distinctive title is transferable without the undertaking.

II. Other Distinctive Signs

864. Trade names which have not been registered but which are used in the transactions as well as 'other distinctive indications' *(diger ayirt edici isaretler)* which have no distinctive ability by themselves may be protected under Turkish law according to the provisions on unfair competition (TComC, Articles 54 et seq., Article 55(1)(a)).

Chapter 5. Designs

§1. Legal Sources

I. Historical Background

865. Previously 'designs' were regulated in Turkish law under the term 'industrial designs' by the 'Decree having the Power of Law for Protection of Industrial Designs, *KHK/*554' (*Endüstriyel Tasarimlarin Korunmasi Hakkinda Kanun Hükmünde Kararname*, *KHK*/554) of 27 June 1995.[150]

866. At present *KHK*/554 was abolished and replaced by provisions of Articles 55–81 of Book Three in 'Industrial Property Law' (*Sinai Mülkiyet Kanunu: SMK*), No. 6769 of 22 December 2016. *SMK* does not use anymore the term 'industrial design' (sinai tasarim), but only 'design' (tasarim).[151]

867. In accordance with *SMK*, the Turkish Patent and Trademark Office [or Authority, i.e. TürkPatent] issued an Implementing Regulation in 2017. Articles 47–70 of this Regulation deal with the details relating to 'designs'.[152]

---

150. On this occasion we would like to list the following novelties *KHK*/554 had introduced into Turkish industrial property law: (i) a system for industrial designs based on registration; (ii) non-examination as to the substance; (iii) publication of industrial designs; (iv) deferment of publication; (v) possibility of multiple applications; (vi) opposition by third parties; (vii) better protection against infringements on the rights of industrial design; (viii) specialized courts for cases relating to industrial designs. *KHK*/554 had been drafted in 1990s in the light of the TRIPs Agreement as well as EC legislation. The principles and solutions of the Proposal for a Council Regulation on the Community Design (EC draft Regulation, Com (93) 342 final COD 463. OJ No. C29 of 31 Jan. 1994, p. 20) and the Proposal for a Council Directive on the Approximation of the Legislation of the Member States on the Legal Protection of Design (EC Directive on Design, Com (93) 344 final COD 464. OJ No. C 345 of 23 Dec. 1993, p. 14). (Cf. Directive 98/71/EC of the European Parliament and of the Council of 13 Oct. 1998 on the legal protection of designs; Council Regulation (EC) No. 6/2002 of 12 Dec. 2001 on Community designs, OJ, L3, 5 Jan. 2002) were examined by the Drafting Commission. The Drafting Commission for Industrial Design Law in which one of the authors served as a member benefited from a previous draft for protection of industrial designs which had been prepared by Prof Dr Ernst E. Hirsch ('Hirsch's Draft'). The Drafting Commission had taken, particularly, into consideration the following foreign laws: Austrian Federal Law on Protection of Designs (*Bundesgesetzüber den Schutz von Mustern, Musterschutzgesetz, MuSchG*) of 7 Jun. 1990; French Law, No. 92-597 of 1 Jul. 1992 on the Intellectual Property Code (Legislative Part) (Loi No. 92-597 relative *au code de la propriétéintellectuelle* [*partielégislative*] as amended by Law No. 94-102 of 5 Feb. 1994); Australian Draft Law on Designs, WIPO Model Law on Designs, Paris and Berne Conventions, former GATT and WTO Agreement (TRIPs).The Drafting Commission had also examined German Law concerning Copyright in Industrial Designs (Designs Law) of 11 Jan. 1876 as amended by the Law of 18 Dec. 1986 (*Gesetzbetreffend das Urheberrecht an Mustern und Modellen* [*Geschmacksmustergesetz*]); Italian Law on Industrial Model Patents (Royal Decree No. 1411 of 25 Aug. 1940 as amended by Law No. 60 of 14 Feb. 1987); Spanish Industrial Property Code (*Estatuto de la Propiedad Industrial*) (Royal Decree, Law of 26 Jul. 1929 as amended by Law No. 12/1975 and Law No. 17/1975) and Swiss Federal Act on Industrial Designs and Models of 30 Mar. 1900 (as amended 16 Dec. 1994) and the Federal Act on Priority Rights for Patents and Industrial Designs and Models of 3 Apr. 1914.
151. *See* Arts 55–81; regarding the common provisions of all industrial property including 'designs' *see* Arts 146 et seq. in Official Gazette, No. 29944 of 10 Jan. 2017.
152. Official Gazette, No. 30047 of 24 Apr. 2017.

II. Structure of *SMK*, No. 6769 Book Three on 'Designs'

868. *SMK*, Book Three has the title 'Design.' This Book is composed of seven Parts and contains 26 articles.

869. Part One deals with 'The Design Right and Its Scope' (Articles 55–60). Part Two is devoted to the matters relating to 'Application, Examination and Registration.' Chapter One in this Part lays down provisions on 'Application, Priority Right and Examination' (Articles 61–64). Chapter Two regulates 'Registration and Publication' (Articles 65–66). Chapter Three covers the matters relating to 'Objection and Examination of Objection' (Articles 67–68). The matters on 'Protection Term and Renewal' are regulated by the provisions of Chapter Four (Articles 69). Part Three is dedicated to the 'Right Ownership and Usurpation' (Articles 70–72). Part Four regulates the matters relating to 'Designs of Employees' (Articles 73–74). Part Five handles the issues concerning 'License' (Articles 75–76). Part Six regulates the matters relating to 'Termination of the Right' on designs. 'Invalidity' of design as a ground of 'termination' has been regulated by Articles 77–79) while the 'Other Termination Grounds and Their Effects' are handled by Article 80). In Book Three 'Infringements of Design Right' are regulated by Part Seven. As regards remedies, legal and penal sanction they are regulated by Book Five on 'Common and Other Provisions' (Articles 146 et seq.).

§2. General Provisions

I. Aims and Scope

870. The aim of *SMK*, No. 6769 Book Three on 'design right' is the protection of designs and development of the industry. According to Article 55(4), a design shall be protected as:

871. A registered design in case it is registered in accordance with the provisions of Book Three and a design shall be protected as a non-registered design in case it is presented to the public for the first time in Türkiye.

872. Protection of designs by *SMK* does not discard the protection provided by the 'Law on Intellectual and Artistic Works' ('*Fikir ve Sanat Eserleri Kanunu*, No. 5846' [*FSEK*]) when the requirements laid down by this law are satisfied (Article 58(3)).

II. Definitions

873. Under *SMK*, 'design' (*tasarim*) means the appearance of the whole or part of a product resulting from the features such as lines, colour, contour, shape, material or texture of the product itself or its ornaments (Article 55(1). Cf. EC Regulation No. 6/2002, Article 3(a)).

874. 'Product' (*ürün*) is defined as any industrial or handicraft item including parts intended to be assembled into a complex product like packaging, presentations of more than one object perceived together, graphic symbols and typographic typefaces but excluding computer programs (Article 55(2)) (Cf. EC Regulation No. 6/2002, Article 3(b)).

875. 'Complex product' is a product which is composed of components which can be replaced or renewed by disassembly and reassembly of the product (Article 55(3)).

III. Persons Entitled to Protection

876. Under *SMK*, the following persons are entitled to benefit from the protection: Turkish nationals; or natural persons and legal entities who are domiciled or engaged in industrial or commercial activities within the territory of the Republic of Türkiye; or persons who have application rights in accordance with the provisions of the Paris or Berne Conventions or the Agreement Establishing the WTO of 15 April 1994.

877. Furthermore, natural persons or legal entities who are nationals of foreign States may benefit from the design protection of *SMK*, in accordance with the principle of reciprocity, if those States confer legal or actual protection on Turkish nationals (Article 3).

§3. Requirements for Protection

I. In General

878. Under *SMK*, No.6769 a design is only capable of protection if it is 'new' and has an 'individual character' (Article 56(1))

879. A design of a product which constitutes a part of a complex item is protected if and when the design of the part itself is *'new'* and has *'individual character'*.

II. Novelty

880. A design is considered *new* if no identical design has been made available to the public before the 'date of reference' or priority but will not be considered new if its features differ only in immaterial details from other designs. Therefore, designs are deemed to be identical if their specific features differ only in immaterial details.

881. Under *SMK*, the design of a part of a complex product shall be considered to be new and to have distinctive character: (a) if the component part is mounted to the complex product, remains visible during normal use of the complex product; (b) if the visible features of the component part fulfil the requirements as to novelty and individual character (Article 56(3)).

882. 'Normal use' means use by the end-user excluding maintenance, servicing or repair work if an identical design is not presented to the public in any part of the world, (a) before the application of priority date for the registered design; (b) before the design is presented to the public for the first time for non-registered design, it shall be accepted as a 'new design'. If the design differs only in immaterial details, it shall also be accepted as identical (Article 56(4)).

883. Under *SMK*, 'made available to the public' is defined as a design which has been published, exhibited, used in trade or otherwise disclosed. It does not include disclosures to third parties under explicit or implicit conditions of confidentiality (Article 6; Cf. EC Regulation No. 6/2002, Article 5).

III. Individual Character

884. According to Article 56(5), a design has an *'individual character'* if the overall impression created by a design on the informed user differs from the overall impression created by any design presented to the public on the same user; (a) before application or priority date for the registered design; (b) before the design is presented to the public for the first time for non-registered design.

885. In the evaluation of the distinctive character, the degree of freedom of the designer in developing the design shall be taken into consideration (Article 56(6)).

IV. Presentation to the Public (Disclosure)

886. 'Presentation or making available to the public' means releasing on the market, use, description, publication, promotion or so on by means of exhibition and sale. Disclosure to a third person under conditions of confidentiality shall not be deemed as making available to the public (Article 57(1)).

887. A disclosure shall not affect the novelty or individual character, if a design for which protection is claimed has been made available to the public during the twelve-month period preceding the application date or, if priority is claimed, the date of priority by the designer, his/her successor in title or a third person in consent with the designer or his/her successor or in abuse of the relation with the designer or his/her successor (Article 57(2)).

§4. SCOPE OF PROTECTION

I. The Scope of Protection and Cases Without Protection

A. *Scope of Protection*

888. According to Article 58(1), a *design owner* may use his/her rights arising out of *SMK*, No. 6769 against *designs* which have no *individual character* compared to his/her own design.

889. In the evaluation of the scope of protection, the *degree of freedom of the designer* in developing his/her design shall be taken into consideration.[153]

B. *Cases outside the Scope of Protection*

890. According to Article 58(4), the following shall not be in the scope of protection:

(a) Designs contrary to public policy or good morals.
(b) Visual characteristics that are mandatory by the technical function of the product.
(c) Visual characteristics of products whose production in definite shape and measures are mandatory for the mechanical montage or connection of the product on which the design is used or applied to another product.
(d) Designs that include the inappropriate use of sovereignty signs taking place in the scope of Article 6ter of the Paris Convention and that covers signs, arms, certificates of achievement or denominations which are outside of this scope but interest the public order and becoming public knowledge in terms of religious, historical and cultural values and for which registration permit shall not be granted by relevant authorities.

891. It should be noted that designs that provide the connection establishment in different ways as finite or infinite with each other of these units in a modular system composed of different or equivalent units provided that the conditions specified in Article 56 are satisfied (Article 58(5)).

II. The Scope of Design Right and Its Limitations

A. *Registered designs*

892. According to *SMK*, a design confers on its holder the exclusive right to use it.

153. Design protection under *SMK*, No. 6769 does not prejudice the protection under *FSEK* (the Law on Intellectual and Artistic Works, No. 5846) if the conditions laid down by this Law are satisfied (*SMK*, Art. 58(3)).

893. Without the consent of the design right holder, *third parties* cannot produce, put on the market, sell, import, use for commercial purposes or keep in stock for those purposes the product in which the design is incorporated or tow which it is applied (Article 59(1)).

B. Unregistered designs

894. Unregistered designs give the right holder the right *to prevent acts* mentioned in the first paragraph, in case of copies of identical designs or in respect of overall impression copies of indistinguishably similar designs are used (Article 59(2)).

C. Limitation of the rights conferred by the design right

895. Under *SMK*, Article 59(3), the rights conferred by a design right shall not extend to:

(1) acts done privately and for non-commercial purposes;
(2) acts done for experimental purposes;
(3) acts of reproduction for the purpose of making citations or teaching, provided that such acts are compatible with fair trade practices and do not unduly prejudice the normal exploitation of the design, and that mention is made of the source;
(4) the equipment on ships and aircrafts registered in a third country, when these temporarily enter the territory of the Republic of Türkiye; the importation in Türkiye of spare parts and accessories for the purpose of repairing such craft and the execution of repairs on such crafts.

896. On this occasion it should be noted that the use of the design of a component part used for the purpose of the repair of a complex product so as to restore its original appearance within three years after the design is released to the market for the first time shall not be deemed as an infringement of the design right provided that no misleading information shall be given about the source of these parts (Article 59(4)).

D. The Right Arising from Previous Use

897. Persons that use the design in the registered scope of protection independently of the registered design in good faith for commercial purposes inside the country or that took serious and true measures in respect of use are given the right to use due to previous use and limited to these preparations to meet the reasonable requirements of the undertaking. Right arising from previous use shall be registered and published in the Bulletin (Article 60(1)).

898. Rights arising from previous use cannot be extended and transferred by granting a licence. Transfer of this right is possible through the transfer of the undertaking (Article 60(2)).

§5. Application, Examination and Registration of Design

I. Application Requirements

A. In General

899. Design application covers (a) the application form containing information about the applicant's identity; (b) a visual explanation that reflects the appearance of the design and that enables reproduction through publication; (c) the name of the product in which the design is incorporated or to which it is applied; (d) the name of the designer or the names of the designers in a group; (e) information containing how registration request right has been obtained from the designer or designers; (f) if any, the request of postponement of the publication; (g) if engaged, the information of the attorney (Article 61(1)).

900. Also, a description of the visual representation or sample of the design can be presented (Article 61(3)).

901. Regarding the classification of the products on which the design is used or applied the provisions of *Locarno Agreement Establishing an International Classification for Industrial Designs* are applied (Article 61(5)).[154]

902. The designer, if his/her name is not indicated in the application form, has the right to request his/her name to be indicated as a designer. Nevertheless, the designer may request his/her name to be secret (Article 61(10); *SMK-Yön*, Article 49).

903. The registration request for multiple designs can be made as multiple applications provided that an additional application fee shall be paid (Article 61(7)–(9)); *SMK-Yön*, Article 55).

904. Spelling (typos) errors or obvious errors in fact are corrected upon the applicant's request provided that no change in the sample of the design shall be made (Article 61(11)).

154. Türkiye is a party to *Locarno Agreement* by the Decree of the Council of Ministers, No. 97/9731 of 5 Aug. 1997.

B. Priority Right Claim and Its Effect

1. Priority Right Claim

905.

- Natural persons or legal entities or their successors that are nationals of one of the contracting countries to the Paris Convention or Agreement Establishing the WTO.
- Natural persons or legal entities or their successors that have a domicile or commercial undertaking in one of these countries, even not being a national of any of these countries, shall benefit from the priority right to make an application in Türkiye for identical design in the scope of the provisions of Paris Convention within six months starting from the date of their application made duly by them to competent authorities for the registration of the design. The priority right not to be used within this period shall be forfeited. To benefit from the priority right, the document of priority from the competent authorities to which the first application has been made shall be obtained (Article 62(1)).
- Natural persons and legal entities mentioned in the first paragraph (Article 62(1)) or their successors benefit from the priority right in the frame of the provisions of the first paragraph based on design application made duly by them in any country that is not party of Paris Convention or Agreement Establishing WTO (Article 62(2)).

906. The subsequent application made in the same country and covering the same subject as the previous first application is deemed as the first application in determining the priority right provided that the previous application is withdrawn or is accepted as withdrawn or refused without presentation to the public for review and without having granted any right as of the date of the subsequent application or forming a basis for a priority right. The previous application is not taken as ground for the demand for a priority right (Article 62(3)).

2. Exhibition Priority

907. Natural persons or legal entities mentioned in Article 3 exhibiting the design for which application has been made or the product to which design has been applied on national or international exhibitions in Türkiye or international official exhibitions or on exhibitions recognized to be official in contracting countries to the Paris Convention or Agreement establishing the WTO, shall benefit from the priority right to make application within six months starting from the date of the exhibition (Article 62(5)).

908. If the design for which the application has been made or the product to which the design has been applied shall be exhibited in a visible way in the exhibition before the official opening date, then the priority right shall commence from the date of exhibition of the product (Article 62(6)).

909. If more than one application is made for a product that is identical or similar to the product exhibited in any exhibition, the first exhibited benefits from the priority right and if the product is exhibited at the same time, the first application benefits from the priority right (Article 62(7)).

3. Request for Priority Right and Its Effect

910. Request for priority right is made with the application. Documents relating to the request are submitted to the Authority within three months after the application date. Otherwise, the request for priority right is deemed unmade (Article 63(1); *SMK-Yön*, Article 56).

911. If more than one priority rights are demanded for a design, the priority right starts as of the first valid priority date. The priority right arising from the display in exhibitions does not extend the priority period date granted according to Article 62 (Article 63(4)).

II. Examination

A. *Examination as to Formal Requirements*

912. The Authority examines the compliance of the application with conditions specified in Articles 61 and 63. An examination is carried out with respect to 'novelty' and 'individual character' of the design. As a result of the examination, if no deficiency in terms of conditions specified in subparagraphs (a) and (b) of Article 61(1) has been determined, application date finalizes as of the date of the receipt of the application by the Authority (Article 64(1)).

B. *Remediable Deficiencies*

913. If deficiencies cannot be remedied in due time, the application shall be deemed invalid (Article 64(4)). Failure to remedy the deficiencies related to priority right in due time shall only cause the loss of priority right (Article 64(5)).

C. *Refusal of Design Registration Request*

914. The Authority rejects the design registration request, (a) not complying with design and product requests; (b) violating public policy or good morals; (c) made by natural or legal persons not included in the scope of Article 3 (*SMK*, No. 6769, Article 3); (d) containing the inappropriate use of sovereignty signs stated in Article 6ter of Paris Convention and sign, coat of arms, orders and naming that are outside this scope but concern the public, became public in terms of religious, historical and cultural value and for which registration permit shall not be granted by relevant authorities; (e) determined not to be *new* (Article 64(6)). If refusal decision is related to only a part of the design, partial refusal decision is given for only that part. In such a case, the remaining part must provide the protection conditions and maintain the design identity to ensure the continuity of registration (Article 64(7)).

D. *Start of the Design Protection*

915. Design protection begins from the date of finalization of the application (Article 64(3)).

III. Registration and Publication

A. *Entry at the Registry*

916. Finalized application shall be recorded in the registry as a registered design and published in the Bulletin (Article 65(1)).

B. *Deferment of the Publication*

917. The applicant along with the application may request the deferment of the publication for a period of thirty-month starting from the application date, if any, the priority date (Article 66(1)). An application demanding the deferment of the publication shall also be recorded in the registry and the demand for deferment shall be published in the Bulletin. The information and documents related to the visual representation of the design and application files shall be made available to third parties for examination (Article 66(2)–(3)).

918. The publishing date of a design for which deferment of publication has been demanded shall be the date of publication of visual representation (Article 66(6)).

§6. Opposition and Examination of Opposition

I. Opposition to Decision and Registration

919. Applicants may raise a justified written objection against decisions of the Authority within two months from the date of notification.

920. Third parties may object in writing against the issuance of a registration certificate within three months from the publication date by paying the fee claiming that the design is not compliant with the definitions specified in Article 55 or does not meet the conditions specified in Articles 55 and 57 or the application has been made in bad faith and contains the unauthorized use of intellectual property rights (Article 67(1)).

II. Examination of the Opposition

A. *In General*

921. *Oppositions* are examined by the *Board* within the framework of the Directorate of *Re-examination and Re-evaluation* (Cf. Article 2 and Article 68(1)). At the stage of examination of the opposition and where it is deemed necessary the *applicant's opinion* is taken. The Board may request the opposing party to submit the additional information and documents within one month after the notification date (Article 68(3)).

B. *Acceptance of Opposition*

922. If the objection is accepted, the registration of the design becomes invalid. If an objection relating to a part of the design is accepted, only that part of the registration shall be deemed invalid (Cf. Article 79). *Invalidity decision* shall be published in the Bulletin (Article 68(5)–(6)).

§7. Term of Protection and Renewal

I. Term of Protection

A. *Registered Designs*

923. Under *SMK*, No. 6769 registered designs are protected for a period of five years from the date of filing of the application. The term of protection is renewable for periods of five years each up to a total term of twenty-five years (Article 69(1)).

B. *Unregistered Designs*

924. The term of protection of *unregistered designs* covers a period of three-year as from the first presentation date to the public of the design for which protection is demanded (Article 69(2)).

II. Renewal of Registration

925. The registration of the design is renewed upon the request of the design owner.

926. Request for renewal shall be made by the design owner within six months before the expiry of the protection date and the information showing payment of the renewal fee shall be submitted to the Authority within the same period.

927. If no request is made, within this period, a renewal request may be made within six months after the expiry of the protection date provided that an additional fee is paid (Article 69(4)).

928. The renewal shall take effect from the day following the expiration of the previous protection period. The renewal is entered in the registry and published in the Bulletin (Article 69(5)).

929. The design right related to the not renewed designs ends as of the date on which the protection term expires (Article 69(6)).

§8. Holder's Right to a Registered Design and Usurpation of Design

I. Holder's Right to Design

A. In General

930. Under *SMK*, No. 6769, the design right belongs to the designer and his/her successors in title (Article 70(1)). The holder of a design has the exclusive right to use the design and to prevent any third party not having his/her consent from using the design. Without the consent of the holder of the right to design, third parties are not entitled to produce to put on the market, sell, offer, import, put in commercial use or keep in stock a product in which such a design is incorporated or into which it is applied.

931. The rights derived from the application and registered design (design right) may be transferred to or inherited by other persons. They can be subject matters of transactions *causa mortis* (i.e., testaments or inheritance contracts). Design rights may be given as security (*rehin*) (Article 148(1)).

932. Moreover, design rights may be levied in execution (*haciz*) (Article 148(1)). On the request of one of the parties, the levy of execution is entered in the register and published in the Bulletin. Regarding security and levy of execution, the relevant provisions of the Turkish Civil Code, No. 4721 (*Türk Medeni Kanunu*) and Code of Enforcement and Bankruptcy (*Icra Iflas Kanunu*) apply.

B. Joint Ownership on Design

933. If more than one person has jointly developed a design, the right to the design belongs to them in accordance with provisions of co-ownership (payli mülkiyet) unless otherwise agreed among the parties (Cf. Turkish Civil Code, No. 4721, Articles 688 et seq.)

934. Each person entitled to a design right may execute the following in his/her own right, (a) he/she can dispose of his/her own share freely and independently of the other joint holders; (b) he/she can make use of the design after having informed the other joint holders. (c) In the event that rights arising from design are infringed in any way, he/she can sue a claim against third persons. In this case, a notification shall be sent by the claimant to the other right holders in order that they can participate in the legal proceedings (Article 70(2)).

935. Licensing of the design to third parties can be granted with the consent of all joint holders. However, the court may taking into account the current circumstances grant this right to one of the joint holders (Article 70(3)).

936. It should be noted that even if more than one person becomes the right owner on it, a design application or design cannot be divided for transfer or for establishing a right on it (Article 70(4)).

II. Usurpation of Design

A. *Situations Relating to Usurpation of Design*

937. If an application for design is made by a person not being a legal right owner or if the design is registered on behalf of this person or if an unregistered design is presented to the public by a person who is not right holder, then the person who claims that he/she is the legal right holder may demand the court to transfer the design ownership to him/her or that he/she is recognized as the design owner without prejudice to his/her rights and demands arising from the design right (Article 71(1)).

938. If these requests are not alleged within three years after the publication of the registered design or the presentation to the public of the unregistered design, they are forfeited (Article 71(3)). Demands alleged in legal proceedings instituted in accordance with Article 71, final decisions given by the court or any other circumstances finalizing the legal proceedings shall be registered and published upon demand in the Bulletin and have an effect on third persons in good faith as of the date of registration in the registry (Article 71(4)).

B. *Effects of Termination of Usurpation*

939. If any change in ownership of the design occurs pursuant to the provisions of Article 71, all rights of third parties related to the design in question terminate when the change is entered in the registry (Article 72(1)–(3)).

§9. EMPLOYEE'S RIGHT TO DESIGN

I. Right to Design Under Employment Contracts

940. Where a design is developed by an employee in the execution of his/her duties or following the instructions given by his/her employer, the right to design belongs to the employer, unless otherwise agreed by contract or understood from the nature of the work (Article 73(1)).

941. If a design is developed by an employee outside the course of his/her duties using the information and equipment available at work, the right to design shall belong to the employer (Article 73(2)). In such cases, the employee shall be awarded the worth which is to be determined on the merits and significance of the design (Article 74(1)).

942. If a design is developed by a member of the teaching staff engaged in scientific research at the universities the provisions regarding employees' designs apply (Article 73(3). Cf. Law on Higher Education, No. 2547 of 4 November 1981, Article 3(1)). The same provisions apply also to designs developed by students as well as designs of interns rendering service free of charge without subjecting to a certain time (Article 73(3)).

943. Sharing the revenue obtained from designs carried out by teaching staff between the higher education institution and the designer is determined by the board of directors of the relevant higher education institution to be given at least half of the revenue to the designer (Article 74/(2)).

II. Right to Design Under Work Contracts

944. If a design is developed within the framework of a contract other than a contract for employment (i.e., work contract; *is görme sözlesmesi*, German: *Werkvertrag*), the right owner shall be determined in accordance with the provisions of the contract between the parties (Article 73(4)).

§10. LICENSING OF DESIGN RIGHT

I. Licensing of Design Right

945. A design right may be subject to a licence agreement (Article 75(1); *SMK-Yön*, Article 69). The licence may be exclusive or non-exclusive (Article 75(1)).

A. Non-exclusive Licences

946. Unless otherwise agreed, the licence is non-exclusive. In case of a non-exclusive licence, the licensor may make use of his/her design right and grant licences to third parties on the same design right (Article 75(2)).

B. Exclusive Licences

947. In case of an exclusive licence, the licensor may not grant licences to other persons. Furthermore, in an exclusive licence, the licensor may not make use of the design right unless it is reserved specifically in the agreement (Article 75(3)).

948. In the event of a breach of conditions of the licence agreement by the licensee, the rights deriving from the application or registered design can be directed against the licensee by the holder of the design right (Article 75(4))

II. Liability Arising from the Transfer of the Right or Granting Licence

949. In case it is subsequently understood that the person who transferred or licensed the design right arising from the registration is not authorized, this person becomes liable against those concerned (Article 76(1)).

950. If a design application is withdrawn or refused or if a design registration is cancelled or deemed invalid, the provisions of Article are applied, provided a more comprehensive liability through agreement in terms of a person transferring his/her design right or licensor has not been foreseen by the parties. The term for claiming compensation arising from the provisions of this Article starts as of the date of the final court decision forming a basis for liability proceedings (Article 76(2)).

§11. Invalidity of Design Right

I. Grounds for Invalidity

951. Under *SMK*, No. 6769, a design may only be declared invalid by a decision of the competent court (Article 77).

952. A registered design can be declared invalid only in the following cases (Article 43(1)):

(1) if the design protected does not fulfil the requirements for protection (novelty, individual character) or is contrary to public policy or principles of morality (Article 77(1)(a));
(2) if it has been proven that the right holder in the design is not so entitled (Articles 77(1)(b));

(3) where there exists a conflicting design, which has been made available to the public at a later date but has an earlier date of filing (earlier rights).

953. Where the invalidity involves only a part of the application or of the registered design, partial invalidity can be ruled with respect to the product or products affected by the part declared invalid (Article 77(2)). The protection continues for the remainder.

II. Claimant and Defendant

A. Claimant

954. Under *SMK*, *any person who* has an interest may request invalidity of design except in cases specified by Article 78(1).

955. In cases of entitlement of design (Article 70), employee designs (Article 73), designs developed by university teaching staff (Article 73(3)) and designs created upon order (Article 73(4)), the invalidity can be requested only by the *'holder of the right'* (Article 78(2)).

956. In case of 'earlier right', only the 'earlier holder of the right' may request invalidity (Article 78(2)).

B. Defendant

957. Action for invalidity of a design is directed against the *holder of a design right registered at the Register* (Article 78(4)).

III. Prescription (Statute of Limitations)

958. Action for the invalidity of a design may be initiated at any time during the term of protection or within five years following the termination of a design right (Article 78(3)).

IV. Effects of Invalidity

A. Retroactive (ex tunc) Effect

959. Under *SMK*, the effect of the final court decision on invalidity is *ex tunc* (retroactive effect) (Article 79(1)).

B. Exceptions

960. The retroactive effects of invalidity do not affect:

(a) any decision on infringement which has acquired the authority of a final decision and been enforced prior to the invalidity decision (Article 79(2)(a));
(b) any contract concluded prior to the invalidity decision, in so far it has been performed before the decision (Article 79(2)(b)).

961. However, partial or total repayment of sums paid under the contract may be claimed on grounds of equity (Article 79(3)).

962. Moreover, claims for compensation for damage caused by negligence or lack of good faith on the part of the holder of the design right, or unjust enrichment are reserved (Article 79(2)).

963. The authority of a final invalidity decision (res judicata) affects all. The court sends its decision to the Authority ex officio. The design is deleted by the Authority and published in the Bulletin (Article 79(4)).

§12. Termination of Design Right

I. Grounds for Termination

964. Design rights terminate in one of the following situations:

(1) expiration of the term of protection;
(2) renouncement of the holder of a design right (Article 80(1)(b); *SMK-Yön*, Article 70).

965. The expiry of the term for protection provided by *SMK*, No. 6769 does not affect the rights provided by other laws.

II. Renouncement of Design Right

966. A design right may be renounced, partly or wholly by the holder (Article 80(1)(b) and (2); *SMK-Yön*, Article 70).

967. Holder of a design right may not renounce, however, his/her right without having the consent of the licensees or holders of rights registered at the registry of the Turkish Patent and Trademark Office [or Authority, i.e. TürkPatent] (Article 80(4)).

968. Where there is a claim by a third party for the design and a court injunction to this effect has been recorded in the registry, renunciation of the design right cannot be requested without the consent of the referred third party (Article 80(5)).

969. The renunciation should be filed in writing to the Authority. It shall have effect as of the date of entry in the registry (Article 80(3)).

§13. Infringements of Design Right and Civil Remedies

I. Infringements of Design Right

970. Under *SMK*, No. 6769, the following situations are regarded as an infringement on a design right:

(a) to make, produce, put on the market, sell, offer, put to use, import or keep in stock for these purposes the identical or substantially similar design without the consent of the holder of the design right;
(b) to extend or transfer to third parties the rights granted by a licence agreement without authorization from the holder;
(c) to seize the entitlement or usurp the design right (Article 81(1)(a)–(c)).

II. Civil Remedies

A. *Requests for Several Remedies*

971. Under *SMK*, the holder of a design right whose rights have been infringed may initiate civil action with the following requests (Article 149):

(a) request for a declaratory judgment relating to the unlawful conduct of the infringer;
(b) request for cease-and-desist and prevention of infringement on design right;
(c) request for removal of infringement and compensation for material and immaterial (moral) damages;
(d) request for confiscation of products produced as the result of the infringement of the design rights and request for confiscation of the equipment and machines used directly to produce such products;
(e) request for ownership on the confiscated products and equipment in return for payment of their values, if possible;
(f) request for provisionary measures with regard to prevention of continuation of the infringement and request for destruction of the confiscated products and equipment in regard to prevention of alterations of such products and prevention of infringement on design rights;
(g) request for disclosure of the court's decision to the persons concerned and its announcement to the public at the cost of the infringer (Article 149(1)(g)).

972. When the court's decision becomes final (res judicata), the holder of the design right (winning party) may request the announcement, in full or in summary, of the final judgment in a daily newspaper, radio, television or by other means of media at the cost of the infringer if there is a justified ground (Article 149(1)(g)).

B. Claimant

973. If the application has been published (Articles 65; 81(2)), the holder of the application right is entitled to initiate civil and penal proceedings against the infringer.

C. Defendant

974. Civil and penal proceedings are directed against the infringer. Where the infringer has somehow been informed of the application and its scope, the infringement is considered to exist even before the publication (Article 81(2)).

975. If the court rules that the infringer has acted in bad faith, the infringement is also considered to exist before publication (Article 81(2)).

976. Lack of any indication on the product, its packaging or in the invoice that the design is registered does not constitute a negation of the infringement. Indications of registration are taken into account with regard to the assessment of negligence (Article 81(3)).

D. Miscellaneous Issues Related to Civil Remedies

1. Compensation

977. *SMK* has laid down several provisions on compensation for damages.

978. Under *SMK*, the infringer of a design right is responsible to compensate the damages caused by his/her negligence (Article 150).

979. In an action for compensation, the holder of the right may request from the infringer the presentation of documents relating to the use of the design right without his/her consent for assessment of the damage he/she suffered (Article 150(3)).

980. In case of infringement on a design right, a request for compensation covers not only *actual damage* (*damnum emergens*) but also *loss of profit* (*lucrum cessans*) (Article 151).

981. With regard to the *assessment of loss of profit*, one of the following calculation methods can be applied. Loss of profit can be calculated (Article 151):

- according to the possible profit that the holder of the design right would have generated if the infringement did not occur; or
- according to the profit obtained by the infringer as a result of the use of the design; or
- according to the licensee fee (royalty) that would have been paid by the licensee if the infringer would have utilized the design in a lawful manner under a license contract.

982. The calculation method to be applied for loss of profit is determined by the holder of the right (Article 151(2)).

983. In the calculation of the loss of profit, in particular, the economic value of the design, the term of protection for the design remaining at the time of infringement, the number and kinds of license agreements related to the design shall be taken into account (Article 151(3)).

984. If the holder of the design right has chosen one of the calculation methods for the loss of profit, the court may add a reasonable amount to the loss of profit, if, in the court's opinion, the design has contributed substantially to the production of the product (Article 151(4)).

985. The economic contribution of the design to the product is determined by taking into account the role of the design with regard to the demand for the product (Article 151(3)).

986. *SMK* has not granted the right to initiate legal proceedings against those who have used the products put on the market by the infringer. The holder of the design may not initiate action for compensation and other legal remedies against such persons (i.e., consumers) unless they acted in bad faith (Article 153).

2. Compensation for the Commercial Reputation of the Design

987. The holder of the design right may request extra damages for the harm incurred to the reputation of the design as the result of poor-quality production and improper marketing (Article 150(2)).

3. Action for Judgment on Non-infringement

988. Under *SMK*, any related person may initiate proceedings against the holder of the design right to obtain a declaratory judgment of non-infringement (Article 154(1)). Such an action can also be initiated together with an action for invalidity of design (Article 154(3)).

989. Prior to the initiation of the action for judgment on non-infringement, the claimant should send a notice to the holder of the design right to express his/her opinions on whether the industrial activities or other related serious actions to be initiated by the requesting party in Türkiye constitute an infringement on the design rights (Article 154(1)).

990. If the holder does not respond within a month of receiving the notice from the interested party or if the interested party does not accept his/her remark, the action for judgment on non-infringement can be initiated (Article 154(1)).

991. This action cannot be initiated by a person against whom an action for infringement of the design right has already been initiated (Article 154(1)).

992. Initiating the proceedings is communicated to all right holders entered in the registry of the Turkish Patent and Trademark Office [or Authority, i.e. Türk-Patent] (Article 154(2)).

4. Action for Security of Evidence

993. Any person entitled to design rights may initiate an action for security of evidence (*delillerin tespiti*) and request the court to ascertain the facts which constitute an infringement on his/her design right (Code of Civil Procedure, No. 6100 (CCP, *HMK*), Articles 400 et seq.).

5. Provisionary (Interim) Measures (Injunction)

994. Any person entitled to initiate legal proceedings may request the court to order provisionary[155] measures (*ihtiyati tedbir*). This request can also be made before the initiation of proceedings (*SMK*, Article 159). The provisions of Code of Civil Procedure (CCP, *HMK*) apply to the matters for which there is no provision in *SMK* (Cf. CCP, *HMK*, Articles 389 et seq.).

995. Under *SMK*, provisionary measures shall be in the nature of helping to secure the effect of the judgment (Article 159).

996. Provisionary measures shall provide the following:

- cessation of the acts of infringement on the design right;
- injunction for the seizure of products produced or imported by using the design within the territory of Türkiye or at customs or free trade areas;
- ordering to give security for damages (Code of Civil Procedure, No. 6100, Article 392).

155. It should be noted that the terms 'interim, interlocutory, precautionary, preliminary and provisional' are used in various legal texts with the same meaning.

6. Seizure at Customs

997. Under *SMK*, customs authorities are authorized to seize imitated products as a provisionary measure which are being imported or exported upon the request of the holder of the design right (Article 159(2)(b)).

III. Specialized Courts and Mediation

998. The relevant procedural provisions of *SMK*, No. 6769 (Industrial Property Law, Article 156) refer to specialized courts. For further explanations including mediation, *see* above paragraphs 653–659 in Chapter 2 – Patents and Utility Models – 'Specialized Courts and Mediation'.

§14. PAYMENT OF FEES AND LEGAL EFFECTS

I. Amount of Fees

999. The fees relating to filing an application, to registering or renewal of design right are paid by the applicant or the holder or his/her agent (Cf. *SMK*, Articles 61(4); 64(3); 65(1); *SMK-Yön*, Article 48(1); 64(3); 69(2)(c)).

II. Legal Effects

1000. If the fee for a certain transaction has not been paid within the period prescribed by the *SMK*, No. 6769 and Implementing Regulation, it shall be deemed that the transaction does not raise any legal effect as of the date of notification in this respect to be made by the Turkish Patent and Trademark Office [or Authority, i.e. TürkPatent] (Article 161(1)).

1001. In case of failure to submit to the Authority within the prescribed period the information that the mandatory fees related to the design right have been deposited for the process related to the grant or registration of the design right, it shall be deemed that the design right application has been withdrawn (Article 161(2)).

1002. If the mandatory fees for the processes related to applications or design rights are deposited deficiently, the deficit amount of fee shall be notified to the requesting party by the Authority. In case of failure to submit to the Authority in due time, the information that the deficient fee has been deposited within one month of the notification date, it is deemed that the application has been withdrawn or the relevant request was not made (Article 161(3)).

1003. Unless stated otherwise, the deposited fees shall not be returned and shall be recorded as revenue by the Authority (Article 161(4)).

§15. Persons and Attorneys Entitled to Carry Out Transactions

1004. Under *SMK*, No. 6769, the transactions and procedures before the Turkish Patent and Trademark Office [or Authority, i.e. TürkPatent] may be carried out only by the following persons:

(1) natural or legal persons who have filed an application;
(2) registered trademark or patent attorneys authorized by those persons (Article 160(1));
    Legal persons may only be represented by those duly empowered by their authorized bodies (Article 160(2));
(3) Natural or legal persons domiciled abroad can only be represented by an authorized trademark or patent attorney (Article 160(3));
(4) If a trademark or patent attorney has been appointed, all transactions are executed through that attorney. All notices made to that attorney are considered to have been made to the principal (Article 160(4)).

Chapter 6. Geographical Indications and Traditional Product Names

§1. Legal Sources

1005. Previously geographical indications were regulated in Turkish law by the Decree having the Power of Law for Protection of Geographical Indications (*Cografi Isaretlerin Korunmasi Hakkinda Kanun Hükmünde Kararname, KHK/* 555) of 27 June 1995.[156]

1006. At present this *KHK* is abolished and replaced by 'Industrial Property Law' (*Sinai Mülkiyet Kanunu: SMK*), No. 6769 of 22 December 2016.[157] Book Two of *SMK*, is devoted to 'Geographical Indication and Traditional Product Name' (cografi isaret ve geleneksel ürün adi). Part One deals with 'Right on Geographical Indication and Traditional Product Name' (Article 33–35). Part Two deals with 'Application and Objections.'

1007. Chapter One lays down the rules on 'Application for Geographical Indication and Traditional Product (specialty) Name' (Articles 36–39); Chapter Two regulates 'Objection and Examination of Objection' (Article 40). 'Request for Registration and Amendments' have been regulated by Part Three (Articles 41–43). Part Four is devoted to the issues related to 'Scope of Right, Its Use and Supervision' (Articles 44–49). Part Five deals with 'Termination of Right' (Articles 50 et seq.). In this Part, Chapter One specifies the grounds of 'Invalidity' and its effects; Section Two regulates 'Withdraw of Right and Liability' (Article 52). Part Six lays down 'Infringement of Right' of the geographical indication. As regards the civil and criminal sanctions they are regulated by Common Provisions in Book Five (*SMK*, Articles 146 et seq.)

---

156. *KHK*/555 had been drafted in the light of the WIPO agreements (Madrid Agreement for the Repression of False or Deceptive Indications of Source on Goods of 14 Apr. 1891 as revised lastly at Lisbon on 31 Oct. 1958; Lisbon Agreement for the Protection of Appellations of Origin and their International Registration of 31 Oct. 1958 as revised at Stockholm on 14 Jul. 1967 and as amended on 28 Sep. 1979). The Agreement Establishing the World Trade Organization: Annex 1/C: TRIPS of 15 Apr. 1994 has been taken into account. Moreover, the draft had been examined in the light of the Council Regulation (EEC) No. 2081/92 of 14 Jul. 1992 on the protection of geographical indications and designations of origin for agricultural products and foodstuffs. Swiss Federal Law on the Protection of Trademarks and Indication of Source of 28 Aug. 1992 had also been taken into account in pre paratory works. *KHK*/555 had introduced to Turkish law several significant concepts and solutions to Turkish law. Among them those can be mentioned: (i) protection of designation of origin and geographical indications; (ii) publication; (iii) opposition by all interested parties; (iv) relations of geographical indications with trademarks; (v) better protection against infringements; (vi) specialized courts.

157. *See* Arts 33–54 for geographical indications and traditional product (specialty) names. Regarding the common provisions for all industrial property *see* Arts 146 et seq. in Official Gazette, No. 29944 of 10 Jan. 2017).

§2. System for Protection of Geographical Indications

I. Purpose and Scope

1008. In *SMK*, No. 6769 provisions of Book Two on protection for geographical indications and traditional product names apply to food, agricultural products, mining and industrial products and handicrafts which comply with the descriptions and conditions laid down in this Book provided that they are registered (Article 33).

II. Definitions

1009. *'Geographical indications'* (cografi isaret) means signs indicating the origin of a product which possesses a specific quality, reputation or other characteristics attributable to a place, area, region or country of origin (Article 34(1)).[158]

1010. For the purposes of Article 33, geographical indications are divided into two groups: *'appellation of origin'* (mense adi) and *'indication of source'* (mahreç isareti) (Article 34(1)(a) and (b)).[159]

1011. Under *SMK*, the concept 'appellation of origin' (mense adi) means the names that identify products, which originate from a locality, a region, or, in exceptional cases, a country with designated geographical boundaries that derive their all or their essential qualities from the natural or human factors exclusively attributed to this geographical area where their production, processing and other procedures are realized (Article 34(1)(a)).

1012. The names identifying products which originate from a locality, region or in exceptional cases a country with designated geographical borders that is associated with this region due to an apparent characteristic, its reputation or other features, where at least one of the steps from production, processing or other operations take place within the borders of the designated geographical area are 'designation of origin' (Article 34(1)(b)).

---

158. The term 'geographical indication' has been chosen by the WIPO to describe the subject matter of a new treaty for the international protection of names and symbols which indicate a certain geographical origin of a given product. The term is intended to be used in its widest possible meaning. It embraces all existing means of protection of such names and symbols, regardless of whether they indicate that the qualities of a given product are due to its geographical origin (such as 'appellations of origin') or they merely indicate the place of origin of a product (such as 'indications of source').

159. This terminology is used by the WIPO agreements or conventions. In this distinction, 'indication of source' means any expression or sign used to indicate that a product or service originates in a country, a region or a specific place, whereas 'appellation of origin' means the geographical name of a country, region or specific place which serves to designate a product originating therein the characteristic qualities which are due exclusively or essentially to a geographical environment, including natural or human factors or both natural and human factors. *See* WIPO, Intellectual Property-Reading Material, 2nd ed., WIPO 1998, p. 116.

1013. Names that are not considered as the appellation of origin or designation of origin but are proven to have been traditionally used in the relevant market for at least thirty years to describe the product and fulfil at least one of the following conditions are identified as tradition product (speciality) name. (i) originating from traditional methods of production or processing or traditional composition; (ii) produced with traditional raw material or ingredients (Article 34(3)).

III. Persons Who May Benefit from the Protection

1014. Regarding the protection of geographical indication and traditional product name the following persons may benefit from the protection provided for by *SMK*, Articles 33 et seq.:

- nationals of the Republic of Türkiye;
- natural or legal persons who are domiciled or engaged in industrial or commercial activities within the territory of the Republic of Türkiye;
- persons who are entitled to the application under the Paris Convention or Agreement Establishing the WTO of 15 April 1994 (Article 2(1));
- natural or legal persons who are nationals of foreign States in accordance with the principle of reciprocity if those States confer legal or actual protection on Turkish nationals (Article 3).

IV. Names That May Not Be Registered as Geographical Indication and Traditional Product (Specialty) Names

1015. Under *SMK*, the following names and signs cannot be registered as geographical indications (Article 35(1)):

(a) names and signs which do not conform with the definitions specified in Article 34 as 'designation of origin' and 'appellation of origin';
(b) names that have become generic names of products;[160]
(c) names of plant varieties, animal breeds or similar names which are likely to mislead the public as to the true origin of the product;
(d) names contrary to public policy and good morals;
(e) names that are not protected, whose duration of protection has expired or not used in their own country although having been applied by persons fulfilling the conditions set out in Article 3;
(f) names that are wholly or partially homonymic with a name that is registered or has already been filed, and which may mislead the public.

160. For the purpose of *SMK*, No. 6769, a name that has become generic means the name of a product which, although it relates to the place or the region where this product was originally produced or marketed, has become the common name of a product. To establish whether or not a name has become generic, account is taken of all factors, in particular, the existing use by the people in the region in which the name originates and in areas of consumption.

1016. Under SMK, the following names or signs cannot be registered as traditional product name (speciality) Article 35(2)):

(a) names not fulfilling the conditions stated in Article 34(3);
(b) names expressing the general feature of the product;
(c) names that may mislead the public about the characteristics of the product;
(d) names contrary to public policy or principle of general public morality;
(e) names that are not protected or used in their own country although their application has been made.

§3. Registration of Geographical Indications and Traditional Product Names

1017. The authority for the registration of geographical indications and traditional product (speciality) names is TürkPatent.

I. Requirements for Registration

1018. Under *SMK*, No. 6769, as earlier under the abolished *KHK*/555, protection for indications of source or appellations of origin of a product are provided by their registration.

A. *Applicants*

1019. Under *SMK*, the following persons are entitled to apply for registration (Article 36(1)):

(a) producer groups: persons or legal entities that produce the product to be protected;
(b) public authorities and institutions and professional institutions accepted as public bodies related to the product or geographical region;
(c) associations, foundations and cooperatives working for public interest in relation to the product or authorized to protect the economic interests of their members;
(d) the relevant producer in case the product is produced by a single producer provided that the proves this fact.

1020. In *SMK*, 'producer' means producers of agricultural, industrial and handcrafted products or processors of natural products or traders of these products (Article 36(2)).

1021. Under *SMK*, the following persons have the right to practice before Türk-Patent in relation to geographical indications and traditional product (speciality) names (Article 160):

- natural or legal persons who are applicants (for legal persons by their authorized organs) (Article 160(1) and (2));
- authorized registered patent and trademark attorneys (Article 160(1)).

1022. Those who are domiciled outside Türkiye can only be represented by trademark or patent attorneys (Article 160(3)). Where an attorney has been appointed, all procedures and formalities are carried out by the attorney (Article 160(4)).

B. Requirements for Application

1023. For *registration of geographical indication,* the following requirements should be satisfied (Article 37(1)):

(a) application form including information on the identity of the applicant and which category he/she is associated with concerning the persons with the right to apply within the meaning of Article 36;
(b) in case the applying natural or legal persons are the only producer of the product, information and documents proving this case;
(c) the name of geographical indication requested to be registered, information and documents about the eligibility of the product as an appellation of origin or as a designation of origin;
(d) description of the product and technical information and documents on the physical, chemical, microbiological and similar characteristics of the product and if necessary, of the raw material;
(e) information on and documents describing the geographical boundaries of the locality, area or region;
(f) description of the method of production; if appropriate, the regional-specific methods of production (local production technics, practices and traditions which give the product its speciality);
(g) evidence that the product is in compliance with the sign requested for registration;
(h) information and documents related to the historical background of the product in the specified geographical area;
(i) information on details of the form of inspection (Cf. Article 49);
(j) information detailing the labellin, marking and means of using the registered designation of origin or geographical indication;
(k) information that the application fee has been paid.

1024. For *registration of a traditional product (speciality) name*, the following requirements should be satisfied (Article 37(2)):

(a) application form including information on the identity of the applicant and which category he/she is associated with concerning the persons with the right to apply within the meaning of Article 36;
(b) the name of the traditional speciality subject to the registration and its product group, and information and documents proving that it is in compliance with the description in Article 34;
(c) description of the product and technical information and documents on the physical, chemical, microbiological and similar characteristics of the product and if necessary of the raw material;
(d) description of the production method where raw material and other components existing within the product are explained together with their features and the product preparation technics which indicate the product characteristic;
(e) information on details of the form of inspection (Cf. Article 49);
(f) information and documents explaining the use of the traditional speciality and detailing the labelling and packaging procedures, if any;
(g) information that the application fee has been paid.

Other procedures and rules regarding applications for geographical indication and traditional product (speciality) names are determined by the *SMK-Yön* (Articles 35–37).

Applications Originating from a Foreign Country

1025. Without prejudice to the international agreements in order to apply the provisions of this Law (i.e., *SMK*) to geographical indications or traditional product (speciality) names originating from foreign countries, in addition to the requirements set out in Article 37, the following requirements are sought (a) the geographical indication or traditional product (speciality) name subject to the application is being protected by the country of origin or the international community of which the country of origin is a member to; (b) establishment of the conditions of supervision set out in Article 49 in the country of origin; (c) provision of equal protection by the country of origin to registration applications for geographical indication or traditional product (speciality) name to be made from Türkiye (Article 39(1)).

C. Examination and Publishing of the Application

1026. The application is examined by TürkPatent (*SMK*, Article 38).

1027. TürkPatent examines the applications in accordance with Articles 33 to 37 and Article 39 (Article 38(1)).

1028. If the information related to the identity of the applicant is not present in the application form, the application is deemed not to have been made (Article 38(2)).

1029. If the conditions set out in Article 37 are not met, TürkPatent requests the remedy of these deficiencies. If the missing information and documents are not submitted in the prescribed period, the application is refused (Article 38(3)).

1030. *TürkPatent* may require the examination of the application by one or more relevant institutions or organizations (e.g., examination of technical features by institutes of universities or independent private institutions) (Article 38(4)).

1031. The applications examined and found eligible by TürkPatent are published in the Bulletin Gazette (Article 38(5) and *SMK-Yön*, Article 38).

D. Objections and Examination

1032. The *applicant* may file an objection with grounds and in writing related to an application refused in the scope of Article 38 within two months of the date of notification of the decision (Article 40(1)).

1033. *Third parties* claiming that the registration application does not conform with Articles 33 to 37 and 39 or the owner of an earlier-dated trademark claiming that the registration application does not conform to Article 48 may file a written objection with grounds within three months of the publication of the application in the Bulletin (Article 40(2)).

1034. The applicant is informed of the objection and his/her opinion is requested (Article 40(2)).

1035. It is mandatory to pay the fee for the objection and to submit information to TürkPatent that it has been paid.

1036. Upon objection, the objection is examined by the *Board within the Re-evaluation and Examination Department* (Kurul) within the framework of the principles laid down in the *SMK-Yön* (Article 40(4); *SMK-Yön*, Article 39(5)). The Board may request an opinion from relevant authorities and bodies (e.g., public institutions or universities or independent private institutions which have expertise in the subject matter) (Article 40(4)).

1037. If TürkPatent considers necessary, it may encourage the parties for *reconciliation* (uzlasma). In such a case the provisions of the Act on Mediation in Civil Law Disputes, No. 6325 (AMedC, *Hukuki Uyusmazliklar Hakkinda Arabuluculuk Kanunu*) (Article 40(5)).

1038. If an amendment is made to the form or scope of the application as a result of the examination of the objection, the final version of the application is published in the Bulletin by indicating the amended part. No objection can be filed for this publication (Article 40(6)). If the application is refused upon objection, the decision is published in the Bulletin (Article 40(7)).

II. Registration and Publication

1039. If no objection is filed within three months of the publication of the application in the Bulletin, the geographical indications shall become effective as of the date of publication and entered in the Register. The registry is public. Upon request a copy of the registration is provided (Article 41; *SMK-Yön*, Article 41).

III. Requests for Amendment and Changes on Applicants and Registrants

Request for Amendment

1040. According to Article 42 in case of *a change in the specifications subject to registration,* an amendment request may be filed by the parties with legitimate interest provided that the amendment fee has been paid. This request shall be examined by the Authority (Article 38) and amendments that are found suitable shall be published in the Bulletin. Objections in writing and with reasons may be filed against the amendment within three months of its publication. The objections shall be examined according to Article 40.

1041. If no objection has been filed or the filed objections have been refused, the amendment is published in the Bulletin and becomes final as the date of its publication The amendments shall be implemented by the related parties within one year at the latest (Article 43(2); *SMK-Yön*, Article 42).

Changes in applicants or registrants

1042. In case the court decides that applicants or registrants for geographical indications or traditional product (speciality) names fail to satisfy the requirements set out in Articles 36 and 49 or if this is determined by the Authority ex officio or if a declaration of the amendment is submitted in writing to the Authority by applicants or registrants, this decision, finding or declaration shall be published in the Bulletin. Within three months of the publication, requests for amendment to the application or registration records may be filed by relevant parties (Article 43(1)).

1043. If no request is submitted or the submitted requests are found not suitable, the rights conferred by the geographical indication or traditional product (speciality) name terminate and this situation is published in the Bulletin (Article, 43(1); *SMK-Yön*, Article 43).

1044. Changes in the name, address, titles or characteristics of the persons who request for or register geographical indications or traditional product (speciality) names are entered in the register and published in the Bulletin (Article 43(3)).

IV. Fees, Payment Periods and Effects

1045. Under *SMK*, natural persons or legal entities and the registered trademark/ patent attorneys authorized by those persons may perform operations before Türk-Patent (Article 160(1)). Legal entities are represented by a natural person or persons assigned by their authorize organs.

1046. Fees for filing, registration, publication, and other fees are payable by the applicants or their agents/attorneys (Cf. *SMK*, Articles 41(1), 161(1)).

1047. An application is considered withdrawn when any of the fees has not been paid within the prescribed period specified in the Implementing Regulation (Article 161(1)).

§4. Scope of Protection

Registered geographical indications

1048. The *protection of geographical indication related to a product* is acquired through registration within the framework of *SMK*, No. 6769 (Article 44(1)).

1049. Registered geographical indications are protected against:

(a) any direct or indirect commercial use of the geographical indication or the emblem foreseen to be used in line with Article 46 to benefit from it's the reputation of the protected name (Article 44(2));
(b) any misleading use or imitation of the registered geographical indication on a product which does not satisfy the product properties specified in the registration;
(c) any use of false or misleading explanations or indications about the origin and the natural or essential qualities of the product stated in the registration;
(d) any deceptive use of the emblem of registered geographical indication (Article 44(2)).

1050. The rights conferred against third parties by the registration of the geographical indication are effective as of its publication date in the Bulletin (Article 44(3)).

1051. If a registered name also contains the generic name of the product, the usage of the generic name does not fall within the scope of protection. Registered geographical indications cannot be the generic name of the product (Article 44(4)). Generic name is the name that has become the common name of the product, although it relates to the region or the locality where this product was originally produced or marketed. In determining whether a name has become generic or not, the use of this name by the public where the product is consumed and other related legislation shall be taken into consideration (Article 44(4)–(6)).

Registered traditional product (speciality) names

1052. Traditional product (speciality) name is acquired through registration within the framework of *SMK*, (Article 45(1)).

1053. Registered traditional product (speciality) names are protected against:

(a) use of the emblem foreseen to be used in line with Article 46 to benefit from its reputation for products which do not carry the properties specified in the registry or its commercial use on products resembling the registered product;
(b) deceptive use of the emblem of registered traditional speciality;
(c) giving any misleading statements or indications on the product's inner or outer packaging, promotional and advertising material (Article 45(2)).

1054. The rights against third parties conferred by the registration of the traditional product (speciality) are effective as of the publishing of the registration in the Bulletin. The registered traditional product names do not provide an exclusive right to the registrant (Article 45(4)).

§5. Use and Inspection of Geographical Indication

I. Indications and Traditional Product (Specialty) Names

A. *Users*

1055. Registered geographical indications and traditional product (speciality) names can be used by *those operating in the production and marketing of products* that comply with the specifications provided in the registration. These persons notify the registrant that they conduct production or marketing aimed at the geographical indication or traditional product (speciality) names (Article 46(1); *SMK-Yön*, Article 44). Persons having the right to use the registered geographical indications or traditional product (speciality) names shall use them together with the emblem on the product or its packaging. It is mandatory to use the emblem for geographical indication (Article 46(2)).

1056. Use of a traditional product (speciality) name without an emblem shall not be governed by *SMK*, No. 6769 (Article 46(4)).

B. Use in Good Faith

1057. The use of the names of natural persons or names of legal entities by these persons or their successors during commercial activities that do not deceive the public is not considered as infringements stated in Articles 44 and 45 (Article 47).

C. Relation with trademarks

1058. After the registration of the geographical indication, a trademark application filed in order to be used in the forms stated in Article 44 or to be used for the goods or services related to geographical indication shall be refused. In case it has been registered, it may be invalidated through a legal proceeding (Article 48(1)).

1059. If a trademark identical with or similar to the geographical indication was registered, in good faith or the rights to use that trademark were acquired through use in good faith before the protection of the geographical indication, rights arising from geographical indication shall not prejudice the registration of the trademark application or the right to use the trademark in good faith (Article 48(2)).

II. Supervision

1060. The supervision is conducted by the supervision institution stated in the application and whose competence is approved by the Turkish Patent and Trademark Office [or Authority, i.e. TürkPatent]. Changes to the supervisory authority in the registry can be made with the approval of TürkPatent (Article 49(2)).

1061. The supervision of use of geographical indications and traditional product (speciality) names covers all kinds of activities regarding the supervision of the conformity of their usage with the features stated in the registration during the stages of production, supply to the market or distribution or during the term the product is on the market (Article 49(1)).

1062. Supervision reports are submitted annually to the Authority starting from the date on which the registration is published in the Bulletin. If a deficiency is found upon examination of the supervision reports the registrant shall be notified and asked to correct the deficiencies within six months (Article 49(4)).

1063. The supervision stated in this Book covers the controls made by the control authority established by the applicant and shall not prejudice the provisions of the Law on Veterinary Services Plant Health Food and Feed, No. 5996 *(Veteriner Hizmetleri, Bitki Sagligi, Gida ve Yem Kanunu)* of 11 June 2010 and other laws related to the supervision of geographical indications and traditional product (speciality) names (Article 49(7)).

§6. TERMINATION IF THE RIGHT: INVALIDITY OF GEOGRAPHICAL SIGNS

I. Invalidity of Geographical Signs

A. *Grounds for Invalidity*

1064. A registered geographical indication can be declared invalid by a court decision in the following cases (Article 50(2)):

(1) where the requirements for protection are not satisfied (Articles 33, 34, 35, 37 or 39);
(2) where it is proved that the registration has not been made by those who have the right to apply in line with Article 36 and the holder of the right is another person;
(3) where it is proved that the supervision has not been carried out duly and properly (Article 49).

B. *Claimant*

1065. Any person who has an interest may request the invalidity of a geographical indication (Article 50(1)).

C. *Defendant*

1066. The legal proceedings relating to invalidity shall be instituted against the person who is registered as the registrant in the registry of the Turkish Patent and Trademark Office [or Authority, i.e. TürkPatent] (Article 50(3)).

D. *Effects of Invalidity*

1. Retroactive (ex tunc) Effect

1067. The decision relating to the invalidity of a geographical indication or traditional product (speciality) name has a retroactive (*ex tunc*) effect. The protection provided by *SMK*, No. 6769 shall be deemed not to have arisen (Article 51(1)).

1068. However, the *ex tunc* effect of invalidity does not extend to the following:

(1) to any final judgment relating to infringement of rights arising out of a geographical indication;

(2) to agreements executed and enforced before the decision of invalidity of the geographical indication. It is possible, however, to demand partial or total reimbursements of the sums paid under such an agreement if equity necessitates this (Article 51(2)–(3)).

2. General Effect

1069. The final judgment of invalidity is effective against everybody. The final court decision is notified to the Authority by the court ex officio. The geographical indication or traditional product (speciality) name deemed as invalid is deleted from the registry of TürkPatent and the information regarding deletion is published in the Bulletin (Article 51(4)).

II. Withdrawal of Right and Liability

1070. The person who registered the geographical indication and traditional product liability may withdraw from his/her rights provided by the registration and the responsibilities related to supervision. The request for withdrawal is published in the Bulletin (Article 52(1); *SMK-Yön*, Article 46).

§7. LEGAL PROTECTION

1071. Protection means the right to prevent unauthorized persons from using geographical indications and traditional product (speciality) names.

1072. Geographical indications and traditional product names are protected under *SMK*, No. 6769 by legal remedies and penal sanctions.

I. Infringements

1073. Under *SMK*, the following uses of a geographical indication by unauthorized persons constitute an infringement on the right of geographical indication (Article 53).[161]

1074. Acts deemed as an infringement of geographical indication right are the following (Article 53):

(a) any direct or indirect commercial use of a registered geographical indication or the emblem whose use is foreseen in accordance with Article 46 for commercial purposes to the products within the scope of the register or comparable

161. Cf. Council Regulation (EC) No. 510/2006 of 20 Mar. 2006on the protection of geographical indications and designations of origin for agricultural products and foodstuffs, Art. 13).

products in a manner to exploit the reputation of the registered geographical sign where they do not carry the features specified in the register;

(b) any misuse, imitation or evocation, even if the true origin of the product is indicated or if the protected name is translated or accompanied by an expression such as 'style', 'type', 'method', 'as produced in' or the like;

(c) any other false or misleading indication as to the provenance, origin, nature of essential qualities of the product on the inner or outer packaging, advertising material or documents relating to the product concerned a false impression of its origin;

(d) any other practice liable to mislead the consumer as to the true origin of the product.

1075. Those who have the right to use the geographical sign may request a claim to be filed before the court by notifying the registrant through a notary public. If the registrant does not accept this request or file a claim within three months from the date of notification, those who have the right to use the geographical sign may file a claim by including the notification made to the registrant (Article 53(2)). The fact that the record of registration of the geographical sign is not presented on the product, packaging or invoice does not exclude the action from being an act of infringement. However, the records and signs related to registration shall be taken into account during the evaluation of the negligence (Article 53(3)).

1076. Acts deemed as an infringement of the right to traditional product names are the following (Article 54(1)):

(a) any commercial use of a registered traditional product name together with the emblem whose use is foreseen in accordance with Article 46 to exploit the reputation of the registered product name for products which do not carry the properties specified in the register or the commercial use of the emblem allocated to the traditional product name on products which resemble the registered product;

(b) any use of the emblem in a deceptive manner to the consumer;

(c) any use of misleading indications or descriptions on the inner or outer packaging, promotional and advertising material or any type of written material related to the product which does not carry the properties specified in the traditional product name register and the emblem.

1077. Those who have the right to use the traditional product name may request a claim to be filed before the court by notifying the registrant through a notary public. If the registrant does not accept this request or file a claim within three months from the date of notification, those who have the right to use the geographical sign may file a claim by including the notification made to the registrant. The legal proceeding shall be notified to the registrant (Article 54(2)).

1078. Where a traditional product name application is published, the applicant is entitled to appeal to the court for acts of infringement stated in this Article. If the infringer has been informed about the application and its scope, the requirement for the application to be published is disregarded. If the court decides that the infringer violates the rights in bad faith, the act of infringement shall be accepted prior to the publication of the application (Article 54(3)).

II. Civil Remedies

A. Remedies

1079. In case of infringement of rights deriving from geographical indications, the following claims can be directed against the infringer (Article 149):

(a) claim for ascertainment of infringement (Article 149(1));
(b) claim for cease-and -desist and prevention of infringement (Article 149(1)(b)-(c));
(c) claim for compensation (Article 149(1)(ç)) and in case of serious infringement of an industrial property right intentionally or by grave negligence, the infringer must also compensate non-material damages (manevi zarar; French: dommage moral) suffered by the owner of the trademark (Article 149(1)(ç));[162]
(d) claim for confiscation of products produced as the result of the infringement of a geographical indication (Article 149(1)(d));
(e) claim for measures to prevent the continuation of infringement and if necessary claim for destruction of products and means of production (Article 149(1)(f));
(f) claim for the announcement of the court's decision to the public at the cost of the infringer (Article 149(1)(g) and (3));
(g) Moreover, an action for provisionary measures *(ihtiyati tedbir talebi)* can also be initiated under *SMK*, Article 159 by persons who have the right to institute a legal proceeding. Provisionary measures cover (i) the prevention and cease-and-desist of the acts infringing the right on geographical indication or traditional product name; (ii) confiscation of products that are produced or imported through infringement of the right on geographical indication or traditional product name; (iii) to submit security in terms of compensation of any damage (Article 159(2)(a)–(c)).

1080. The provisions of Code of Civil Procedure, No. 6100 (CCP, *HMK*) apply to matters for which there is no special rule in SMK regarding provisionary measures. (*SMK*, Article 159(3)).

162. The harm of respectability of the trademark as the result of improper use of the infringer is the typical aspect of non-material damages. In cases related to infringements on the right on geographical indication or traditional product name compensation for non-material damages cannot be claimed (Art. 149(4)).

B. Claimant

1081. Civil remedies may be claimed by the *holder of the right* whose rights deriving from the geographical indication or traditional product name have been infringed (Article 149(1)).

C. Defendant

1082. Civil actions may normally be directed against the *infringer.*

1083. Civil remedies may not be claimed, however, against the *persons using or benefiting from the products marketed by the infringer.* The persons who may not be sued are, generally, consumers (Article 153).

D. Means of Proof

1084. Under *SMK*, the holder of a geographical indication right may request the *presentation of documents* related to the use of geographical indication by the infringer in order to prove the amount of compensation (Article 150(3)).

E. Specialized Courts and Mediation

1085. The relevant procedural provisions of *SMK*, No. 6769 (Industrial Property Law, Article 156) refer to specialized courts. For further explanations including mediation, *see* above paragraphs 653–659 in Chapter 2 – Patents and Utility Models – 'Specialized Courts and Mediation'.

F. Prescription: Statute of Limitation

1086. The claims relating to infringements on the right on a registered geographical indication or a traditional product name are subject to the provisions on the prescription of the Turkish Code of Obligations Article 146 (*SMK*, Article 157). Under the Turkish Code of Obligations, the usual prescription period is ten years unless another limitation period has been provided by law (Article 146).

Chapter 7. Plant Variety Protection

§1. In General

1087. Plant variety rights are confined to the protection of the reproductive or propagating material of a variety.

1088. Plant variety rights (or plant breeder's rights as they are often called) have a twofold purpose.

1089. First, they provide a mechanism of reward and incentive to plant breeders.

1090. Second, they provide a method of controlling the reproduction of varieties which breeders have created.

1091. 'Varieties' should be distinguished from genera and species which are higher orders.

1092. In some countries, plant variety rights have been regulated by specific laws: e.g., the UK: Plant Varieties and Seeds Act 1964; German: *Sortenschutzgesetz* 1985; France: French Code for Intellectual Property (Article Law 623–1/35).

1093. In 1961, the *International Convention for the Protection of New Varieties of Plants* ('the UPOV Convention') was concluded in Paris and signed by most European countries. The Convention was revised at Geneva on 10 November 1972, on 23 October 1978 and on 19 March 1991.

1094. In the *EU, Regulation* (EC) No. 2100/94 of the Council of 27 July 1994 regulates the protection of plant variety rights.

§2. The UPOV Convention 1991

I. Purpose of the Convention

1095. The 1991 Convention does not alter the fundamental principles of the previous conventions (1961 Convention and its amendments), namely that Contracting Parties are to grant and protect breeders' rights in the reproductive and propagating material of plant varieties.

1096. Under the system of the 1991 Convention, breeders who have produced a new variety may apply for registration of this variety at a national level. If registration is obtained, the proprietor has the exclusive right to commercially exploit the reproductive or propagative material of the variety.

1097. Under the UPOV Convention, the protection shall last for a minimum of twenty years and shall not be shorter than twenty-five years for trees and vines.

1098. Under some circumstances, the rights can last up to thirty years (e.g., potatoes).

1099. Under the UPOV Convention, the Contracting Parties shall constitute a Union for the Protection of New Varieties of Plants (Article 1(2)).

II. Conditions for the Protection

1100. Under the UPOV Convention, breeders' rights can be granted where the variety is new, distinct, uniform and stable and has been designated by a denomination which is called its generic designation.

1101. Protection is only granted to plant 'varieties'.

III. National Treatment and Reciprocity

1102. The UPOV Convention has accepted the *principles of national treatment* and *reciprocity* (Article 3). The Contracting Parties shall not discriminate in the granting of breeders' rights between their own nationals and nationals of another Contracting State (Article 4).

IV. Rights Protected and Scope of Protection

1103. The owner of plant variety rights under the 1991 UPOV Convention has the exclusive right in relation to the reproductive or propagating material of the protected variety, to produce or reproduce; condition for the purposes of propagation; offer for sale, market, export, import or stock for any of these purposes (Article 14(1)).

§3. PROTECTION OF PLANT VARIETY UNDER TURKISH LAW

1104. In Türkiye breeder's rights on new varieties of plants are protected by the 'Protection of Rights of Breeders on New Varieties of Plants Law', No. 5042 (PPlantL; *Yeni Bitki Çesitlerine Ait Islahatçi Haklarinin Korunmasi Hakkinda Kanun*) of 8 January 2004.[163]

163. Official Gazette, No. 25347 of 15 Jan. 2004.

1105. The details of the breeder's rights can be found in the 'Regulation on Protection of Breeder's Rights on new Varieties of Plants' *(Yeni Bitki Çesitlerine Ait Islahatçi Haklarinin Korunmasina Dair Yönetmelik).*[164]

1106. Further, there is another 'Regulation on Enjoyment of Public Servants Employed in Public Institutions and Entities from the Breeder's Rights' *(Kamu Kurumu ve Kuruluslarinda Çalisan Görevlilerin Islahatçi Hakkindan Yararlanmasina Iliskin Yönetmelik).*[165]

1107. Türkiye is a party to International Convention for the Protection of New Varieties of Plants, known as 'The *UPOV Convention*', ratified by Law, No. 5601 of 13 March 2007.[166]

1108. Conditions for plant variety protection: Under Law, No. 5042 the breeder's right is protected where the variety is new, distinct, uniform and stable (Article 3).

1109. Plant type: Plant type means the plant group that is defined with some of its features revealed by one or multiple genotypes, that is distinguished from the other genotypes in the same species with at least one typical feature and that is in the smallest taxonomic section which is accepted as a unit in terms of suitability for unchanged multiplication (*SMK*, No. 6769, Article 2(b)). Under Law, No. 5042 *variety* means a plant grouping within a single botanical taxon of the lowest known rank, which grouping, irrespective of whether the conditions for a grant of a breeder's right are fully met, can be (i) defined by the expression of the characteristics resulting from a given genotype or combinations of genotypes, (ii) distinguished from any other plant grouping by the expression of at least one of the said characteristics and (iii) considered as a unit with regard to its suitability for being propagated unchanged (Article 2(e)).

1110. Breeder: *Breeder* means the person who bred, or discovered and developed, a variety (Article 2(c)).

1111. Distinctness: The variety is deemed to be distinct if it is clearly distinguishable from any other variety whose existence is a matter of common knowledge at the time of the filing of the application (Article 6(1)).

1112. Uniformity: The variety is deemed to be uniform if, subject to the variation that may be expected from the particular features of its propagation, it is sufficiently uniform in its relevant characteristics (Article 7).

---

164. Official Gazette, No. 25551 of 12 Aug. 2004.
165. *See* Official Gazette, No. 25801 of 30 Apr. 2005. This Regulation has been amended by the Amendment Regulations in Official Gazette, No. 26453 of 5 Mar. 2007 and No. 26997 of 14 Sep. 2008.
166. Official Gazette, No. 26465 of 17 Mar. 2007.

1113. Entitlement to variety protection: The breeder of the variety or his/her successor in title is entitled to variety protection (Article 11(1)).

1114. Duration of variety protection: The protection period is twenty-five years as of the registration of the breeder's right. This period is thirty years for trees, grapevines and potatoes (Article 10).

1115. Scope of breeder's right: Under Turkish Law the breeder's right grants the breeder the following exclusive entitlements, (i) production or reproduction; (ii) conditioning for the purpose of propagation; (iii) offering for sale; (iv) selling or other marketing; (v) exporting; (vi) importing; (vii) stocking (Article 14).

1116. Exceptions to the breeder's right: The effect of variety protection does not extend to the acts where carried out (i) privately and for non-commercial purposes; (ii) for experimental purposes in relation to the protected variety; (iii) for the breeding of new varieties (Article 16).

1117. Exploitation rights and legal succession: The right to variety protection, the claim to granting of variety protection and the variety protection itself can be transferable. They can be inherited by the heirs of the breeder. Moreover, they can be subject matter of pledges and attachments (Article 49). Application for the breeder's right and the right itself can be the subject matter of an exclusive or non-exclusive licence agreement (Article 50).

1118. Legal remedies in case of infringement of breeder's right: If the breeder's right has been infringed the breeder may direct the following claims to the infringer: (i) cease-and-desist of infringement; (ii) prevention of infringement; (iii) compensation for damages and immaterial damage (Article 57(1)(a)–(c)).

1119. The claims relating to infringements on registered trademarks are subject to the provisions on the prescription of the Turkish Code of Obligations Article 146 (*SMK*, Article 157). Under the Turkish Code of Obligations, the usual prescription period is ten years unless another limitation period has been provided by law (Article 146).

1120. Regarding subject-matter jurisdiction (görev), under *PPlantL*, actions in the first instance relating to legal remedies or penal sanctions are heard by '*specialized*' civil and criminal courts. These are determined by the Council of Judges and Prosecutors upon the recommendation of the Ministry of Justice (*PPlantL*, Article 68).

1121. As for territorial jurisdiction (yetki), civil actions under *PPlantL* are initiated at the court of the domicile of the claimant or at the place where the offense has been committed or at the place where the infringement had its effects (Article 57(2)). Where the claimant does not have domicile in Türkiye, the courts of Ankara, the Capital shall have jurisdiction (Article 57(3)). As for civil actions initiated by third parties against the holder of the relevant right, the competent court is the court where the defendant is domiciled. If the defendant is not domiciled in Türkiye, the provisions of Article 57(3) apply as above (Article 57(4)). If there are several competent courts, the court where the first action was initiated shall have jurisdiction (Article 57(5)). Where the claimant or the defendant is the Ministry of Agriculture and Forestry, the competent court shall be courts of Ankara, the Capital (Article 57(6)).

1122. Regarding procedurals rules on mandatory mediation attempts as well as prospects under 'the Singapore Mediation Convention' which may also apply to plant variety protection, *see* the explanations in paragraphs 658–659 in Chapter 2 – Patents and Utility Models – 'Specialized Courts and Mediation'.

Chapter 8. Chip Protection

§1. In General

I. Special Regulations

1123. In some countries, semiconductor chips are protected by special regulations.

A. USA

1124. The US pioneered this field. To protect semiconductor chips, the US in 1984 enacted the *Semiconductor Chip Protection Act* ('SCPA') as an amendment to the *Copyright Act* (17 USC sections 901–914).

B. EU

1125. The *EC Directive* No. 87/54 of 16 December 1986 *on the legal protection of integrated circuits* was a response to the US Semiconductor Chip Protection Act 1984.[167]

1126. According to Directive No. 87/54, a *semiconductor product means* the final or an intermediate form of any product consisting of a body of material which includes a layer of semi-conducting material; and having one or more other layers composed of conducting, insulating or semi-conducting material, the layers being arranged in accordance with a predetermined three-dimensional pattern; and intended to perform, exclusively or together with other functions, an electronic function (Article 1(a)).

1127. '*The topography of a semiconductor product* means a series of related images, however fixed or encoded' (Article 1(b)).

1128. The Directive required EC Member States to pass legislation at the national level by 7 November 1987 (Article 11).

C. WIPO

1129. Within the framework of the WIPO, the 'Treaty on the Protection of Intellectual Property in Respect of Integrated Circuits' was executed on 26 May 1986.

167. *See* Council Directive on the legal protection of topographies of semiconductor products, No. 87/54/EEC in OJ 1987 No. L 24/36.

1130. The provisions of this Treaty are based on the principle of national treatment of foreign citizens of countries which have signed and ratified the Treaty.

D. TRIPS Agreement

1131. Under Article 35 of the TRIPS Agreement, 'Members agree to provide protection to the layout-designs (topographies) of integrated circuits in accordance with Articles 2 through 7 (other than paragraph 3 of Article 6), Article 12 and paragraph 3 of Article 16 of the *Treaty on Intellectual Property in Respect of Integrated Circuits'* and in addition to comply with Article 36 through Article 38.

E. Germany

1132. In accordance with EC Directive No. 87/54, Germany enacted the *'Semiconductor Protection Act'* (Halbleiterschutzgesetz, HalblSchG) on 22 October 1987.

1133. Under this Act, 'three-dimensional structures of microelectronic semiconductor products (topographies) are protected if and insofar as they have originality' (section 1/1).

1134. German *HalblSchG* does not protect concepts, processes, systems or techniques embodied in the chip.

1135. A *topography* has originality if it is the result of intellectual effort, not commonplace and not just a copy of another topography.

1136. Where a *topography* consists of a combination of commonplace parts, it is protected to the extent that the combination taken as a whole is original.

F. Austria

1137. In Austria, semiconductor chips are protected by the *'Semiconductor Chip Protection Act'* (Bundesgesetzüber den Schutz der Topographies von mikroelektronischenHalbleitererzeugnissen, Halbleiterschutzgesetz, HlSchG) which was enacted on 23 June 1988. This law was also modelled upon the EC Directive.

1138. Under the Austrian law, three-dimensional structures of microelectronic semiconductor chip products (i.e., topographies) can be protected if and insofar as they are original.

1139. A *topography* is original if it is the result of the creator's own intellectual effort and if the topography is not common and usual in the semiconductor industry.

1140. If the topography consists of several common parts, it may nevertheless be protected insofar as the arrangement of these parts in its entirety is original.

II. Scope of the Right to Chip Protection

1141. The *chip protection right* grants its owner the exclusive right to exploit the topography and to prevent any third person from reproducing and exploiting the topography or its parts or from making descriptions in order to produce topography from offering, distributing, etc.[168]

1142. Industrial copying, marketing or offering for sale and importation for marketing purposes are prohibited acts.

1143. Any person who infringes the *chip protection right* can be sued by the owner of the right (prevention, cease-and-desist, compensation, announcement of the court's decision, etc.).

§2. Protection of Chips under Turkish Law

I. In General

1144. In Türkiye, the integrated circuit topographies are protected by the Protection of Integrated Circuit Topographies Law (PICTopoL, *Entegre Devre Topografyalarinin Korunmasi Hakkinda Kanun),* No. 5147 of 22 April 2004[169]

1145. The aim of the PICTopoL is not only to protect the integrated circuit topography but also to encourage the development of industry and technology in this field. This Law covers the principles, rules and requirements for the protection of registered integrated circuit topographies (Article 1).

1146. Integrated circuit: *Integrated circuit* means a product in its final form or an intermediate form in which the elements, at least one of which is an active element and some or all of the interconnections are integrally formed in and/or on a piece of material and which is intended to perform an electronic function (Article 2(a)).

1147. Layout-design (topography): *Layout-design* (topography) means the three-dimensional disposition of the elements, at least one of which is an active element

168. Cf. TRIPS Agreement, Art. 36.
169. Official Gazette, No. 25448 of 30 Apr. 2004. This Law has been amended by Industrial Property Law, No. 6769 (Arts 188(c) and 191(2)). Article 39 of the Law, No. 5147 was abolished by Art. 191(2) of the Law, No. 6769.

and of some or all of the interconnections of an integrated circuit or such a three-dimensional disposition prepared for an integrated circuit intended for manufacture (Article 2(b)).

1148. Holder of the right: The right for protection of integrated circuit topography belongs to its *creator or his/her successors in title* (Article 7(1)). The right on integrated circuits created by researchers at universities belong to their authors (Article 9(1)). If the educational institution has made expenses to provide certain tools and equipment for studies which led to the integrated circuit topography, the academics are responsible for reporting to the educational institution that the integrated circuit topography is evaluated, and to provide information about the method of evaluation and the revenues accrued if requested. The educational institution may ask for an acceptable share of the revenue collected in three months from the receipt of the written notification. However, the amount to be claimed cannot exceed the expenses made by the educational institution (Article 9(2)).

1149. The holder of the right of the integrated circuit topographies designed within the agreements other than the contract for service is the person who assigned the job (Article 10).

1150. Exclusive rights on layout-designs: The right holder of a layout-design enjoys the following exclusive rights: (i) reproducing the protected layout-design in its entirety or for any creative part thereof; (ii) commercially exploiting the protected layout-design, an integrated circuit in which the layout-design is incorporated (Article 11).

II. Formalities of Protection

1151. Protection provided by PICTopoL, No. 5147 is applicable to the nationals of the Republic of Türkiye, physical persons and legal entities that are resident and engaged in industrial and commercial activity in Türkiye and those who are entitled to file applications within the scope of international treaties (Article 3).

1152. Registration: Registration of layout-design (integrated circuit topography) is carried out by the Turkish Patent and Trademark Office [or Authority, i.e. Türk-Patent] (PICTopoL, Article 13 as amended by *SMK*). Registration applications are made in written and separately for each integrated circuit topography (Article 13). Formalities relating to the registration of integrated circuit topography are regulated in Articles 14–16.

1153. Duration of protection: The protection term of the exclusive rights of integrated circuit topography is as a rule ten years starting from the date of filing the application for registration (PICTopoL, Article 6(2)).

1154. Transactions related to integrated circuit topography: Under Turkish law, the application for registration of integrated circuit topography and rights deriving from the registration can be transferred and inherited. They can be the subject matter of a security transaction and transactions by will. They can be attached by creditors (Article 17). *All transactions inter vivo* related to integrated circuit topography are subject to written form (Article 17(3)). Moreover, the application and rights deriving out of registration can be licensed (Article 18 as amended by *SMK*, No. 6769).

1155. Cancellation of the right on integrated circuit topography: An integrated circuit topography can be cancelled by a court judgment. The suit for cancellation can be initiated by persons who have a legal interest, consumer associations (Article 19(1)), and chambers of commerce and industry (Cf. Law, No. 5590 of 8 March 1950 as amended). In case of cancellation of an integrated circuit topography, the court judgment has '*ex tunc*' effects. The cancellation judgment is announced at the Register and has effects towards every person (PICTopoL, Article 20).

1156. Grounds for termination of the right on integrated circuit topography: The right on integrated circuit topography comes to an end by the termination of the protection period or upon waiver of the right holder (Article 21(1)). As soon as the termination of the protection period the subject matter of the right belongs to the public domain (Article 21(2)).

III. Infringement and Remedies

1157. Infringements on the right on integrated circuit protection: The typical infringements on the right on integrated circuit topography are the following acts: (i) reproducing the whole or any original part of a protected layout-design and (ii) importing, selling or providing in any other form for commercial purposes, any protected layout-design, an integrated circuit in which the layout-design is incorporated without the authorization of the right holder (Article 11).

1158. In case of infringements on the application for integrated circuit topography or on the right, the applicant or the right holder can initiate the following lawsuits: *action for cease-and-desist of the infringement, compensation for damages including loss of profit* (*lucrum cessans*) and *immaterial damage* (Articles 26, 28). The winning party is also entitled to request the *announcement of the court judgment* in daily papers (Article 32).

1159. The claims relating to infringements on registered trademarks are subject to the provisions on the prescription of the Turkish Code of Obligations Article 146 (*SMK*, Article 157). Under the Turkish Code of Obligations, the usual prescription period is ten years unless another limitation period has been provided by law (Article 146).

1160. Under PICTopoL, initiating an *action for the non-existence of an infringement* is possible (Article 33).

1161. An *action for the security of evidence (*declaratory order from the court) can be initiated (Article 26). Moreover, in actions initiated or to be initiated under PICTopoL, a *decision for provisionary measures* can be claimed from the court (Article 34).

1162. Regarding subject-matter jurisdiction (görev), under PICTopoL, actions in the first instance relating to legal remedies or penal sanctions are heard by *'specialized'* civil and criminal courts. These are determined by the Council of Judges and Prosecutors upon the recommendation of the Ministry of Justice (PICTopoL, Article 31).

1163. As for territorial jurisdiction (yetki), all actions against the decisions of TürkPatent and by third parties who suffer damages arising from TürkPatent's decisions are initiated before 'specialized' courts of Ankara (Article 31(2)). Civil actions under PICTopoL are initiated at the court of the domicile of the claimant or at the place where the offense has been committed or at the place where the infringement had its effects (Article 26(3)). Where the claimant does not have domicile in Türkiye, the competent court is the court at the place where his/her registered patent or trademark attorney has his/her office and if the attorney's record has been deleted, the court where TürkPatent is located (Article 26(4)), i.e., Ankara, the Capital. As for civil actions initiated by third parties against the holder of the relevant right, the competent court is the court where the defendant is domiciled. If the defendant is not domiciled in Türkiye, the provisions of Article 26(4) as above apply (Article 26(5)). If there are several competent courts, the court where the first action was initiated shall have jurisdiction (Article 26(6)).

1164. Regarding procedurals rules on mandatory mediation attempts as well as prospects under 'the Singapore Mediation Convention' which may also apply to chip protection, *see* the explanations in paragraphs 658–659 in Chapter 2 – Patents and Utility Models – 'Specialized Courts and Mediation'.

Chapter 9. Trade Secrets and Confidential Information

§1. In General

I. Concepts of Know-how and Trade Secrets

1165. Usually, a distinction is made between *technical or manufacturing secrets* (German: Fabrikationsgeheimnisse) and *trade secrets* (German: Geschaeftsgeheimnisse). The first category deals with *manufacturing process* (know-how) while the latter is related to organizational matters and commercial operations.

1166. 'Know-how means a body of technical information that is secret, substantial and identified in any appropriate form'.[170]

1167. Trade secrets are not only restricted to technical data. Information of a non-technical nature, such as lists of suppliers or customers, distribution policy or commercial organization may also be protected as trade secrets.

II. Protection of Know-how and Trade Secrets

1168. Know-how and trade secrets are under the protection of the law.

A. *National Laws*

1169. In some national laws, for the protection of trade secrets, the following three conditions should be met:

(1) First, the know-how must really be secret, in contrast to publicly known.
(2) Second, the manifest intention of maintaining confidentiality must be proved.
(3) Third, the commercial value of the secret must be shown.[171]

B. *TRIPS Agreement*

1170. The TRIPS Agreement imposes on the States to effectively safeguard the 'non-disclosed information' (commercial secrets) on the condition that the relevant information, is on the one hand, confidential, namely that it is not widely known and that it cannot be easily known to third parties and on the other hand that it has a commercial value which results from its confidential nature (Article 35).

---

170. Compare Commission Regulation (EC) 940/96 of 31 Jan. 1996 on the application of Art. 85(III) of the Treaty to certain categories of technology transfer agreements, Art. 10.

171. *See* Rüster, Bernd, (Gen. Ed.), World Intellectual Property Guidebook, Federal Republic of Germany, Austria, Switzerland, Bender, Matthew, 1991. For Germany: Ch. 3; for Austria: Ch. 4; for Switzerland: Chapter.

§2. PROTECTION OF TRADE SECRETS UNDER TURKISH LAW

I. Concepts of Know-how

1171. Trade secrets and confidential information, as legal concepts, have not been defined by any positive legal norm in Turkish law. They are usually included in the notion of 'know-how'.

II. Protection of Know-how

1172. A specific law does not exist for the protection of know-how, trade secrets and confidential information. They are protected, however, by the provisions of the Turkish Commercial Code (TComC), No. 6102 of 13 January 2011 on unfair competition (*haksiz rekabet*, Articles 54 et seq.)

1173. When an individual utilizes or passes on to others the manufacturing secrets (know-how) or the trade secrets that he/she unlawfully obtained, this conduct constitutes an act of unfair competition (TComC, Article 55(1)(d)).

1174. Likewise, to seduce employees, agents or other auxiliary persons of a competitor to reveal or search out manufacturing or trade secrets of their employers or principals is also an act of unfair competition (TComC, Article 55(1)(b); (3)).

1175. In case of infringement on know-how, the provisions of TComC relating to civil remedies (prevention, cease-and-desist of infringement, claim for compensation, etc.) (TComC, Articles 56–57) and penal sanctions for acts of unfair competition (Article 62) apply.

III. Protection of Trade Secrets

1176. The provisions of TComC, No. 6102 of 13 January 2011 on unfair competition *(haksiz rekabet)* (Article 55(1)(b); (3) and (d) and Article 64) also apply for the protection of trade secrets.

1177. Under Turkish law, the protection of trade secrets is also provided by other specific provisions. For instance, in joint stock companies *(anonim sirket, A.S.)*, the members of the Board of Directors are obliged not to disclose the trade secrets of the undertaking and not to compete with the company (TComC, Articles 395–396).

Selected Bibliography

Turkish Intellectual Property Law in General

Dericioglu, Kaan, *Fikri Haklar Klavuzu*, (Intellectual Property Guide), ISO Yayini, 2003.

Dericiooglu, Kaan, *Fikri Haklar Sözlügü*, (Intellectual Property Dictionary), TÜSIAD, 2010.

Kaya, Ahmet Göktug, *Sinai Mülkiyet Kanunu*/Industrial Property Law, onikilevha, Istanbul, 2018.

(This work contains the English translation of Industrial Property Law, No. 6769)

Kaya, Arslan / Varol, Reyhan / Okutan, Gül, *Fikri Mülkiyet Hukuku ve Radyo Televizyon Hukuku Mevzuati, 1. Basi* (Compilation of the Legislation on Intellectual Property Law and Radio Television Law, 1st ed.), Istanbul, 1998.

Oguz, Arzu / Yilmaztekin, Hasan Kadir / Üner, Ezel, *Fikri Mülkiyet Hukukunda Uzman Arabuluculuk* (FMHUArb, Specialized Mediation in Intellectual Property Law), Ankara, 2020.

Özsunay, Ergun, In Product Fraud: Counterfeit Goods Suppression: TURKEY: Unfair Competition, Patent Law, Copyright Law, Trademark Law, Enforcement of Foreign Judgments, Arbitration, Civil Procedure, edited by John P. Sinnott General Editor (Gen. Ed.), Oceana Publications, New York, London, Rome, Release 94-1, issued August 1994, 101 pages.

Özsunay, Ergun, Intellectual Property Rights, In Business Guide to Turkey, edited by T. Kayacikli & F. Karakeçili. Universal Dil Hizmetleri ve Yayincilik A.S., Istanbul, 1998.

Özsunay, Murat R., The Turkish 2009 Draft Code of Civil Procedure, Eight Decades after the Voluntary Adoption of the Swiss-Neuchatel Code of Civil Procedure, Common Law, Civil Law and the Future of Categories, in J. Walker & O.G. Chase, Common Law, Civil Law and the Future of Categories, Lexis Nexis, Canada, 2010.

Özsunay, Murat R., Civil Procedural Systems: Pro and Contra (Turkey), in Civil Procedure in Cross-Cultural Dialogue: Eurasia Context, IAPL 2012 World Conference on Civil Procedure in Moscow, Conference Book, Ed. by Dimitry Maleshin; International Association of Procedural Law, Moscow: Statut, 2012.

Tekinalp, Ünal, *Fikri Mülkiyet Hukuku, Güncellestirilmis ve Genisletilmis 5. Basi* (Intellectual Property Law, Updated and Enlarged 5th ed.), Istanbul, 2012.

Selected Bibliography

Turkish Copyright Law

Aksu, Mustafa, *Bilgisayar Programlarinin Fikri Hukukta Korunmasi* (Protection of Computer Programs in Intellectual Property Law), Istanbul, 2006.

Arkan, Azra, *Eser Sahibinin Haklarina Baglantili Haklar* (Neighbouring Rights attached to the Author's Rights), Istanbul, 2005.

Arslanli, Halil, *Fikri Hukuk Dersleri,* C. II, (Textbook on Intellectual Law), Istanbul, 1954.

Ates, Mustafa, *Fikri Hukukta Eser* (Work in Intellectual Property Law), Ankara, 2007.

Ates, Mustafa, *Fikir ve Sanat Eserleri Üzerindeki Haklarin Kapsami ve Sinirlandirilmasi* (Scope and Limitations of Rights on Intellectual and Artistic Works), Ankara, 2002.

Ayiter, Nusin, *Hukukta Fikir ve Sanat Ürünleri* (Intellectual and Artistic Works in Law), 2nd ed., Ankara, 1981.

Baspinar, Veysel-Kocabey, Dogan, *Internette Fikri Haklarin Korunmasi* (Protection of Intellectual Property Rights on Internet), Ankara, 2007.

Besiroglu, Akin, *Düsünce Ürünleri Üzerinde Haklar* (Rights on Intellectual Property), 3rd Edition, Istanbul, 2004.

Bozbel, Savas, *Fikir ve Sanat Eserleri Hukuku* (Law on Intellectual and Artistic Works), Istanbul, 2012.

Bozkurt, Yüksel / Armagan, Ebru, *Dünya Fikri Mülkiyet Örgütü* (WIPO) *Tahkim Sistemi* (WIPO Arbitration System), Ankara, 2010.

Börü, Safak Parlak, *Fotograf Üzerindeki Haklar* (Rights on Photograph), Ankara, 2013.

Dalyan, Sener, *Bilgisayar Programlarinin Fikri Hukukta Korunmasi* (Protection of Computer Programs in Intellectual Property Law), Ankara, 2009.

Dayioglu, Sadettin, *Fikir ve Sanat Eserleri Hukuku Bakimindan Müzik Edisyon Faaliyeti ve Edisyon Sözlesmeleri* (Musical Edition Activity and Contracts for Edition from the Viewpoint of Law on Intellectual and Artistic Works), Fikri Mülkiyet Yilligi 2010, Istanbul, 2011, p. 179.

Deren-Yildirim, Nevhis, *Haksiz Rekabet Hukuku ile Sinai Mülkiyet Hukukunda Ihtiyati Tedbirler* (Interim Measures in Unfair Competition Law and Industrial Property Law), 2nd Edition, Istanbul, 2002.

Erel, Safak N., *Türk Fikir ve Sanat Hukuku,* 3. Baski (Turkish Intellectual and Artistic Law, 3rd Ed.), Ankara, 2009.

Fikri Mülkiyet Haklari ve Uluslararasi Uyum Sorunlari Semineri (Seminar on Intellectual Property Rights and International Harmonization), Istanbul, 9 October 1995, Istanbul, 1996, Publication No. 1996–1998.

Giritlioglu, Necla, *Yayin Sözlesmesi* (Publishing Contract), Istanbul, 1967.

Gökyayla, Emre, *Telif Hakki ve Telif Hakkinin Devri Sözlesmeleri* (Copyright and Contracts on Assignment of Copyright), 2nd Edition, Ankara, 2001.

Hirsch, Ernst E., *Das neue Urhebergesetz der Türkei*, UFITA, 1954, pp. 24 et seq.

Hirsch, Ernst E., *Fikri ve Sinai Haklar* (Intellectual and Industrial Rights), Ankara, 1948.

Keyder, Virginia Brown, *Fikri Mülkiyet Haklari ve Gümrük Birligi* (Intellectual Property Rights and Customs Union), Intermedia, Istanbul, 1996. (This work contains the English translation of the Turkish Law on Intellectual and Artistic Works [*FSEK*], No. 5846).

Marmara Üniversitesi Avrupa Toplulugu Enstitüsü, Gümrük Birligi Çerçevesinde Türkiye'de Fikri ve Sinai Haklarin Korunmasi (Protection of Intellectual and Industrial Rights in Türkiye within the Framework of the Customs Union), *Avrupa Arastirmalari Dergisi*, Vol. 4, Nos. 1–2, 1995–1996.

Misir, Mustafa Bayram, *Fikri Haklarin Korunmasinda Meslek Birliklerinin Yeri* (Role of Collecting Societies regarding Protection of Intellectual Rights), Ankara Barosu Fikri Mülkiyet ve Rekabet Hukuku Dergisi (FMR) 2002/4, 2002, p. 15.

Nal, Temel, Das türkische Urheberrecht-Grundlagen und gegenwaertiger Entwicklungsstand, GRUR ınt., 2000, p. 1.

Okutan, Gül, *Türk Milletlerarasi Özel Hukukunda Fikir ve Sanat Eserleri* (Intellectual and Artistic Works in the Turkish Private International Law), in Essays in Honour of Prof. Dr Nihal Uluocak, Istanbul, 1999, pp. 213 et seq.

Özsunay, Ergun, Copyright Law in Turkey, In Product Fraud: Counterfeit Goods Suppression, TURKEY, edited by John P. Sinnott (Gen. Ed.), Oceana Publications, Dobbs Ferry, New York, Release 94–91, Issued August 1994, 101 pages.

Özsunay, Ergun, Copyright Law in Turkey, Managing Intellectual Property, No. 24, November 1992, pp. 29–32.

Özsunay, Ergun, *5846 sayili Fikir ve Sanat Eserleri Kanunu'nun Uygulanmasinda Ortaya Çikan Belli Basli Sorunlar ve Kanunda Yenilemeler Yapilmasini Gerektiren Nedenler* (Major Issues in the Practice of the Law on Intellectual and Artistic Works, No. 5846 and the Grounds necessitating Amendments in this Act), in The Istanbul Chamber of Commerce (ITO = ICOC), *Fikri Mülkiyet Haklari ve Uluslararasi Uyum Sorunlari Semineri* (Seminar on Intellectual Property Rights and International Harmonization), 9 October 1995, Istanbul, 1996, Publication No. 1996–1998, pp. 28–40.

Öztan, Firat, *Fikir ve Sanat Eserleri Hukuku* (Law on Intellectual and Artistic Works), Ankara, 2008.

Öztrak, Ilhan, *Fikir ve Sanat Eserleri Üzerindeki Haklar* (Rights on Intellectual and Artistic Works), 2nd ed., Ankara, 1977.

Sahin, Büsra, *Türk Hukukunda Sinema Eserlerine iliskin Lisans Sözlesmesi* (License Agreement Relating to Cinematographic Works in Turkish Law), Seçkin, Ankara, 2018.

Tekinalp, Ünal, *Fikir ve Sanat Eserleri Kanununun Eser Sahipleri Açisindan Yer ve Kisi Itibarile Uygulanmasi* (Application of the Law on Intellectual and Artistic Works in respect of Territory and Person with regard to the Owner of the Work), In [*Festschrift*] Essays in Honour of Prof. Dr Nihal Uluocak. Istanbul, 1999, pp. 367–379.

Tekinalp, Ünal, *Fikri Mülkiyet Hukuku, Güncellestirilmis ve Genisletilmis Besinci Basi* (Intellectual Property Law, Updated and Enlarged 5th ed.), Istanbul, 2012.

Tekinalp, Gülören & Ünal, *Fikri Mülkiyet Hukukuna Iliskin Kanun Hükmünde Kararnamelere Göre Korumadan Yararlanabilecek Kisiler ve Elverisli Hükümler (Asgari Haklar) Ilkesi* (Persons who can benefit from the Protection within the

Governmental Decrees on Intellectual Property and the Principle of Available Provisions (Minimum Rights), in Essays in Memoriam of Prof. Dr Bülent Davran, Istanbul, 1998, pp. 155–166.

Topaloglu, Mustafa, *Bilgisayar Programlari Üzerindeki Haklar ve Bu Haklarin Korunmasi* (Rights on Computer Programs and Protection of These Rights), Türkiye Bilisim Vakfi Yayinlari, Istanbul, 1997.

Tosun, Yalçin, *Sinema Eserleri ve Eser Sahibinin Haklari* (Cinematographic Works and Author's Rights), Istanbul, 2009.

Tüysüz, Mustafa, *Fikri Haklar Üzerindeki Sözlesmeler* (Contracts on Intellectual Rights), Yetkin, Ankara, 2007.

Yarsuvat, Duygun, *Türk Hukukunda Eser Sahibi ve Haklari, Genisletilmis 3. Basi* (Author of the Work and His/Her Rights under Turkish Law, enlarged 3rd ed.), Istanbul, 1984.

Turkish Patent, Utility Model and Design Law

Ayiter, Nusin, *Ihtira Hukuku* (Invention Law), Istanbul, 1968.

Bas, Erdal, *Bulusun Faydali Model Belgesiyle Korunmasi* (Protection of Invention by Utility Model Certificate), Ankara, 2013.

Çolak, Ugur, *Türk Patent Hukuku* (Turkish Patent Law), Ankara, 2022.

Erdem, B. Bahadir, *Patent Hakkina Iliskin Sözlesmelere Uygulanacak Hukuk* (Applicabler Law to Agreements on Patent Right), Beta, Istanbul, 2002.

Erdem, Bahadir, *Fikri Hukukta Türk Mahkemelerinin Milletlerarasi Yetkisi* (International Jurisdiction of Turkish Courts in Intellectual Property), Seçkin, Ankara, 2002.

Hirsch, Ernst E., *Hukuki Bakimdan Fikri Say*, I.C.: *Nazari Esaslar, Sinai Haklar (Ihtira Beratlari ve Sinai Modeller)*, Turkish Translation by V. Çernis [(Intellectual Work from the Legal Viewpoint, I. Vol.: Theoretical Principles, Industrial Rights (Patents and Industrial Designs)], Istanbul, 1942.

Kaptekin, Deniz, *Patentin Hükümsüzlügü* (Nullity of Patent), Istanbul, 2013.

Kaya, Ahmet Göktug, *Sinai Mülkiyet Kanunu* (Industrial Property Law), Oniki Levha, Istanbul, 2018 (Translation of Industrial Property Law, No. 6769).

Keskin, Serap, *Fikri (Düsünsel) Mülkiyet Haklarinda Patent ve Markanin Ceza Normlari ile Korunmasi* (Protection of Patent and Trademark through Penal Norms in Intellectual Property Rights), Seçkin, Ankara, 2003.

Noyan, Erdal, *Patent Hukuku, Genisletilmis ve Gözden Geçirilmis 2. Baski* (Patent Law, Enlarged and Revised 2nd ed.), Ankara, 2011.

Ortan, Ali Necip, *Avrupa Patent Sistemi* (European Patent System), C. I, Ankara, 1991; C. II, Ankara, 1992.

Ortan, Ali Necip, *Isçi Buluslari Hukuku* (Law on Employees' Inventions), Izmir, 1987.

Ortan, Ali Necip, *Patent Lisansi Sözlesmesi* (Patent Licensing Agreement), Ankara, 1979.

Özsoy, Saadet Hande, *Türk Hukukunda Patent Lisansi Sözlesmesi* (Patent Licensing Agreement in Turkish Law), Ankara, 2011.

Özsunay, Ergun, In Product Fraud: Counterfeit Goods Suppression: TURKEY: Patent Law, edited by John P. Sinnott (Gen. Ed.), Oceana Publications, New York, London, Rome, Release 94–91, issued August 1994.

Öztek, Selçuk, *Son Degisikliklerden Sonra Türk Patent Hukukunun Anahatlari* (Outlines of the Turkish Patent Law after the Last Amendments), Paper submitted to the Seminar on Intellectual and Industrial Property Rights within the Framework of the Customs Union organized by the Marmara University European Law Institute on 15 May 1996, published in *Avrupa Arastirmalari Dergisi, Özel Sayi*, Vol. 4, No. 1–2, 1995/1996, pp. 56 et seq.

Öztürk, Özgür, *Türk Hukukunda Patent Verilebilirlik Sartlari* (Requirements for Patentability in Turkish Law), Istanbul, 2008.

Saraç, Tahir, *Patentten Dogan Hakka Tecavüz ve Hakkin Korunmasi* (Infringment on the Right Arising out of Patent and Protection of the Right), Ankara, 2003.

Sehirali, Feyzan Hayal, *Patent Hakkinin Korunmasi* (Protection of Patent Right), Ankara, 1998.

Tamer, Ahmet, *Patent ve Faydali Model Hakkina Aykiriligin Sonuçlari* (Consequences of Infringement of Rights on Patent and Utility Model), Ankara, 2013.

Tekinalp, Ünal, *Fikri Mülkiyet Hukuku, Güncellestirilmis ve Genisletilmis Besinci Basi* (Intellectual Property Law, Updated and Enlarged 5th ed.), Istanbul, 2012.

Tüzüner, Özlem, *Faydali Modelin Korunmasi ve Faydali Modelin Korunmasina Uygulanacak Hukuk* (Protection of Utility Model and Law Applicable to the Protection of Utility Model), Istanbul, 2011.

Utku, Doruk, *Sinai Haklarin Rehni* (Pledge of Industrial Property Rights), Ankara, 2009.

Turkish Trademark Law

Arkan, Sabih, *Grup Markalari* (Group Marks), in *Festschrift* for Firat Öztan, Ankara, 2010, pp. 275 et seq.

Arkan, Sabih, *Marka Hukuku* (Trade Mark Law), C. I, Ankara, 1997; C. II, Ankara, 1998.

Bilgili, Fatih, *Marka Hukukunda Hakkin Kötüye Kullanilmasi* (Abuse of Right in Trademark Law), Ankara, 2006.

Çolak, Ugur, *Türk Marka Hukuku* (Turkish Trademark Law), Istanbul, 2023.

Dirikkan, Hanife, Taninmis Markanin Korunmasi (*Protection of Well-known Marks*), Seçkin, Ankara, 2003.

Karahan, Sami, *Garanti Markasi* (Guarantee Mark) in *Festschrift* for Firat Öztan, Ankara, 2010, pp. 1201 et seq.

Karahan, Sami, *Marka Hukukunda Hükümsüzlük Davalari* (Cases for Nullity in Trademark Law), Konya, 2002.

Karahan, Sami, *Ortak Marka* (Collective Mark), in *Festschrift* for Huseyin Ülgen, Istanbul, 2007, pp. 1097 et seq.

Kaya, Ahmet Göktug, *Sinai Mülkiyet Kanunu* (Industrial Property Law), Oniki Levha, Istanbul, 2018 (Translation of Industrial Property Law, No. 6769).

Kaya, Arslan, *Marka Hukuku* (Trademark Law), Istanbul, 2006.

Keskin, Serap, *Fikri (Düsünsel) Mülkiyet Haklarinda Patent ve Markanin Ceza Normlari ile Korunmasi* (Protection of Patent and Trademark through Penal Norms in Intellectual Property Rights), Seçkin, Ankara, 2003.

Keyder, Virginia Brown, *Fikri Mülkiyet Haklari ve Gümrük Birligi* (Intellectual Property Rights and Customs Union), Intermedia, Istanbul, 1996, pp. 25 et seq.

Selected Bibliography

Meran, Necati, *Marka Haklari ve Korunmasi* (Rights on Trademark and Their Protection), Ankara, 2008.

Okutan, Gül, *Sesler, Renkler ve Kokular Marka Olarak Tescil Ettirilebilir mi? Avrupa Topluluklari Mahkemesinin Üç Karari* (Can Voices, Colors and Scents Be Registered as Trademark? On three Judgments of the EC Court), in *Festschrift* for Gülören Tekinalp, Istanbul, 2003, pp. 579 et seq.

Özarmagan, Müge, *Marka Hakkinin Kullanmama Nedeniyle Sona Ermesi* (Termination of Right on Trademark on the Ground of Non-Use), Istanbul, 2008.

Özsunay, Ergun, The New Turkish Trademark Law, Fordham International Law Journal 19, No. 4, April 1996, pp. 1542–1577.

Özsunay, Ergun, *AB'de Marka Hukukunun Uyumlastirilmasi: AT Yönergesi Üzerine Düsünceler* (Harmonization of Trade Mark Law in EU: Considerations on Council Regulation (EC) No. 40/94 of 20 December 1993 on Community Trademark), in Essays in Memoriam for Selim Kaneti, Istanbul, 1996, pp. 119–129.

Özsunay, Ergun, Trademarks in Turkey, Managing Intellectual Property, Vol. 18, March 1992, pp. 38–39.

Özsunay, Ergun, New Turkish Trademark Law (Some Remarks on the System of the Decree Having the Power of Law, *KHK*/556 for Protection of Trademarks dated 24 June 1995), ITO (ICOC), Publication No. 1995-30.

Öztek, Selçuk, *Ilaç Markalari Arasinda Iltibas ve Türk Markalar Hukukunun Çözümlenmemis Bazi Genel Sorunlari* (Confusion among Pharmaceutical Trade Marks and Some Unsolved General Issues of the Turkish Trade Mark Law) in *Hukuk Arastirmalari*, Vol. 6, Nos. 1–3, January–December 1991, 15 pages.

Öztek, Selçuk, *Marka Terkini Davalarinda Yargi Yolu (Görevli Mahkeme)* (Judicial Means in Actions for Erasure of Trademark, Competent Court with regard to Jurisdiction'), in *Istanbul Barosu Dergisi* (Review of the Istanbul Bar Association), April-May-June 1993, Vol. 67, Nos 4–5–6, pp. 237–242.

Rüzgar, Eser, *Marka Hakkinin Internet Reklamciligi Yoluyla Ihlali ve Sorumluluk Rejimi* (Violation of Right on Trademark through Internet Advertising and the Liability Regime), Istanbul, 2013.

Sanal, Osman, *Markanin Hükümsüzlügü* (Nullity of Trademark), Ankara, 2004.

Tekinalp, Ünal, *Fikri Mülkiyet Hukuku, Güncellestirilmis ve Gelistirilmis Besinci Basi* (Intellectual Property Law, Updated and Enlarged 5th ed.), Istanbul, 2012.

Tüzüner, Özlem, *Marka Rehni Sözlesmesi ve Uygulanacak Hukuk* (Contract of Pledge on Trademark and Applicable Law), Istanbul, 2007.

Uysal, Erkan, *Probleme des türkischen Markenrechts aus der Sicht des deutschen und europaeischen Rechts*, Dissertation, Köln, Berlin, Bonn, München, 1998.

Uzunalli, Sevil, *Markanin Korunmasinin Kapsami ve Tazminat Talebi* (Scope of Protection of Trademark and Claim for Compensation), Ankara, 2012.

Yalçiner, Ugur G. / Karaahmet, Erdogan, *Marka Tescilinin Temel Ilkeleri, Genisletilmis Baski* (Basic Principles of Registration of Trademark), Enlarged ed., Ankara, 2011.

Yasaman, et al. *Marka Hukuku, 556 sayili KHK Serhi*, C. I-II (Trademark Law, Commentary of Governmental Decree No. 556, Volumes I-II), Istanbul, 2004.

Yasaman, Hamdi, *Marka Hukuku ile Ilgili Makaleler, Hukuki Mutalaalar, Bilirkisi Raporlari* (Articles, Legal Opinions and Experts' Reports on Trademark Law), Volumes I-IV, Istanbul, 2003–2012.

Yasaman, Hamdi, *Paris Anlasmasi Anlaminda Taninmis Markalar* (Well-Known Trademarks in the Paris Convention), in *Festschrift* for Kemal Oguzman, *Galatasaray Hukuk Fakültesi Dergisi*, 2002, pp. 300 et seq.

Trade Names and Confidential Information

Arkan, Sabih, *Ticari Isletme Hukuku* (Law of Commercial Enterprise), Revised 5th ed., Ankara, 1999.

Bilge, Mehmet Emin, *Ticari Sirlarin Korunmasi* (Protection of Commercial Secrets), in *Festschrift* for Mehmet Somer. Istanbul, 2006.

Domaniç, Hayri, *Ticaret Hukukunun Genel Esaslari* (General Principles of Commercial Law), Enlarged 4th ed., Istanbul, 1988.

Imregün, Oguz, *Kara Ticareti Hukuku Dersleri: Genel Hükümler, Ortakliklar, Kiymetli Evrak, 12. Basi* (Textbook on Trade Law: General Principles, Partnerships, Negotiable Instruments, 12th ed.), Istanbul, 2001.

Karayalçin, Yasar, *Ticaret Hukuku Dersleri, I: Giris-Ticari Isletme* (Textbook on Commercial Law, I: Introduction–Commercial Enterprise), 2nd ed., Ankara, 1961.

Mimaroglu, Sait K., *Ticaret Hukuku, Birinci Cilt: Isletme Hukuku* (Commercial Law, Vol. I: Law of Commercial Enterprise), 2nd ed., Ankara, 1970.

Özsunay, Ergun, Know-How in Turkish Law and Practice, Managing Intellectual Property, No. 18, March 1992, pp. 38–39.

Poroy, Reha / Yasaman, Hamdi, *Ticari Isletme Hukuku* (Textbook on Commercial Undertaking), Istanbul, 2012.

Saka, Zafer, *Ticaret Hukuku, Ticari Isletme* (Commercial Law, Commercial Enterprise), Istanbul, 1988.

Yesiltepe, Salih Önder, *Ticari Sir-Is Sirri* (Commercial Secret-Business Secret), in [*Festschrift*] Essays in Honor for Mehmet Somer, Istanbul, 2006.

Protection of Plant Varieties and Chips

Boztosun, Ayse Odman, *Entegre Devre Topografyasi Hakkinda Elestirel Bir Bakis* (A Critical View on Integrated Circuits Topography), *Atatürk Üniversitesi Erzincan Hukuk Fakültesi*, C. VIII, 2004, No. 3–4, pp. 309–338.

Boztosun, Ayse Odman, *Islahçi Hakki* (Breeder's Right), Ankara, 2006.

Tekinalp, Ünal, Fikri Mülkiyet Hukuku, *Güncellestirilmis ve Genisletilmis Besinci Basi* (Intellectual Property Law, Updated and Enlarged 5th ed.), Istanbul, 2012.

Tüysüz, Mustafa, *Fikri Mülkiyet Haklari Çercevesinde Yeni Bitki Çesitleri Üzerindeki Islahçi Hakki* (Breeder's Right on New Varieties of Plants within the Framework of Intellectual Property Rights), Ankara, 2007.

Yüce, Özden, *Fikri ve Sinai Haklar Hukukunda Entegre Devre Topografyalari* (Integrated Circuits Topography in the Law on Intellectual and Industrial Rights), Istanbul, 2010.

Foreign Laws

Intellectual Property Law in General

Abbott, Frederick / Cottier, Thomas / Gurry, Francis, International Intellectual Property in an Integrated World Economy, 2nd ed., Wolters Kluwer, New York, 2012.

Selected Bibliography

Antons, Christoph, The Enforcement of Intellectual Property Rights-Comparative Perspectives from the Asia-Pacific Region, Kluwer Law International, 2011.

C.K. Chow, Daniel / Lee, Edward, International Intellectual Property Problems, Cases and Materials, West Group, 2006.

Campbell, Denis, (Gen. Ed.) / Cotter, Susan, (ed.), International Intellectual Property Law. European Jurisdictions, published under the auspices of the Centre for International Legal Studies, Salzburg, Austria, John Wiley & Sons Ltd., 1995.

Campbell, Dennis, (Ed.), International Protection of Intellectual Property. FT, Law & Tax, Vol. 1 and 2.

Cornish, William, Intellectual Property-Omnipresent, Distracting, Irrelevant? Oxford University Press, 2004.

D'Amato, Anthony / Estelle Doris, Long, (Ed.). International Intellectual Property Law, Kluwer Law International, 1997.

D'Amato, Anthony / Estelle Doris, Long, A Coursebook in International Intellectual Property, West Academic, 2000.

Dessemontet, François, *La propriété intellectual*, Lausanne, 2000.

Gilliéron, Philippe, *Propriété intellectuelle et Internet*, Lausanne, 2003.

Govaere, Inge, The Use and Abuse of Intellectual Property Rights in E.C. Law (Intellectual Property in Practice), London, Sweet & Maxwell, 1996.

Götting, Horst-Peter, *Gewerblicher Rechtsschutz und Urheberrecht, 2. Auflage, Verlag* C.H.Beck, 2008.

Gray, Josephine / Phillips, Jeremy / Waelde, Charlotte, International Encyclopaedia of Laws, Volume 3: Intellectual Property, United Kingdom, 1998, Kluwer Law International (The Hague, London, Boston), Suppl. 3 (June 1998).

Groves, Peter, et al. Intellectual Property and the Internal Market of the European Community. London, Dordrecht, Boston: Graham & Trotman, 1993.

Lieber, Helmut / Zimmermann, Axel, *Die einstweilige Verfügung im Gewerblichen Rechtsschutz. Verlag* C.H.Beck, 2009.

Metaxas-Maranghidis, George, (Ed.), Intellectual Property Laws of Europe, John Wiley & Sons, Chichester, 1995.

Phillips, Jeremy / Firth, Alison, Introduction to Intellectual Property Law, 4th ed., London, Oxford University Press, 2001.

Rehbinder, Manfred / Vigano, Adriano, (Hrsg.) *URG Kommentar, Urheberrechtsgesetz, Orell Fuessli, 3. Auflage*, 2008.

Rüster, Bernd, (Gen. Ed.). World Intellectual Property Guidebook, Federal Republic of Germany, Austria, Switzerland, Matthew Bender, 1991.

Schmidt-Szalewski, Joanna, International Encyclopaedia of Laws, Vol. 2: Intellectual Property, France, 1999, Kluwer Law International (The Hague, London, Boston), Suppl. 10 (June 1999).

Schnopfhagen, Richard / Heine, Dietrich / Katanic, Vladan, Intellectual Property Law in Austria, Kluwer Law International, 2011.

Steiger, Martin / Birkhauser, Nicolas / Aschmann, David, *Immaterialgüterrecht, 4. Auflage,* Helbing & Lichtenhahn Verlag, 2012.

Torremans, Paul, Holyoak / Torremans, Intellectual Property Law, 7th ed., Oxford, 2013.

Tritton, Guy, Intellectual Property in Europe, London, 3rd ed., Sweet & Maxwell, 2007.

Troller, Alois, *Immaterialgüterrecht: Patentrecht, Markenrecht, Muster und Modellrecht, Urheberrecht, Wettbewerbsrecht, Band I-II, 3rd ed.*, Basel/Frankfurt am Main, 1983–1985.

Troller, Alois, *Précis du droit de la propriéte immateriale* (Traduit par K. Troller et V.J. Vesely), Helbing & Lichtenhahn, 1977.

Troller, Kamen, *Manuel du droit suisse des biens immatériels*, 2 Vol., 2nd ed., Basel, Frankfurt am Main, 1996.

von Büren, Roland / David, Lucas, (Hrsg.), *Rechtsschutz in Schweizerisches Immaterialgüter-und Wettbewerbsrecht, Vol. I/2, 2. Auflage*, Basel, Frankfurt am Main, 1998.

von Büren, Roland / David, Lucas, (Hrsg.), *Schweizerisches Immaterialgüter-und Wettbewerbsrecht, Bd. I/1, Grundlagen, zweite, erweiterte und teilweise neu gefasste Auflage*, Basel, Frankfurt am Main, 2002.

von Büren, Roland / Marbach, Eugen / Ducrey, Patrick, *Immaterialgüterrecht-und Wettbewerbsrecht*, Staempfli, Bern, 2008.

WIPO (Ed.), Introduction to Intellectual Property, Kluwer Law International, 1997.

WIPO, Intellectual Property Handbook, WIPO Publication, 2nd ed., Reprinted 2008.

Copyright Law

Barrelet, Denis / Egloff, Willi, *Das neue Urheberrecht. Kommentar zum Bundesgesetz über das Urheberrecht und verwandte Schutzrechte, 2. überarbeitete Auflage*, Bern, 2000.

Bellefonds, Xavier Linant de, *Droit d'auteur et droits voisins*, Paris, Dalloz, 2.édition, 2004.

Bertrand, André, *Le droit d'auteur et les droit voisins*, Paris, Dalloz, 1999.

Colombet, Claude, *Propriété littéraire et artistique: et droits voisins*, Paris, Dalloz-Sirey, 9.édition, 1997.

Dessemontet, François, *Le droit d'auteur*, Lausanne, 1999.

Dreier, Thomas / Schulze, Gernot, *Urheberrechtsgesetz, 3. Auflage*, Verlag C.H.Beck, 2008.

Gautier, Pierre-Yves, *Propriété littéraire et artistique*, Paris, PUF, coll. *Droit fondamental*, 8.édition, 2012.

Grages, Jan-Michael, *Verwaiste Werke*, Mohr Siebeck, 2013.

Hertin, Paul W., *Urheberrecht, 2. Auflage*, Verlag C.H.Beck, 2008.

Hillig, Hans-Peter, (Hrsg.), *Europaeisches und internationals Urheberrecht*, Verlag C.H.Beck, 2006.

Laddie / Prescott / Vitoria, The Modern Law of Copyright and Designs, 4th ed., London: Butterworths, 2011.

Lucas, Andre / Lucas, H.-J., H.-J. Lucas & A. Lucas-Schloetter. *Traité de la propriété littéraire et artistique, 4. édition*, LexisNexis, 2012.

Luo, Li, *Verwertungsrechte und Verwertungsschutz im Internet nach neuem Urheberrecht*, Verlag C.H.Beck, 2004.

Müller, Barbara K. / Oertli, Reinhard, (Hrsg.), *Urheberrechtsgesetz (URG)*, Staempfli, Bern, 2012.

Nimmer, Melville B. / Nimmer, David, Nimmer on Copyright, Matthew Bender, 1998.

Rehbinder, Manfred, *Urheberrecht, 16. Auflage*, C.H.Beck, 2010.
Sterling, J.A.L., Protection of Authors Works, Performances, Phonograms, Films, Video, Broadcasts and Published Editions in National, International and Regional Law, In World Copyright Law, London, Sweet & Maxwell, 2003.
Straub, Wolfgang, *Softwareschutz*, Dike Verlag AG, Zürich, 2011.
Sucker, Reinhard, *Der digitale Werkgenuss im Urheberrecht*, Mohr Siebeck, 2013.
Wandke, Artur-Axel / Bullinger, Winfried, *Praxiskommentar zum Urheberrecht, 4. Auflage*, Verlag C.H.Beck, 2011.

Patent, Utility Models and Designs Law

Benkard, Georg / Dobrucki, Barbara, *EPÜ-Europaeisches Patentübereinkommen*, Verlag C.H.Beck, 2002.
Benkard, Georg, *Patentgesetz, Gebrauchsmustergesetz, 10. Auflage*, Verlag C.H.Beck, 2006.
Bertrand, A., *Marques et Brevets. Dessins et Models*, Paris, Delmas, 1995.
Chisum, Donald S. / Nard, Craig Allen, et al., Principles of Patent Law (Cases and Materials), Foundation Press 2004 (U.S.A.).
Chisum, Donald S., Chisum on Patents, LexisNexis, 2011.
Fitzner, Uwe / Lutz, Raimund / Bodewig, Theo, (Hrsg.), *Patentrechtskommentar, 4. Auflage*, Verlag C.H.Beck, 2011.
Greffe, Pierre / Greffe, François, *Traité des dessins et modeles*, France, Union Européenne, Suisse, Paris, LITEC, 8.édition, 2008.
Gruber, Stephan, Thomas Adam & Andreas Haberl, *Europaeisches und internationales Patentrecht, 6. Auflage*, Verlag C.H.Beck, 2008.
Harguth, Alexander / Carlson, Steven, Patents in Germany and Europe, Procurement, Enforcement and Defence-An International Handbook, Kluwer Law International, 2011.
Hilti, Christian, *Europaeisches und schweizerisches Patent-und Patentprozessrecht, 3. vollstaendig überarbeitete Auflage des Lehrbuchs von* Mario M. Pedrazzini, Bern, 2008.
Hubmann, Heinrich / Götting, Horst-Peter, *Gewerblicher Rechtsschutz, 7. Auflage*, C.H.Beck, 2001.
Klitzsch, Gottfried / Stockmair, Winfried, The Protection of Technical Innovations and Designs in Germany, 2. *Auflage*, Verlag C.H.Beck, 2001.
Krasser, Rudolf, *Patentrecht–Ein Lehr- und Handbuch, 6. Auflage*, C.H.Beck, 2009.
Laddie / Prescott / Vitoria, The Modern Law of Copyright and Designs, 4th ed., Vol. 1, Chapter 29, London: Butterworths, 2011.
Macciacchini, Sandro, *Urheberrecht und Meinungsfreiheit*, Bern, 2000.
Muir, Ian / Brandi-Dohrn, Matthias / Gruber, Stephan, European Patent Law, Law and Procedure under EPC and PCT, 2nd ed., Oxford University Press, 2002.
Nieder, Michael, *Die Patentverletzung*, Verlag C.H.Beck, 2004.
Osterrieth, Christian, *Patentrecht*, 3. Auflage, C.H.Beck, München, 2007.
Paterson, Gerald, The European Patent System (Intellectual Property Library), 2nd ed., London: Sweet & Maxwell, 2001.
Pedrazzini, Mario M., *Patent-und Lizenzvertragsrecht*, 2. Auflage, Bern, 1987.
Schulte, Reiner, *Patentgesetz mit EPÜ, Kommentar, 9. Auflage*, Verlag Carl Heymanns, 2014.

Singer, Margarete / Staude, Dieter, *Europaeisches Patentübereinkommen, 4. Auflage*, Verlag Carl Heymanns, 2007.

Singer, Romuald / Singer, Margarete, The European Patent Convention, A Commentary, Revised English (1995) Ed. by Ralph Lunzer, London, Sweet & Maxwell, 1995.

Staub, Roger / Celli, Alessandro L., (Hrsg.), *Designrecht*, Schulthess, 2003.

Suthersanen, Uma, Design Law in Europe, London: Sweet & Maxwell, 2000.

von Büren, Roland, *Patentrecht und Know-How unter Einschluss von Gentechnik, Software und Datenschutz*, Helbing & Lichtenhahn, *1. Auflage*, 2006.

Trademark Law

Althammer, Werner / Ströbele, Paul / Klaka, Rainer, *Markengesetz, 5. Auflage*, Köln, Berlin, Bonn, München, 1997.

Annand / Norman. Blackstone's Guide to the Community Trademark, Blackstone Press Limited, 1998.

Annand / Norman. Blackstone's Guide to the Trademarks Act 1994, London, Blackstone Press Limited, 1994.

Becker, Guido M., *Zur Konkurrenz von Marken und Geschmacksmusterschutz*, Mohr Siebeck, 2013.

Berlit, Wolfgang, *Markenrecht, 9. Auflage*, C.H.Beck, 2012.

Blumenthal, Corsin, *Der strafrechtliche Schutz der Marke: Unter besonderer Berücksichtigung der Piraterie*, Bern, 2002.

Davies, Isabel M., (Gen. Ed.), Sweet & Maxwell's European Trademark Litigation Handbook, London, Sweet & Maxwell, 1998.

Fezer, Karl-Heinz, *Markenrecht, 4. Auflage*, Verlag C.H.Beck, 2009.

Gilson, Jerome, Trademark Protection and Practice, Matthew Bender, 1997 (USA).

Görlich, Daniel, *Die anlehnende Markennutzung für nicht aehnliche Produkte*, Mohr Siebeck, 2013.

Hacker, Franz, *Markenrecht, 3. Auflage*, Carl Heymanns Verlag, 2013.

Hacker, Franz, *Markenrecht-Das Deutsche Markensystem, 2. Auflage*, Carl Heymanns Verlag, 2010.

Hubmann, Heinrich / Götting, Horst-Peter, *Gewerblicher Rechtsschutz*, 7 Auflage, C.H.Beck, 2001.

Ingerl, Reinhard / Rohnke, Christian, *Markengesetz, 3. Auflage*, Verlag C.H.Beck, 2010.

Lange, Paul, (Hrsg.), Internationales Handbuch des Marken- und Kennzeichenrechts, Verlag C.H.Beck, 2009.

Lange, Paul, *Marken- und Kennzeichenrecht, 2. Auflage*, Verlag C.H.Beck, 2011.

Lucas, David, *Kommentar zum Schweizerischen Privatrecht: Markenschutzgesetz*, Basel, Frankfurt am Main, 1994.

Marbach, Eugen, *Markenrrecht, Schweizerisches Immaterialgüter-und Wettbewerbsrecht*, Vol. III, 2. Auflage, Helbing & Lichtenhahn Verlag, Basel, 2009.

Mathély, P, *Le nouveau droit français des marques*, Paris, *Journal des Notaires et des Avocats*, 1994.

Pedrazzini, Mario M. / von Büren, Roland / Marbach, Eugen, *Immaterialgüter- und Wettbewerbsrecht*, Bern, 1998.

Repenn, Wolfgang / Weidenhiller, Gabriele, *Markenbewertung und Markenverwertung, 2. Auflage*, Verlag C.H.Beck, 2005.

Ströbel, Paul / Hacker, Franz, *Markengesetz, 10. Auflage*, Carl Heymanns Verlag, 2012.

Tatham, David / Richards, William, ECTA (European Communities Trademark Association) Guide to E.U. Trade Mark Legislation, London, Sweet & Maxwell, 1998.

Troller, Alois / Troller, Patrik, *Kurzlehrbuch des Immaterialgüterrechts, 2. Auflage*, Helbing & Lichtenhahn Verlag, Basel, Frankfurt am Main, 1981.

Troller, Alois, *Immaterialgüterrecht: Patentrecht, Markenrecht, Muster und Modellrecht, Urheberrecht, Wettbewerbsrecht, Band I-II, 3rd ed.*, Basel, Frankfurt am Main, 1983–1985.

von Schultz, Detlev, (Hrsg.), *Kommentar zum Markenrecht, 3. Auflage*, 2012.

Protection of Plant Variety Rights and Chips

Derzko, Natalie, M. Plant Breeder's Rights in Canada and Abroad: What Are These Rights and How Much Must Society Pay for Them? McGill Law Journal 39 (1994): 144–178.

Groves, Peter, et al. Intellectual Property and the Internal Market of the European Community, London, Dordrecht, Boston: Graham & Trotman, 1993.

Rüster, Bernd, (Gen. Ed.). World Intellectual Property Guidebook, Federal Republic of Germany, Austria, Switzerland, Matthew Bender, 1991 (Chapters 7 section 7C; 8 section 8/G).

Würtenberger, G., Plant Breeders Rights and Patents: An Effective Legal Protection for Plant Varieties, International Society for Horticultural Science, XXI. International Eucarpia Symposium on Classical versus Molecular Breeding of Ornamentals – Part I, Acta Horticulturae 612, 2003, pp. 187–193.

Codes, Las, Governmental Decrees, and other Regulations

Codes and Statutes

Act on Evaluation, Classification and Support of Cinematographic Works (*Sinema Filmlerinin Degerlendirilmesi ve Siniflandirilmasi ile Desteklenmesi Hakkinda Kanun*), No. 5224 of 14 July 2004, Official Gazette, No. 25529 of 21 July 2004 as amended by Law, No. 7163 of 18 January 2019, Official Gazette, No. 30671 of 30 January 2019.

Press Law (*Basin Kanunu*), No. 5187 of 9 June 2004, Official Gazette, No. 25504 of 26 June 2004.

Protection of Breeder's Rights on New Varieties of Plants Law *(Yeni Bitki Çesitlerine Ait Islahçi Haklarinin Korunmasina Iliskin Kanun),* No. 5042 of 8 January 2004, Official Gazette, No. 25347 of 15 January 2004.

Protection of Integrated Circuit Topographies Law (*Entegre Devre Topografyalarinin Korunmasi Hakkinda Kanun*), No. 5147 of 22 April 2004, Official Gazette, No. 25448 of 30 April 2004.

Law on Intellectual and Artistic Works (*Fikir ve Sanat Eserleri Kanunu – FSEK*), No. 5846 of 5 December 1951, Official Gazette, No. 7891 of 13 December 1951, as amended by Act, No. 2936 of 1 November 1983, Act, No. 4110 of 7 June 1995,

Act, No. 4630 of 21 February 2001, Act, No. 5101 of 3 March 2004, Act, No. 5217 of 14 July 2004, Act, No. 5571 of 28 December 2006, Act, No. 5718 of 27 November 2007 and Act, No. 5728 of 23 January 2008, Act, No. 7346 of 21 December 2021.

Act on Private International Law and Procedural Law (APIL – *Milletlerarasi Özel Hukuk ve Usul Hukuku Hakkinda Kanun – MÖHUK)*, No. 5718 of 27 November 2007, Official Gazette, No. 26728, 12 December 2007.

Code of Criminal Procedure (CCrimP – *Ceza Muhakemesi Kanunu - CMK*), No. 5271 of 4 December 2004, Official Gazette, No. 25673 of 17 December 2004.

Code of Civil Procedure (CCP – *Hukuk Muhakemeleri Kanunu – HMK*), No. 6100 of 12 January 2011, Official Gazette, No. 27836 of 4 February 2011.

Code of Enforcement and Bankruptcy (CEB – *Icra ve Iflas Kanunu – IIK*), No. 2004 of 9 June 1932 as amended several times, last by the Law, No. 6352 of 2 July 2012, Official Gazette, No. 2128, 19 June 1932.

Expropriation Act (*Kamulastirma Kanunu*), No. 2942 of 4 November 1983, Official Gazette, No. 18215 of 8 November 1983, as amended by the Law, No. 4650 of 24 April 2001; Law, No. 6306 of 16 May 2012; Law, No. 6487 of 24 May 2013; Law, No. 6495 of 12 July 2013.

Law on Entry into Force and Implementation of the Turkish Commercial Code (*Türk Ticaret Kanununun Yürürlügü ve Uygulama Sekli Hakkinda Kanun*), No. 6103 of 14 January 2011, Official Gazette, No. 27846 of 14 February 2011.

Law on Patent and Trademark Attorneys and Some Arrangements (*Patent ve Marka Vekilligi ile Bazi Düzenlemeler Hakkinda Kanun*), No. 5000 of 6 November 2003, Official Gazette, No. 25294 of 19 November 2003 as amended by Decree Having the Power of Law, No. 703 of 2 July 2018, Official Gazette, No. 30473 of 9 July 2018.

Law on Industrial Property, No. 6769 (*Sinai Mülkiyet Kanunu – SMK*) of 22 December 2016, Official Gazette, No. 29944 of 10 January 2017.

Turkish Civil Code (TCC – *Türk Medeni Kanunu – TMK*), No. 4721 of 22 November 2001, Official Gazette, No. 24607 of 8 December 2001.

Turkish Code of Obligations (TCO – *Türk Borçlar Kanunu – TBK*), No. 6098 of 11 January 2011, Official Gazette, No. 27836 of 4 February 2011.

Turkish Commercial Code (TComC – *Türk Ticaret Kanunu – TTK*), No. 6102 of 13 January 2011, as amended, Official Gazette, No. 27846 of 14 February 2011.

Turkish Penal Code (TPC – *Türk Ceza Kanunu – TCK*), No. 5237 of 26 September 2004, as amended, Official Gazette, No. 25611 of 12 October 2004.

Governmental Decrees Having the Power of Law (Repealed)

KHK/551: Decree No. 551 Having the Power of Law on Protection of Patent Rights (*Patent Haklarinin Korunmasi Hakkinda Kanun Hükmünde Kararname*), Official Gazette, No. 22326 of 27 June 1995. Amended by *KHK*/566, Official Gazette, No. 22412 of 22 September 1995 and Act, No. 4128, Official Gazette, No. 22456 of 7 November 1995. For correction of printing errors, *see* Official Gazette, No. 22330 of 1 July 1995. (It was repealed and replaced by Industrial Property Law, No. 6769 of 22 December 2016, Article 191).

KHK/554: Decree No. 554 Having the Power of Law on Protection of Industrial Designs (*Endüstriyel Tasarimlarin Korunmasi Hakkinda Kanun Hükmünde*

Kararname), Official Gazette, No. 22326 of 27 July 1995. (It was repealed and replaced by Industrial Property Law, No. 6769 of 22 December 2016, Article 191).

KHK/555: Decree No. 555 Having the Power of Law on Protection of Geographical Signs (*Cografi Isaretlerin Korunmasi Hakkinda Kanun Hükmünde Kararname*), Official Gazette, No. 22326 of 27 June 1995. (It was repealed and replaced by Industrial Property Law, No. 6769 of 22 December 2016, Article 191).

KHK/556: Decree No. 556 Having the Power of Law on Protection of Trademarks (*Markalarin Korunmasi Hakkinda Kanun Hükmünde Kararname*), Official Gazette, No. 22326 of 27 June 1995. (It was repealed and replaced by Industrial Property Law, No. 6769 of 22 December 2016, Article 191).

Other Regulations

Implementing Regulation Concerning the Protection of Integrated Circuit Topographies Law (*Entegre Devre Topografyalarinin Korunmasi Hakkında Kanunun Uygulama Seklini Gösterir Yönetmelik*), Official Gazette, No. 25686 of 12 December 2004.

Implementing Regulation of Industrial Property Law, Official Gazette, No. 30047 of 24 April 2017.

Regulation on Commercial Registry (*Ticaret Sicili Yönetmeligi*), Official Gazette, No.28541 of 27 January 2013.

Regulation on Emblem Regarding Geographical Indications and Tradition Product Names (Cografi Isaret ve Geleneksel Ürün Adi Amblem Yönetmeligi), Official Gazette, No. 30285 of 29 December 2017.

Regulation on Employees' Inventions, Inventions Made in Higher Education Institutions and Inventions Arising from Publicly Supported Projects (*Çalisan Buluslarina, Yüksekögretim Kurumlarında Gerçeklestirilen Buluslara ve Kamu Destekli Projelerde Ortaya Çikan Buluslara Dair Yönetmelik*), Official Gazette, No. 30195 of 29 September 2017.

Regulation on Marking of Intellectual and Artistic Works (*Fikir ve Sanat Eserlerinin Isaretlenmesi Hakkinda Yönetmelik*), Official Gazette, No. 23172 of 16 November 1997.

Regulation on Protection of Breeder's Rights on New Varieties of Plants (*Yeni Bitki Çesitlerinin Korunmasina Dair Yönetmelik*), Official Gazette, No. 25551 of 12 August 2004.

Regulation on Protection of Integrated Circuit Topographies (*Entegre Devre Topografyalarinin Korunmasi Hakkinda Kanunun Uygulanma Seklini Gösterir Yönetmelik*), Official Gazette, No. 25686 of 30 December 2004 as amended by the Regulation issued by Turkish Patent and Trademark Authority, Official Gazette, No. 30341 of 23 February 2018.

Communiques

Communiqué on Tariff of Fees to be applied in Year 2023 by the Turkish Patent and Trademark Authority (*Türk Patent ve Marka Kurumunca 2023 Yilinda Uygulanacak Ücret Tarifesine lliskin Teblig*), BİK/TÜRKPATENT: 2023/1, Official Gazette, No. 32060 (5. Mük.) of 31 December 2022.

Index

The numbers here refer to paragraph numbers.

Index

Index

www.ingramcontent.com/pod-product-compliance
Lightning Source LLC
Chambersburg PA
CBHW071437230926
51846CB00001B/258
9789403529875